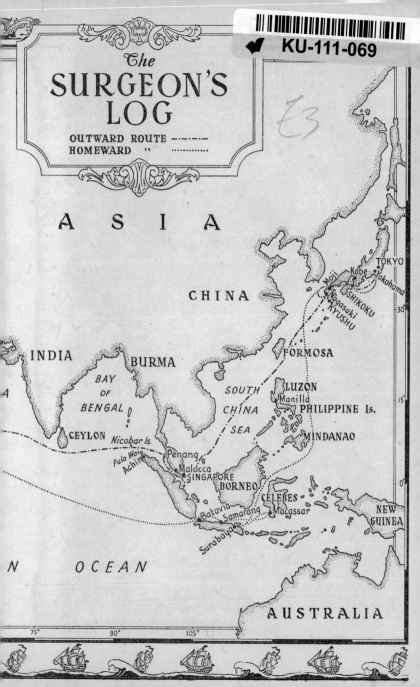

The
SURGEON'S LOG

OUTWARD ROUTE —·—·—
HOMEWARD   "   ············

E3

ASIA

CHINA

TOKYO
Kobe ·Yokohama
Moji ·SHIKOKU
Nagasaki· KYUSHU
30°

FORMOSA

INDIA

BURMA

BAY
OF
BENGAL

SOUTH
CHINA
SEA

LUZON
Manilla
PHILIPPINE Is.
15°

CEYLON   *Nicobar Is.*
Pulo Wai
Achin   Penang
Malacca
SINGAPORE
BORNEO

MINDANAO

CELEBES
Macassar
NEW
GUINEA
0°

Batavia· Samarang
Surabaya

OCEAN

AUSTRALIA

75°   90°   105°

THE SURGEON'S LOG

THE
SURGEON'S LOG

Impressions of the Far East

By

J. JOHNSTON ABRAHAM

Author of "The Night Nurse"
etc.

REVISED EDITION WITH NEW PREFACE AND
ADDITIONAL CHAPTER.

LONDON
CHAPMAN & HALL LTD.
37 ESSEX STREET, W.C.2

Registered at the G.P.O., Melbourne, for transmission by post
as a book.

First Edition September 1911
Second Edition October 1911
Third Edition November 1911
Fourth Edition January 1912
Fifth Edition March 1912
Sixth Edition October 1912
Seventh and Cheaper Edition May 1913
Eighth and Cheaper Edition May 1914
Ninth and Cheaper Edition January 1916
Tenth and Cheaper Edition March 1918
Eleventh and Cheaper Edition April 1919
Twelfth and Cheaper Edition May 1921
Thirteenth and Cheaper Edition February 1922
Fourteenth Edition, Reset and with New Illustrations June 1926
Fifteenth and Cheaper Edition June 1927
Sixteenth and Cheaper Edition August 1929
Seventeenth and Cheaper Edition November 1931
Reset and Reissued in Pocket (Eighteenth) Edition August 1933
Nineteenth (Pocket) Edition April 1935
Twentieth (Cheap) Edition May 1935
Twenty-first (Cheap) Edition July 1936
Twenty-second Edition November 1936
Twenty-third Edition March 1937
Twenty-fourth Edition May 1937
Twenty-fifth Edition July 1937
Twenty-sixth Edition May 1938
Twenty-seventh Edition September 1939
Twenty-eighth Edition May 1940
Twenty-ninth July 1943
Thirtieth Edition 1947
(Revised with new Preface and additional Chapter)

Wholly set up and printed in Australia for the Oxford University
Press, Leighton House, Melbourne, by Wilke & Co. Pty. Ltd.,
19 Jeffcott Street, Melbourne.

To

My Australian Wife

PREFACE TO THE THIRTIETH EDITION

It is thirty-six years since "The Surgeon's Log" was first published; it has been reprinted almost unchanged twenty-nine times; and now that I have been asked to write an introduction to the revised thirtieth edition I feel that my readers might like to hear something of its early adventures in search of a publisher.

Originally I wrote these impressions of the sea and of the men who do business in great waters mainly for the joy of savouring in tranquillity the pleasure my experiences had given me. But when the manuscript was finished I had an intense desire to share my memories with others less fortunate.

The great publishing houses, however, to whom I sent it did not seem to share this desire. The script came back monotonously, generally after three weeks, sometimes with a polite note of regret, sometimes without. Once a famous house kept it six months and my hopes rose steadily. But again one morning it came back, dog-eared and tattered in its brown paper parcel—the ninth refusal; and I was in despair.

It was a very bitter moment. I nearly threw the script into the fire. But that afternoon, as it happened, I went to St. Peter's Hospital, Henrietta Street, Covent Garden; and, sitting in the house-surgeon's room looking casually out of the window, I saw the name "Chapman and Hall" on a building across the way.

"Dickens's publishers," I thought. "I'll try them and if they fail me I'll give it up."

So once more the dog-eared script with the first three pages re-typed was parcelled up and posted. I didn't expect to hear anything for a month; I was used to delays; so I arranged to do some medical work in the North of England.

My breath was therefore rather taken away when I found a letter only a week later on the breakfast table, sent on from my London address, with "Chapman and Hall" on the envelope. Eagerly I tore it open. I could scarcely believe my eyes: they wanted it! It seemed too good to be true after the endless months of waiting.

What had happened was that Arthur Waugh, the Managing Director, saw it on his desk the day it arrived, opened it, read a bit and liked it. That night he took it home with him and read it through. Next day he wrote offering me terms. He was cautiously optimistic as a publisher has to be, for the fate of a book lies in the hands of the public not the publisher. But he had hopes, and naturally I shared them.

Well, those hopes have been more than realised. The book has appeared in many different forms year after year ever since 1911. It has lived through two major wars, is now approaching its half millionth copy, and has made me thousands of friends all over the world.

I have written a number of books since—some, I think, better. But none the less, I am quite content that they should be forgotten if this one, "The Surgeon's Log," is remembered.

London, W.1.   Jan. 1947.

CONTENTS

CHAPTER I

CHAPTER II

CHAPTER III

CHAPTER IV

CHAPTER V

CHAPTER VI

CHAPTER VII

CHAPTER VIII

CHAPTER IX

CHAPTER X

CHAPTER XI

LIST OF ILLUSTRATIONS

CHAPTER I

FINDING A SHIP: LIVERPOOL TO PORT SAID

WHEN the Pathologist discovered what was the matter with me, I think he felt it more acutely even than I did; for I had an inkling that something was wrong for weeks before I asked him to overhaul me; and it therefore did not come as so much of a shock to me when he diagnosed what I had already shrewdly guessed.

We had been through a lot of things together; and so the discovery distressed him very much.

"Of course it means you'll have to go away," he said. "I don't know how on earth I'll get along without you."

The Pathologist and I are supposed to share a flat. As a matter of fact the place is dominated by the Pathologist's impedimenta: a microtome, two incubators, bottles of every shape and size, flasks, two microscopes under bell-jars, bundles of slides and boxes of coverslips, test-tubes, and Petri dishes, books and monographs, on chairs, on the table, on the floor—anywhere. Any space not occupied by these the Pathologist and I share. I made a firm stand a year previously when he suggested keeping four "control" guinea-pigs in the flat—that I decided was too much.

The day after the examination, when we were sitting over the fire at night, smoking our last pipes, he said:

"Well! Have you decided anything?"

"I don't know what to do," I answered.

"What you want," he said sharply, "is to get away from all this sort of thing," waving his arm around. "You want to get clear of this atmosphere of 'wounds and bruises and putrefying sores.' You want to do nothing but eat,

1

drink, and sleep—in fact, you want to play the complete
cow and chew grass. In polite society, I should say go
for a rest cure, but you know what I mean."

"But who's going to pay for all this?" I said dolefully.

"Ass! It's a ship you want."

It was curious. I had never thought of that; but it
was obviously the right thing. I felt my depression melting like mists before the morning sun. Of course, that
was it. A ship—I had always wanted a ship; but circumstances had never seemed favourable. So many seemingly important things were ever pressing that the idea,
once strong, had gradually faded to the shadow of a
dream. Now grim necessity had settled it. The important things seemed somehow to dwindle into nothingness before the spectre we had raised.

A ship. Already my spirits began to revive.

"You've hit it, old man," I said with conviction.

"That's better," he answered with a satisfied smile.

We got a *Daily Telegraph*, and commenced to go
through the list of shipping companies. Tacitly we agreed
that only boats going to the Tropics were suitable. A
kind of reaction-hilarity took possession of us. The very
names of the ports of call were as good as a volume of
Kipling on that drear November night. We forgot the
rain outside, the sloppy London streets, the taxis, and the
motor- buses crowded with damp humanity. In our minds
we were sailing over a moonlit summer sea, along a
darkly outlined coast, with palm-trees sharply silhouetted
against a sky of palest aquamarine, and the indescribable
smell of jungle vegetation coming to us on the land
breeze as we hung idly leaning o'er the rail.

"Now, which of these should I apply to?" I said.

"Try them all, and any more you can find," said the
Pathologist.

.   .   .   .   .

Next morning I went into the City, to find, like
Columbus, that I had got into a new world. It was all

very strange and different. Imagine someone who has been accustomed to working only with a certain class of mind for years, who has merely to mention his name amongst that class, whereupon he is looked up in the "Directory," labelled and judged as to capabilities to a nicety—in short, someone whom the expert eye immediately recognises as the correct wheel, or rod, or lever for a certain position, great or small as the case may be, in the intricate scientific machinery of London hospital life. Then imagine such an individual suddenly finding himself in the position of having to seek a post from someone whose occupation for years has been overseeing bills of lading, thinking of insurance risks, watching markets, and discussing rebates with turtle-fed directors. It was like talking to a man in a foreign language.

I was asked was I a teetotaller, could I speak Spanish, what companies had I been in before, had I a Discharge Book; and again was I a teetotaller? They wanted to know could I organise concerts, did I understand music, could I give references to two people of recognised position in Society, was I a British subject, had I an English qualification; and again was I a teetotaller? There were no questions as to my scientific abilities—that seemed to be of no consequence—but was I a teetotaller? In a vague sort of way I began to feel as though I had descended in the social scale. Apparently ships' surgeons were not drawn from the highest ranks in the profession. Was I a teetotaller?

· · · · · ·

The sum total of the first morning's impressions was distinctly depressing. It seemed there was no great demand for ships' surgeons. One person asked me how much I was prepared to pay for the round trip. I stared at him, and rapidly took my departure. He had my address, however, and next morning I had a letter from him offering me a housemaid's wages, should I care to go. I ignored that letter. Afterwards when I came to know the sea and shipping, I discovered that that company paid no dividend to its deluded shareholders, but supported a baronet in affluence.

Another individual seemed to be quite eager to have me. That made me wary. I was beginning to know the ropes. Inquiries led me to discover it would be part of my duties to vaccinate some thousands of Portuguese immigrants before they could land at certain South American ports. When I inquired how much extra I should get for this, I was told it was all in the day's work. In addition I found out that cases of yellow fever, small-pox, etc.—anything likely to detain the ship in quarantine —it was suggested, should be signed up as "Malaria," or something else innocuous. In other words, I was to perjure my professional soul, in addition to working overtime, for the wages of a street-scavenger.

This person also asked if I were a teetotaller, but, only in a half-hearted sort of way, as if that were too much to expect. I informed him I was a dipsomaniac and left.

.   .   .   .   .

Some companies I went to had no vacancies for months; others I found required uniforms which would absorb six months' pay, and compelled their surgeons to supply themselves with instruments which may have been used in the time of Nelson, but had been antiquated ever since—instruments which, however, an omniscient Board of Trade still required ships to carry, and the companies had managed, somehow or other, to squeeze their surgeons into paying for themselves.

Eventually a man I met in one of the offices put me on the right tack.

"Why should you bother with passenger companies at all?" he said. "What you want is a ship bound East, a ship with no fixed itinerary, which may be away four, six, eight months, whose course is not known once it has discharged its outward-bound cargo. It's got to be a big ship with plenty of space to be comfortable out East, and one belonging to a good company, otherwise the food will be poor. You'll not find such a company in London."

"Where then?" I said.

"Liverpool's the place! London's not in it with Liverpool when it comes to shipping!"

So it was, as the result of much inquiry, several letters, and a hasty personal interview, that one winter's afternoon, some weeks later, I found myself in Liverpool in response to the following summons:—

"You are hereby appointed surgeon to the s.s. *Clytemnestra*. The vessel will sail from Liverpool on or about the 12th Jan., and you will please, unless otherwise notified, arrange to attend at the Birkenhead shipping office at 10.30 a.m. on the 10th Jan. to sign articles for the voyage.

I am, etc.,
MEDICAL SUPT.,
————— S.S. Co."

.   .   .   .

Liverpool is frankly a jumping-off place for anywhere and the people are not ashamed of it. The place lives and moves and has its being in ships and shipping. Everywhere one sees the signs of shipping companies; and all the trams seem to run to the pier-head.

It is impossible to avoid ships and shipping in Liverpool. One might be in London for years and then not discover it was a shipping port. But in Liverpool everyone talks "ship"; half the population in the streets seem to have a rolling gait; in the cafés the pretty waitresses ask what company you belong to when they have seen you twice; and at the music-halls the artistes invariably sing as encores songs purporting to be of the sea.

The sailor is the real king of Liverpool. Everybody in Liverpool loves the sailor, and is only too anxious to show him how to have a good time and spend his money while he is ashore; and it is he who is the great man there till he has spent it.

Then he goes to sea again to earn more.

At the old-fashioned hotel in Birkenhead, where I was advised to stop, again the flavour of the sea was very much in evidence. A picture of a full-rigged ship sailing over carefully regulated waves was prominent in the hall. Faded photographic groups of officers in the Mercantile Marine adorned several of the public rooms. Curious shells and corals formed the usual mantel ornaments. I walked into a room which I thought was public, to find I had invaded the den of an old retired sea-captain. Everyone knew I was a ship's surgeon, and took a friendly interest in me, which, to one used to the distant service of city caravanseries, was at first almost embarrassing. My pale student complexion and general washed-out appearance, I discovered afterwards, had been put down by them to malaria. They were used to wrecks of men returning from the fever-zones of the Amazon, West Coast and the Malay Archipelago.

Scottish engineers, Welsh mates, captains of steamships, their wives and daughters, made up the hotel's clientele.

Everyone and everything was very intimate. The Welsh "boots" and general factotum was a mine of information on all things nautical. I drew upon him continually. The morning after my arrival he gave me minute directions how to find the Shipping Office; but of course I went wrong; and, after wandering a devious way amongst dreary-looking buildings, past scrap-heaps of old iron, and broken-down boats, over railway lines, till I thought I was utterly lost, it was a corresponding relief when I suddenly came on a building labelled Mercantile Marine Office.

There was a crowd of men hanging round outside, several boys, and a decrepit old fellow in uniform, with a Board of Trade badge on the collar of his coat. The lounging crowd made way for me; and I found myself in a bare sort of office, with a long counter at one side and a railed-off place at the upper end. An American stove stood in the middle of the office, and gave out a feeble wave of heat. All round the walls notices to mariners, warnings, regulations, etc., were stuck up. Two young clerks sat on stools behind the counter, taking no notice of anyone, and apparently having some great joke between themselves. Nothing seemed to be going to happen. I walked aimlessly round the room, staring at the notices. A youngish, fair-looking man stood at the stove warming his hands. Our eyes crossed.

"Excuse me, are you the doctor?" he said.

I confessed.

"Pleased to meet you," he said.

I answered rather uncertainly, not knowing whom I had got.

"First voyage?" he queried.

Again I confessed, feeling amateur was written all over me.

Just then there was a noise outside; and another man came hurrying in, and went behind the counter. After him the whole crowd strolled leisurely in. The two clerks woke up. One of them yawned. My new acquaintance nodded at the man who had come in.

"That's Mr. Thomas," he said.

I felt my ignorance. Doubtless the remark was illuminating; but I was none the wiser. I liked the look of Mr. Thomas, however. One of the clerks looked over at me.

"Are you the doctor?"

I admitted it; and he rushed away, and brought a Medical Register, looked me over, asked my name, looked it up, asked my address, looked that up, looked me over again, and finally appeared to be satisfied. Then he collected a pile of documents together. Everyone was now assembled; and at a nod from Mr. Thomas he began to read in a monotonous sing-song voice from the document before him:—

" . . . . s.s. Clytemnestra, *bound from Liverpool to Yoko-hama, and (or) any other port or ports within the limits of 72 degs. N. latitude, and 65 degs. S. Latitude, trading to or from; as may be required, till the ship arrives at a port, or final port of discharge, in the United Kingdom, or Continent of Europe, between the River Elbe and Brest, for a period not exceeding eighteen months, as the Master may require. . . ."*

I was listening intently, but, looking around, saw that no one else was paying the least attention. It was all the same to them whether they signed on for San Francisco, Sydney, or Shanghai. It was a twice-told tale to them. And truly it mattered little whether they listened or not: for from the wording it was obvious we might legally be sent anywhere a ship could sail.

The sing-song voice seemed to act on them like a soporific. It went on indefinitely, reading more and more rapidly and indistinctly.

Suddenly it stopped; and then in a natural voice the clerk said:

"All members of the crew to be on board before midnight on the 12th Jan."

This seemed to be the part they were waiting for. They all woke up. "Twelve o'clock Saturday night, mates," said one of them. The rest nodded.

"Get ready to sign now," said the clerk briskly.

"Officers first." Someone signed. Then the clerk said:

"You, doctor!" and pointed to a column. In five seconds I had signed away my liberty for eighteen months, agreed to abide by a mass of regulations I did not understand, and to sail on a ship I had never seen.

Mr. Thomas appeared suddenly then to become aware of my existence.

"How are you, doctor? Happy to meet you."

We shook hands cordially; and still I did not know.

Apparently that was all. The long queue were signing as I passed out. I had become a "seaman," a person whom the Board of Trade made elaborate regulations for, passed Acts of Parliament to protect, devised penal codes to punish, and other laws equally stringent to save from the rapacity of "owners."

It was my duty now to report myself to the Liverpool office.

A wooden-faced clerk took my name, asked me to be seated, and telephoned to the department.

Doors opened and shut, people came in and out, clerks popped heads through compartments and answered questions. I watched it all in a detached way. It did not concern me. Presently there was an irruption.

A little wrinkled Chinaman in full dress of ceremony—black skull-cap, carefully braided queue, wide black alpaca jacket and trousers, and black silk shoes with thick white soles—came into the office, and marched straight to one of the compartments. For the first time in my life I heard "pidgin" English. Up to then I had thought it more or less a product of the novelist's imagination; but here it was in all its native impurity.

"Belong No. 1 *Clytemnestlla*. Wanchee pleeceman," he said.

The clerk behind the counter smiled.

"All right, No. 1, what for?"

"Two-thlee piecee men makee talk, lun away alleesame one piecee," he said very earnestly.

The clerk tried to look grave.

"And you want a policeman to keep them from leaving the ship?"

The No. 1 nodded; and just then my friend of the morning—Mr. Thomas—came in. He looked at the No. 1 and then at the clerk.

"What's our No. 1 up to?" he said.

"Says some of your Chinamen want to break ship, and comes here to ask us to get a policeman to stop them, Mr. Thomas."

The No. 1 nodded in confirmation.

"All right, No. 1; pleeceman come to-night. Maskee," said Mr. Thomas.

But the No. 1 was not satisfied with that. He knew if any of his crew escaped he would suffer in pocket; and when a Chinaman thinks his dollars in danger he is difficult to satisfy. Eventually they had to take him into an inner office and relieve him of all responsibility.

In the meanwhile Mr. Thomas came over to me.

"I suppose you're waiting for old Farquharson, Doc?" he said.

Then, with the characteristic, naive, ever-present contempt which the man of his hands always has for anyone or anything pertaining to the art of the scrivener, he added:

"I hate coming to offices. They're bothering me now about some hides lost in Macassar last voyage. It's annoying when you want to be at home every minute you can before you sail."

I caught at the last half of his sentence.

"Then we sail together?" I said.

He laughed. "Of course! You didn't know then that I'm Chief Officer of the ship you've 'signed on' for?"

"I'm jolly glad to hear it," I said. He nodded.

"Well, since we're on the subject, here's another of your shipmates, the Chief Engineer," he added as a large rubicund figure appeared in the doorway, and came over smiling to us.

"Mr. Halahan—our new Doc."

Mr. Halahan said he was "pleased to meet" me in a strong Belfast accent that my heart warmed to immediately.   .   .   .   .   .

I went on board finally the evening before we sailed. It was close upon midnight. A solitary policeman at the dock gates directed the cabman, pointing to the far-off oblong outline of a shed black against the glare of the great arc lamps beyond.

"They're loading still. Good night, sir! Thank you! Pleasant voyage, sir!"

In the morning I was awakened by a steward tapping at my door. He had brought my morning coffee.

"What time would you like your bath, sir? Doctor usually has it at seven bells."

"All right. That'll suit me," I said composedly, successfully concealing, I hoped, my total ignorance of what "seven bells" meant.

Later, as I stood watching the long line of docks that in the morning mist represented England, I heard a voice at my elbow.

"We're leaving God's own country, Doc." It was the Chief Engineer, who had come up from below as soon as we had got clear into the Mersey. He had a piece of waste in his hand. An engineer is never quite happy unless he has a piece of waste or a sweat-rag handy.

"I'm always glad to get back, and I'm always glad to get away again," he said. "Queer, isn't it! When you're in the East you feel sorry for the poor devils who have to live there, and know they envy you the fact that you soon will be homeward bound. When you've passed the 'Rock' (Gibraltar) you count every hour till you've sighted England. When you've been home a few days you begin to dread the thought of leaving again so soon, and make up your mind to look out for a shore billet at once. But you never do take that shore billet. When you've been home a fortnight, and have seen your mother or your wife and one or two other people that matter, you begin to feel restless again. You want the sun, the sky, the vivid colours, the long calm days at sea, the quiet of the deck, the regular monotonous sound of the screw—you ache for it all again; you want the Oriental deference you have been accustomed to; you want—you don't know what you want, but you do know you want to get out of England. You laugh at yourself after a few voyages; but it's got into your blood by then, and you can't help yourself. You're ruined for shore life. You'll know all about it when you come back, Doc."

We were leaning on the rail, looking for'ard.

"Just look at Thomas," said Halahan (whom I shall call the Chief in future); "he's coming aft now. Everything is wrong with him this morning. Homesick. Young wife. A sailor should never marry."

Certainly Mr. Thomas was in a pessimistic mood. He stopped on his way to us to make some disparaging remark to the bo'sun.

"Call himself a pilot," he said, apropos of nothing, coming up to us from the main deck. "He's let that Shire boat and the *Circe* through in front of us. The *Circe* thinks she's faster than us. Now he's given her two hours' start."

"Pilots," he muttered, "think they own the earth. You bring a ship all round the world in safety; they take her up the Mersey, and then claim credit for the whole voyage."

The Chief laughed. "All mates, and most masters, can't stand pilots," he said to me in a stage whisper.

"How would you like a stranger coming down and messing about in your engine-room?" retorted the mate.

"I should tell the No. 1 greaser to pour oil over him till his bearings cooled down," he answered grimly.

"H'm. We can't tell the quartermaster to throw him off the bridge—worse luck. That's where you have the pull over us."

"Mr. Thomas!" came a voice from the bridge-deck above. The mate straightened up sharply.

"Yes, sir!" he said, and disappeared up the ladder.

"That's the Old Man. Have you seen him yet?" said the Chief.

"No," I answered.

"He's all right," he said simply. It is the greatest commendation one sailor can give another.

A burly form came down from the bridge-deck above,

followed by the mate. I had never met John Bull in real life; and, though I was familiar with him in political cartoons, had come to think of him as rather a mythical person—a creature of the imagination. It was therefore somewhat of a shock to meet him face to face, disguised as a captain in the Mercantile Marine. Instead of a curly-brimmed silk hat he wore the company's regulation cap. I looked for the Union Jack waistcoat. It was not there. But the one that was, covered an equally expansive chest. The top-boots were absent, as was also the hunting crop. I regretted the top-boots, but penetrated the disguise at once.

The mate presented me.

"This is our doctor, Captain Tucker."

He nodded. It was just the sort of nod John Bull would be expected to give. It meant: "I don't quite know what sort of fellow you are yet; but, if I make up my mind to like you, I don't care care what anyone else says about you."

"Can't make your name out, Doc," he said. "You write such a confounded bad hand, dashed if I could read it in the articles."

I confessed the name my father had saddled me with, and apologised for my cryptic handwriting.

"It's part of the training of a doctor to write badly," I explained. "A prescription is a mysterious enough thing in itself; but when it is written by a first-class bad hand, like mine, it becomes a talisman."

His eyes twinkled, and I felt we had got *en rapport*.

"Oh, that's it," he said, and passed on into his cabin.

On the bridge the quartermaster struck "one bell." On the fo'castle head the man on the look-out repeated it. A few seconds later the second steward appeared at the companion hatch and violently rang a hand-bell.

"Breakfast," said the Chief. "Come on, Doc," and he led the way below.

At the mess-room door we paused. The captain had

not yet entered; and I discovered it was etiquette to wait until he arrived. It was the first glimpse I had of the majesty of the master of a ship, representing as he does the King, the Law, and the British Constitution on the high seas.

Presently he came, and took the head of the table. My place I found was on his right, opposite the mate. The other officers had places further down. The engineers with the exception of the Chief, who dined with us, had a mess-room of their own. I looked round curiously to see the place that was to be our home for the next six months, and wondered how we should all get on in the enforced intimacy so unavoidable on a ship.

Half an hour after breakfast I was just finishing my last letters, as I found it would be the only opportunity we should have until we reached Port Said, when I heard a voice coming down my ventilator:

"Hurry up, Doc. The pilot's going. Got your letters?"

I rushed on deck to find we had slowed down for a steam-tug which was rapidly approaching us on the starboard bow. Presently she sheered off a point; and a boat putting out from her drew alongside. One of our crew caught the rope thrown to him, the pilot swung down the ladder, waited for the swell to rise, and dropped neatly into the boat. Away he went with a wave of his arm to the Old Man on the bridge, down came the pilot flag, the ladder was hauled up, and soon the boat and tug were dancing specks in the wake.

"Now we've got the ship to ourselves," said the mate with a grunt of satisfaction.

After tiffin I went on deck again. On the bridge the second mate walked stolidly to and fro. Close to me two Chinamen, black with coal-dust, clad in thin blue dungarees, each with his pig-tail rolled in a tight knot behind and his bare feet hooked in wooden sandals, dumped ashes down the shoot into the sea, accompanying each heave with guttural cries. On the fo'castle head the man on the look-out tramped steadily backwards and forwards. The rest of the ship seemed dead. No one was about, and the cold soon drove me below again. Here everything was still. I looked into the cabin next to mine, to find the third mate fast asleep. It was his watch below, and he was taking advantage of it to get as much sleep as possible. As for me, I had no watch to keep, no night bell to rouse me in the darkness, no ward telephone to bring me, half awake, half clothed, in the small hours of the morning to watch the last agonies of the dying in the dim-lit long white ward, where shrouded figures slept in rows unconscious of the shadowy wings of Azrael hovering over them.

Snuggled down on my settee, the chant of the screw came to me with a faint monotonous regularity, infinitely soothing. The water swished murmurously alongside, like a lullaby in an unknown tongue of liquid vowel sounds. The peace of the sea fell over me as with a mantle. Time melted into nothingness—to-day, to-morrow, yesterday. Time! What was time?

The entrance of the steward woke me. He had brought my tea. My book was on the floor. There were sounds of movement overhead, of feet shuffling. A rough staccato voice said:

"Relieve the wheel, and look-out!"

It was the watch changing. Presently the shuffling died away, and the monotone of the screw slipped again into the unconscious rhythm of life. An interval elapsed, then sounds came again. The third mate had wakened and was singing softly, for company, to himself:

"Oh, Whisky made me pawn my clothes,
    Whisky, Johnny?
Oh, Whisky gave me a purple nose.
Whisky for my honey.

Oh, Whisky killed my poor old dad.
　　Whisky, Johnny?
And took away all the sense he had.
　　Whisky for my honey."

A hoarse voice here interrupted him. "One bell, sir!"
It was the quartermaster notifying the approaching
change of watch. "All right, quartermaster! I'm coming!"
I heard him answer.

A few minutes later the round shining face of the
Second Officer appeared in my doorway. He looked at
me cautiously, as if he were expecting something.

"All right, Doc?" he queried.

"Yes. Quite all right."

"Feeling up to dinner?"

As a matter of fact I wasn't. The hours for meals
seemed to come round with startling rapidity. I stated
this to the Old Man in explanation of my want of
appetite. He waved it aside politely but firmly, and
stated his opinion that I was "sickening for something."

"Never mind, Doc," he said encouragingly; "we'll
make a sailor of you yet." And to illustrate what he
meant proceeded to get the better of an enormous menu.

It was an astonishing feat. Undoubtedly he was a
mighty trencherman. The others, good men and true,
were not in it with him. He made me think of all sorts
of incongruous things—beef, beer, and the British Constitution, City dinners and the Lord Mayor's coachman,
prize Shorthorns and the Agricultural Hall, gout and
dyspepsia—all in one breath.

"My appetite's not what it was," he admitted at the
end of dinner. "I don't feel a bit hungry now."

He talked all the time he was eating, keeping the
conversation going. When there was a lull everyone kept
quiet till he re-started. The mate stared solemnly at the
cloth. The Chief smiled quietly to himself, or looked over
at me. I gathered that it was not etiquette for a sub-
ordinate to start any new subject of conversation in the

presence of the Old Man. The doctor was the only one who could afford to neglect his opinion, or differ very violently from him in argument. The Chief also might venture to disagree, though not with the same freedom. But an executive officer—no, it was better not. These things slowly dawned upon me during the course of this my first day.

Presently the Old Man sighed comfortably, the sigh of repletion.

"I suppose, Doc, we'll have to get back to work," he said.

"I suppose so," I echoed.

This was the invariable signal that dinner was over. He said it to me every night at sea for the following six months; and I made the invariable response. The mate told me he had been saying it to every doctor for years. We followed him slowly out of the mess-room, each to his own quarters.

.   .   .   .   .

It was not until we had passed the Bay of Biscay that I found my sea legs and made my appearance in the mess-room. The Old Man's eyes twinkled when on the third day I turned up at breakfast. The mate nodded solemnly; the second mate, grinning cheerfully, made way for me to pass.

"Try some dry hash, Doc," said the Old Man. "Must have some dry hash. No man can call himself a sailor who doesn't like dry hash."

He proceeded to help himself to about a quarter of the dish, added two fried eggs and several slices of bacon, and fell to. Previously he had had fish. Afterwards he had a mutton chop and fried potatoes. This, with sundry cups of coffee, toast and marmalade, made up his breakfast.

"Always have dry hash on the menu whenever possible," he explained. "Reminds me of the old sailing-ship days when I was a boy. What do you think of it, Doc?"

"Fine," I said. I could have eaten anything that morning.

"Thought we'd make a sailor of you," he remarked in a gratified tone. "It's the greatest test of a sea-cook I know, to be able to make dry hash right. This man's a treat. What do you think, Mr. Thomas?"

"Quite good," replied the mate laconically.

"Ever taste 'dog's body,' Doc?" continued the Old Man.

"No," I answered promptly.

"Oh, it's not so bad as that," he laughed. "Don't suppose our cook would know how to make it," he added regretfully. "Only a real old 'shell-back' would."

On the question of food the Old Man was inexhaustible. The subject interested him profoundly. He was always ready to experiment on anything new. When we were ashore in port together, later, he was ever willing to investigate any dish he had not tasted before. His reputation, I found, was known all over the Far East. His delight in eating was so naïvely transparent that people asked him everywhere, and usually contrived to have something new for him to sample, much to my profit, as we were invariably asked out together. That he was quite aware of the amusement he caused I was soon quick to discover. But it affected him not at all. Like Falstaff, he was content to be a source of wit in others. In reality he secretly enjoyed leading them to believe they were poking fun at his expense, unknown to him. When I grasped the situation it caused me infinite joy. The Machiavellian-Gilbertian ponderosity of it was so ruminatingly droll. It pleased them; it pleased him, if possible, more—everyone was pleased. What more could one wish for?

Amongst the Chinese I discovered he was vastly esteemed on account of his Gargantuan prowess. Merchants waited to send their cargo home by his ship simply because, when invited to their table, he had done them the honour of out-eating every other European present. To be fat is to look like a mandarin in the Celestial Empire; and no one could deny his pre-eminence in that respect. He certainly was immense. I have seen his great bulk overawe truculent Japanese coolies in a way nothing else could; for the Japanese, too, by heaping honours upon their enormously fat wrestlers, show the same curiously Oriental reverence for obesity as a sign of power which the European mind vainly tries to understand.

In spite of these facts, however, he was beginning to get seriously alarmed by his continual increase in weight, as I discovered a few days later, when he had made up his mind to confide in me. But at the time, of course, I knew nothing of that.

Breakfast was almost over. The second mate had gone to relieve the third when the Old Man rose.

"We'll start inspection this morning if you're all right, Doc."

"Quite all right," I hastened to assure him.

So I had my first initiation into work; and morning inspection became a daily routine for the rest of the voyage, every day at sea. The Old Man, the mate, the Chief, and I formed the inspecting body. First we went for'ard to the forecastle. Here the petty officers and quartermasters had their cabins—the carpenter, familiarly known as Chips, the bo'sun, the lamp-trimmer, known as Lamps, the four quartermasters, and a deck boy, who acted as their steward. The Old Man peered in everywhere and remarked about several things to the mate. Then we went aft again, and inspected the cook's galley to see that everything was clean. After that down to the well-deck aft, to the seamen's quarters, in the stern. The English sailors were quartered on the starboard side, the Chinese firemen to port. These latter had a special rice-cook of their own; and the Old Man gave him a dressing-

down about the filthiness of his galley without ever looking inside.

"Sure to be dirty," he remarked to me. "A Chinaman
isn't healthy unless he's dirty. The Japanese are clean
but dishonest. The Chinaman is honest but filthy.
Cleanliness doesn't go with honesty in the East. In fact,
most things go by contraries to the West."

So he gave the rice-cook a thorough rating as a stimulus; and the man took it all with the inscrutable face of
the Oriental. It was impossible to tell whether he even
knew he was being censured. Then we went into the
Chinamen's fo'castle.

It was there, for the first time, I smelt the indescribable
smell of the East—the smell of every inhabited place
beyond Suez, the smell of fœtid narrow streets, of teeming populations, of temples and joss-sticks, of jealously
guarded houses, of tropical suns beating upon rotten vegetation, of palm oil and patchouli, of sandal-wood and
copra, dried fish and all the thousand-and-one abomina-
tions that make up the sum total of it all.

It is a smell you loathe at first, get used to, grow to
like, and finally, when you are back in clean, fresh
England, at intervals have a hungry longing for that you
would do almost anything to satisfy—a nostalgia that
starts an unrest in your blood, sends you down to the
docks to watch the great ships outward bound, and
makes you envy the faces looking over the rail saying
good-bye to England.

It was a long, narrow, dim-lit place, with two tiers of
box-like bunks around three of its walls. Some of the
men were lying asleep in their bunks; others, clad only in
thin dungaree trousers, their lean, naked yellow bodies
otherwise exposed, were playing some noisy game in
which wooden blocks were banged with much chatter on
the rough deal bench that served them for a table. One
man was having his head shaved by the barber of the
company, with a razor that looked like a pen-knife.

Gibraltar

Coaling at Port Said

Crouched beside the stove a thin worn figure sat smoking from a long brass pipe, which he put stealthily away when we entered.

"Opium!" said the Chief quietly to me.

Littered all round, in corners, in bunks, everywhere, were quaint-looking boxes fastened with elaborate locks, clothes, sandals, rubbish in buckets, vegetables, bits of dried fish and herbs hanging from the roof, gaudy almanacs fastened to the walls, and quantities of cheap English umbrellas tied up in bundles in every corner—the Chinaman has a passion for collecting one-and-sixpenny umbrellas. In the sternmost corner a few joss-sticks, burning in a tin of sand before a tiny tinsel-gauded shrine, cast a faint pervasive odour all around.

The Old Man stumped resolutely to the centre of the fo'castle; and we followed silently. Suddenly he snorted:

"This place is like a d——d pigsty. Where's the No. 1?"

The Chief picked out a man.

"Tell No. 1 Captain wanchee."

Presently the little squat Chinaman I had seen in the Liverpool office asking for a policeman appeared. His face was absolutely immobile; but his little black eyes had the furtive look of a rat's.

The Old Man fell on him with a loud voice. His language about the state of the fo'castle was vitriolic. He seemed to be in an ungovernable rage. He cursed in English. He also made remarks in Chinese which, the Chief told me, were not complimentary to the female relatives of the listeners. They had been learnt in the process of years from many hands, and were constantly being added to, as he found them much more effective than Billingsgate. He vituperated till we were half way across the deck again; and the little man following said never a word. Once or twice he squirmed slightly at some specially choice bit in Chinese; but the English left him undisturbed.

Once on the saloon-deck the Old Man turned to me with a faint twinkle in his eye.

"Exhausting, isn't it, Doc? Got to sling it into them hot. Same every voyage. Filthy ruffians, aren't they?"

"They're a lot cleaner than plenty of English firemen I have sailed with," said the Chief, who felt this to be an oblique reflection on the engine-room staff, and, like every man worthy of his salt, wanted to stick up for his own.

"Never could see any good in any d——d foreigner, German, Dago, Nigger, or Chink," said the Old Man sturdily.

"Good old John Bull!" I murmured to myself.

"Don't you think so, too, Doc?" he said, turning to me.

"Thinking so is the secret of England's greatness," I answered diplomatically.

It was a beautiful clear day, with just a suspicion of chilliness in the air. The little wavelets lapped lovingly alongside. Ships passed us on either side, for we were in the regular ocean thoroughfare. Far out the white wings of a wind-jammer rose like a cloud on the horizon. The mate was busy for'ard. The Chief and I hung listlessly over the rail. One of the crew was getting the ship's sails out from the fore-peak to air them in the sun.

"Fat lot of good they'd be," said the mate, coming aft. "In the old days," he added regretfully, "they took the *Nestor* into Bombay under sail, when she broke down off Sokotra. We don't need sailors now. Look at those fellows for'ard. They might as well be painters."

Half a dozen A.B.s under the orders of the bo'sun were squatting on the main deck, with chipping hammers and cold chisels in their hands. They were all clothed in much-worn dungarees; and each carried the inevitable sailor's knife, in its sheath, stuck in his belt behind the right hip. In their headgear alone they showed variety of taste. Caps were predominant. Two wore broad-brimmed hats of what I afterwards came to know as

Samarang bamboo plait. The bo'sun, a morose, inarticulate Welshman with wild Celtic eyes, was resplendent in a tropical helmet, once white, and brass earrings. Months later, when I came to know him well, and caught him in a moment of expansion, I asked him what he wore the earrings for; and he told me they had cured him of moon blindness got on a "down-easter" sailing from 'Frisco to Montevideo. Now he was marshalling his men to start chipping the inside of the bulwarks; and soon the steady click, click, click of hammers resounded throughout the ship.

"She'll be painted three times over before we get back to Liverpool," said the mate.

"Why?" I inquired in surprise.

"Rust," he answered tersely. "Got to keep on painting. Salt water plays the deuce with iron. We took her into Liverpool a month ago, spotless, shining like a bride. In a week, with coal, and cargo, and careless handling, they made her look like a dirty old 'Geordie' (Newcastle tramp)."

"The soul of a mate is eaten up with paint. He thinks, dreams, and talks paint and nothing else from port to port," said the Chief.

"When I think of an engineer I think of oily smudges," retorted the mate.

"There you are, Doc. He divides the world into those who paint and those who spoil that paint. Didn't I say his mind was 'paintish'?"

.   .   .   .   .   .

All the next morning we were running down the coast of Portugal. The Old Man was in great form; we had stolen a march on the *Circe* in the night, keeping closer in, and he said we'd probably be able to signal Sagres before her.

As the morning grew we kept running closer and closer in, till at one o'clock we sighted Cape St. Vincent, with its Moorish-looking lighthouse on the top, perched on the extreme edge of the promontory. Painted bright yellow, with a tower at either corner, it looker for all the world like a child's wooden toy house at our distance from the shore.

But it was not the lighthouse we were making for. Round the corner, past the lighthouse, we came upon a round drum of a building with a flagstaff. The Chief and I gazed intently at it with our glasses.

"Sagres," he said.

As we swung round, the Old Man had had four coloured flags run up from the flying bridge. It was the ship's name in international code. We watched intently for the response. In the afternoon sun the station seemed as dead as the dodo till just as we came abeam, when suddenly a pennant of brilliant red and white broke and fluttered at the top of the flagstaff, stayed a few seconds, and then came slowly down again.

"That's the answer," said the Chief. "Your mother and mine, the Old Man's wife, and the Mate's will read in to-morrow's paper; 's.s. *Clytemnestra,* Liverpool for Yokohama, passed Sagres.' They won't know how it's done; but that's it. Let's go below. It's deuced cold."

Early in the grey of morning we passed the town of Gibraltar crouching below the dimly seen outline of the great rock fortress, Point Europa sending a half-seen questioning finger out towards us.

We were in the Mediterranean; and in a few hours I came to the conclusion it was distinctly warmer.

"It's no use thinking of deck-chairs yet," said the Chief, who, like most engineers, was a cat for comfort.

.   .   .   .   .

It was in the middle watch that night I got my first case.

"You there, Doc?" It was the third mate's voice.

"Yes. What's the row?"

"Captain's compliments, and one of the quarter-masters is delirious. Would you mind seeing him?"

I tumbled out shivering from the warm bunk, and hurried into some clothes.

"Where is he?" I said.

"For'ard. Port side. Third cabin!"

It was a little man from Inverary. He was crooning away to himself in the Gaelic, tossing his arms about. He felt like a furnace. I held the thermometer up to the light.

"How much?" said the third mate.

"104° F," I answered.

Together we went back, feeling our way along the deck. The night was very dark. An odd star peeped at us between the hurrying clouds. The square blackness of the deck-houses amidships loomed like the head of a threatening monster over us, the two forward lights of the captain's cabin glaring at us like lidless eyes unwinking from their midst. Above two smaller lights, closer together, showed dimly the towering height of the flying bridge, and the spectral figure of the officer on watch pacing steadily backwards and forwards across them. A faint glare at intervals shot up to the sky from the great funnel behind. Over the side we could hear the angry gurgling of unseen waters. We were like a ghost ship upon an unknown sea.

Something like this I said to the mate.

"Alone?" he said phlegmatically. "Not we! Look there!"

He pointed out to starboard; and there far out we saw a clear white light, with another behind it; whilst low down, appearing and disappearing at intervals between them, was a third light, dull red. It was the mast-head and port lights of a ship making the same course as ourselves.

I reported to the Old Man and turned in again.

．　　．　　．　　．　　．

In the night we passed Algiers. In the morning I found my patient much better. During the round that day I made up my mind there was something the matter with the Chinese cook. Had I breathed my suspicion to the Old Man, he would have ordered him up for inspection; but that was exactly what I did not want. Instead, I asked the Chief's advice. He was, in a way, the guardian of the Chinamen, and felt responsible for them.

"No," he said, "you're quite right. I think I understand Chinks. They have very little faith in European doctors; but they try every new ship's doctor at least once. If he happens to cure his first case, then the word goes round, This doctolh bolong good pidgin'; and everyone will come to him with any ailment he has. If he fails, in their opinion, they'll never come near him again, but will wait till we strike some Chinese port, and bundle off to one of their own men. They've got lots of queer stuff of their own in the fo'castle to dose themselves with, and of course, there's always opium."

"I see," I said.

Strolling for'ard again, I was captured by the Old Man. For some days previously we had been taking a two-mile walk together, measured as so many turns on the saloon deck. His idea was to reduce his weight, mine to get some exercise. But I had cooled off. He rolled so in his walk that we constantly impinged, a fact of which he was blissfully unconscious, being sixteen stone, and having the elasticity of an indiarubber man. I, on the contrary, was battered. It was not a fair contest. I began to make excuses. For a stout man he was unnaturally active; so during our walk I explained to him, between the collisions, that it was not exercise he wanted to reduce his weight—he took enough of that—but dieting. Accordingly I put him on a regimen that very day; and at tiffin he ate only about enough for two men. The mate was mildly sarcastic about it all. The Chief, on the other hand, was somewhat troubled, because the Old Man stated that he would be the lighter of the two before we reached Penang. To start fair we rigged up a bo'sun's chair on deck, had ourselves weighed, and I was appointed official "keeper of the records." The Chief affected disbelief in dieting, and gave it as his opinion that "Antadipose" was the stuff.

On the morning of the twelfth day we sighted Port Said. First came a lighthouse, and then some low-lying land.

"That's Damietta," said the Chief.

Then the land disappeared, as though it had been a mirage; and there was nothing but sea and horizon again, till quite suddenly another lighthouse flashed up. "That's it," said the Chief.

Straining our eyes in the dim morning light, we saw the Pharos, and surrounding it the dim irregular outline of low-lying houses. Picking up the pilot, we slowly approached, steaming in past the breakwater and the great statue of Lesseps, pointing with outstretched arm to the canal his genius had made possible. It might have been the Port of London. But no—suddenly we came on a scene the East alone could have evolved. It was a P. & O. coaling. Around the queenly long dark hull, with its lines on lines of port-holes punched out, as it were, and strung like pearls along the sides, clustered irregular rows of squat and grimy low-lying lighters; and up and down the improvised gangways from them to the ship, and back again, an ant-like stream of basket-carrying figures, dark brown, grimy, turbaned, petticoated, barefooted, swarmed endlessly, whilst all the time a murmuring shout ran with them. At the top of one of the gangways a tall white-robed figure stood reciting, in a loud monotone, verses from the Koran. It was this the swarming hive took up, and shouted as they ran: "La ilaha ill' Allah Mohammedu rasul Allah."

Slowly we moved past, and presently a steam launch, flying the Crescent and Star, with a crew in tall red tarbushes, came towards us. The crew gesticulated wildly, and shouted *"Docteur! Docteur!"* With true British phlegm no one took any notice. The gesticulations then grew more and more frantic; they drew alongside, and hooked eagerly on to the gangway. Then from the cabin of the launch a little Frenchman, swathed to the eyes in a huge overcoat, tripped aboard us, looking very cold and miserable in the raw morning. He was vastly polite, got our Bill of Health, bowed profusely, tripped down to his launch again, and steamed away. Down came the yellow flag from the foremast; and immediately on that signal a number of motionless bumboats pulled vigorously towards us. From every side they came —men in turbans, tarbushes, fezes, wide-trousered, long-coated, lean, brown-faced, brown-eyed, oily rascals, rowed by piratical-looking boatmen. They scurried up the gangway with their bundles, and fell on us, particularly me. They knew I was the doctor at once, my air of never-having-been-there-before giving me completely away. They wanted to sell me cigarettes, post-cards, Maltese lace, ostrich feathers, Florida water, Turkish delight. They wanted to cut my hair, mend my boots, guide me ashore, do anything or everything for me. They followed me round the deck. There was no peace from them.

"Say that Jock Ferguson is looking after you," said the Chief.

I did so.

It acted like a charm. They melted away. It was like the magic faery word that calmed the demons of the underworld.

"Who is Jock Ferguson?" I inquired.

"Ask me another," said the Chief. "Nobody knows who Jock Ferguson is. They're all Jock Ferguson. That fellow over there, talking to the chief steward, is the particular rascal I know as Jock. I don't believe there's any such person."

Certainly nothing could have been more unlike the name than the man. He was a tall, thin, coppery fellow, with exceedingly dark eyes. He wore a fez with a turban round it, a long grey overcoat, wide trousers, and long French boots.

"He's the most polished rogue I know. He cheats me every time I come here; and still I get everything I want from him. I owe him money now; and yet he will never ask me for it. He is an artist. You talk to him," said the Chief.

I did. He had a fluent command of both French and English. He told me in broad Scotch that he came "frae Pitlochry." He also got a prescription out of me for a cold in the head from which he was suffering. I bought two porous water-bottles (chatties) from him, for use in the Indian Ocean. One of them was cracked and use-less, I discovered, when I had reason to use it. He insisted on presenting me with a box of cigarettes. Sub-sequently I found I had bought 500 from him, though I do not care for Egyptians. I suppose he hypnotised me into buying them.

"Going ashore, Doc?" said the mate.

"Think so. How long have we?"

"Eight hours," he answered. "We've got to take in a thousand tons of coal, and we have six hundred tons of cotton alongside for Kobe."

"Anyone coming with me?" I inquired.

No one could. Everyone was busy. Jock Ferguson promptly offered me a guide; and presently I found my-self in a boat rowed by a picturesque old ruffian in a patched blue coat, wide blue trousers, bare legs and feet. Round his hoary old head he had wrapped what looked like the remnants of a Paisley shawl. My guide, who was very proud of his English, was somewhat more re-spectable. He wore a red knotted muffler round his fez, petticoats, and elastic-sided boots.

On shore I was guided past the Sudanese sentry—a most dignified black person in khaki marching to and fro with fixed bayonet—into the main street. Here my

dragoman, who had a vituperative acquaintance with
many similarly clad persons, rescued me from several
who wished to press their acquaintance and wares on my
notice. He wanted, evidently, to do all the cheating for
his master, and, if he could, for himself.

The shops were filled with the usual tourist rubbish.
They all looked like pawnbrokers' places. Everywhere
the notices were in French, the official language of Egypt.
The guide hailed a carriage for me. It looked as if it
had previously been used as a hen-roost. The horses
were mules, the harness an intricate mass of strings and
knots. The guide informed me it was the end of the
Ramadan—a month of fasting enjoined on all Mohammedans—and that everyone was holidaying in consequence. He advised going to see the Arab fair. This
was on the sands, past the new mosque, against the outer
wall of which one decrepit old gentleman was squatting
darning his trousers, taken off for the purpose, and several
others were lying apparently asleep. Presently we came
on the fair. There were boat-swings and roundabouts,
and a circus tent from which came the sound of frequent
pistol firing, and much shouting. It might have been an
English village green on a Bank Holiday save for the
boys in bright new tarbushes, and sloe-eyed little girls
very conscious of their new muslin frocks and the flowers
in their carefully braided long black hair, who ran about,
rode on the roundabouts, and hung around the stalls of
the sweetmeat vendors. Sugar-cane cut into lengths of
about a foot seemed to be especially appreciated by the
boys, who each chewed his piece as he scampered now
ahead, now behind his father. The little girls walked
sedately alongside their parents nibbling Turkish delight.

From the fair we drove to the native quarter, a place
of narrow streets, dilapidated lath-and-plaster buildings
teeming with multitudinous life, small native shops, laun-
dries, and little open cafés, where grave old men sat
cross-legged playing chess and smoking interminable cigar-

ettes. Most of the women seen about were old and wrinkled. They wore the veil in a negligent manner—it was no longer necessary to hide their beauties from the eyes of men. Once a young woman passed in the disfiguring yashmak, with its ugly brass cylinder over the nose and forehead. Girls in plenty were running around; but this was the only young woman seen. It is this scarcity of female charm that strikes the European so much at first, used as he is to the crowds of idle women gaping in the shop windows and blocking up the thoroughfares in the regions where "sales" (so called with sardonic humour) abound. From these narrow streets we came to a part where the houses looked mysterious, and the streets were curiously empty. It was the middle of the afternoon; and the place seemed buried in Sabbatical gloom. All the houses were alike, square, flat-sided, pierced by monotonous rows of windows, heavily guarded by strong Venetian shutters, each storey having its own verandah.

Suddenly, as we drew near one house, the strains of music came echoing into the empty sandy street. As if at a signal the decrepit chariot stood still, my guide got down, and suggested I should go in.

I thought rapidly, and then followed him. It was queer, and I wanted to know. He led the way upstairs into a large room where several men were playing roulette. No one took any notice of me; but apparently the bank were having a very bad time of it. Everyone was winning. The music from the automatic piano was deafening. I looked on silently for some time, and then made a move for the door. An oily-looking Greek intercepted me.

"Won't you try your luck?" he said.

"I'm not drunk enough," I answered.

He shrugged his shoulders, and I passed out. On the stairs I paused, and then stole quietly back. The music had ceased; and all the confederates who had been playing so feverishly, and winning so much, had ceased also, and were preparing to resume the *siesta* my advent had so fruitlessly interrupted.

The guide seemed disappointed. He climbed up slowly to the box beside the driver again, and we ambled on. Turning a corner, a woman's low laugh came soft and clear in the stillness of the sandy street; a face appeared for a moment on the verandah; and then there was a discreet cough.

Automatically the driver stopped. The guide turned round inquiringly; but I looked straight ahead. He said something, probably not complimentary; and the rickety old carriage with its two skinny mules ambled on again.

•   •   •   •   •

There are ugly stories about Port Said—it has an unsavoury reputation: stories of men winning large sums at the gambling hells and then mysteriously disappearing —the desert sand is a convenient place for the disposal of dead bodies; stories of drunken sailors supposed to be drowned on the way to their ships; stories of innocent English girls, eager to buy curios, setting out under the guidance of such a rascal as I had, and never appearing again—the secrets of the harem are well kept. Probably most of these stories are apocryphal.*

•   •   •   •   •

All day long we had been loading cotton for Japan. The coolies were very slow at it. It was the day of rejoicing after the fast; and extra inducements had had to be held out to them to make them work. It was also very cold and raw; and Egyptian coolies do not love the cold. Consequently it was late in the afternoon before it was all stowed.

Then we started coaling. Coaling is a nightmare. Plug your ventilators, fasten the doors of your cabin, screw up your ports hermetically, and yet the coal dust gets in.

* Later in the first World War we cleaned it up and made it as safe as Bayswater.

It came alongside in lighters; and from each boat two big heavy planks were raised to the bunker doors. Up one of these planks the half-naked coolies ran, each with his basket full of coal, after dumping which he ran down the other plank to the lighter again. We, too, had a long-robed patriarch chanting verses from the Koran. It seems the men work quicker under the inspiration of the chant, and the coaling company keeps a special reciter constantly employed. But the row is something indescribable. Night fell, and still the coaling went on. The lights from the cafés on shore came in long rippling streaks across the water; and through the windows could be seen figures passing and repassing. Sometimes, the sound of music, too, would come—but very rarely for the din of the coolies seemed to increase as the coal in the lighters sank lower and lower. Huge cressets burning on the lighters cast a lurid glare over the grimy, perspiring figures. It was like a scene out of the Inferno. They seemed to be working faster and faster; the voice of the chanter rose wilder and wilder; the coal in the lighters sank lower and lower. There was a sudden last shout, a sound of hurrying feet, everyone rushed to leave the ship, the planks were withdrawn, ropes cast loose, the empty lighters with their burning flares drifted into the night, and all was still.

Coaling was over. The Chief passed me, negroid with dust, where he had been measuring. I went on deck again. We looked like a Newcastle tramp. Grimy black hands had left their mark all over the spotless white paint of the deck-houses. The mate was snorting round, cursing softly to himself.

The stillness after the din was wonderful. Near the canal mouth a big German mail-boat, which had been coaling all day, had hoisted three lights on her foremast. That was the signal for the pilot to come aboard. Her three great decks were all aglow with serried rows of lights; and as she slipped silently past us, her huge searchlight throwing a blinding glare in front, a hose-pipe jerking water over the stern to shake off persistent bumboats, the music of her band came clear across the water.

"What are we waiting for?" I asked.

Our signal lights had been up some time, the pilot had come aboard, the electrician had got his searchlight going. The pilot explained that there were two mail-boats and a troopship just coming out of the Canal, and we could not start until they passed.

Presently the "stand-by" rang; the great searchlight in the bow burned bright; the ship seemed to wake up suddenly; and in another minute we were moving into night in the Canal.

CHAPTER II

THE INDIAN OCEAN

MIDNIGHT in the Canal is a sensation. There is an air of ghostly unreality about it. No sound is heard except the sizzling of the enormous searchlight hung over the bow close down near the water. Everything is dark save in the region of the cone of light. There is nothing to see but a narrow strip of illuminated water, fluorescent green, bounded on either side by unlimited dun-coloured sand. The ship crawls slowly on, raising scarce a ripple, following the line of buoys as they appear in the area of light, one after another endlessly in an interminable shadowy chain, making one count, owing to the absence of other objects, till sheer futility kills by inanition. I watched it all as a dream till suddenly a hoarse voice came from the bridge:

"All hands on deck. Make fast."

The telegraph rang clearly from the depths of the engine-room; and figures appeared in the darkness, fore and aft. The native boatmen rowed silently ashore, and made us fast to posts on the left bank. A bright light like a star, low down, appeared far in front of us, grew steadily larger, and at last showed as the searchlight of an approaching vessel, which itself looked like a gigantic glowworm in the faint halo rising from its dim-lit ports. There was not room for us both to keep our course; so we had had to tie up. It was a troopship homeward bound; and she passed so close that we could see the men through the open ports playing cards in the ease of un-buttoned tunics.

35

After that the course was clear, and we proceeded un-interrupted through the silent night.

In the morning I woke to find the sunlight streaming through my ports. It was a glorious day. The light air from the desert gave one a peculiar feeling of buoyancy. The land itself seemed forgotten of man—nothing but sand, far as the eye could reach—sand in ridges, sand in little flat plains, sand in hummocks and miniature moun-tains, with here and there a few solitary scrub acacias, adding, if possible, to the desolation.

Every now and then we would pass a big slate-coloured canal dredger, with its long arm erect, and its native crew lolling about, regardless of the inevitable Greek skipper.

Sometimes a little fussy C.S. tug-boat would steam cheekily past us at full speed, the native crew one wide-mouthed grin at us as we crawled painfully along at five miles an hour.

Suddenly we came on an Arab encampment on the edge of the Canal. Some dozen camels were kneeling, groaning audibly under the weight of their burdens in the foreground; further back were four ragged tents and one or two white-robed figures; whilst between, more camels, silhouetted against the skyline, were stringing off, driven by diminutive sturdy turbaned figures with shrill, important voices. One imp saw me preparing to photo-graph the scene, and posed himself in what he assumed was a dignified position, getting so excited that he fell into the shallow water on the edge of the Canal, from which he was rescued with much laughter by his com-panions.

In the early forenoon the Canal suddenly widened into a reach of shallow water; and the white roofs and minarets of a town appeared on the right, some miles away. This was Ismailia; and here we found the German mail-boat just ahead of us.

A steam launch heading across the lake circled round to us, took off our pilot, and gave us a second in his place. It is supposed to be too great a strain for one pilot to bring a ship the whole way through the Canal.

Soon we were off again between the narrow banks, proceeding slowly until we saw a clump of palm-trees, and low-lying houses, in the distance. A little jetty projected into the water; and overhead on the flagstaff we could see two black balls suspended.

"That's Deservoir, the last station before the Bitter Lakes, and the message is, 'All clear,'" said the mate.

As we came opposite we could see the stationmaster, his wife and daughter, sitting in the verandah under the shade of the palm-trees, dressed in their Sunday best, enjoying the Sabbath calm.

In another minute we had reached a broad expanse of water; the telegraph rang sharply; the ship seemed suddenly to wake; the orders were, "Full speed ahead"; and presently we were dashing across the lake for all we were worth, so that, looking back shortly afterwards, the station was a mere clump of feathery palm-trees on the horizon, with the white triangular sails of two *dahabeeyahs*, rising one on either side, a framework for the picture, against an azure sky fading to an opalescent green as it touched the desert sand beyond the edge of the horizon. All around was a flatness of water. It was an hour's run across the lakes.

"We should make Port Tewfik at four o'clock," said the skipper.

Accordingly everyone retired after tiffin to finish up his mail; and so things became distinctly ruffled when the unexpected order came: "Turn out. Make fast."

"Dash it all! We're only four miles from Suez," said the mate. There was a Canal station about a hundred yards ahead; Madame was its name.

"Just like a woman to do the unexpected," said the Chief. It was some consolation, however, to find that the German mail-boat was also held up.

"Half an hour," said the mate.

An hour passed. "Soon now," said everyone. Another hour passed. "Deuced odd," was the general comment. Another hour fled. There was nothing to do except stare at the mail-boat ahead. She was decorated with flags in honour of some German Royalty's birthday; and to while away the time the band discoursed sweet music of the Fatherland.

Drowsily the afternoon wore slowly on. A man came leisurely along the Canal bank and talked to our Greek pilot. Then we learnt that a lighter, loaded with stone, had most inconsiderately sunk in the middle of the channel, and it would be impossible to pass her till the tide rose.

"If England were at war and I were an enemy, the first thing I'd do would be to block the Canal," said the Chief. "It's as easy as falling off a log."

We paced slowly up and down the deck. Above us was a sky of luminous turquoise stretching in one huge vaulting arch from pole to pole of the horizon. On either side the hot and yellow sands, making the air vibrate above, tremulous in hazy, blurred outlines, stretched to the uttermost limits of vision, cleft only by the long green opalescent ribbon of the Canal. Surrounding us was an infinite quiet. Even the German orchestra had been abashed to silence by a feeling of the presence of the spirit of the Infinite—or perhaps because the music had run out. The Chief and I, too somnolent to walk any more, drowsily discussed the two hypotheses, lying in our deckchairs, our feet high over our heads on the taffrail. But even when we laughed, we laughed softly, for the feeling of immensity was over us, and we could in-tuitively understand how, nurtured in such great vast-nesses, the Semitic mind had risen above the futile poly-theism of the Greeks, and evolved the grand conception of a vast, omnipotent, omniscient and omnipresent God, with its necessary corollary, "There is no God but God."

On the fo'castle head the Arab boatmen, dressed in gaberdines of faded blue, brown-faced, white-toothed, with brilliant orange turbans, squatted round a hookah in somnolent content, waiting with the infinite patience of the East till it was the will of Allah that we should proceed further.

By this time the swift kaleidoscope of sunset was imminent. Above, the blue was still of an intensity; but towards the west it faded to the green of sea-encircled caverns lit by a morning sun along a chalk-cliff coast. Wisps of long-drawn cloudlets sailed slowly, rosy-pink in the middle heights; whilst on the ruddy path between us and the sinking sun the sands glowed golden, rose and jasper, and the ribbon of the Canal became a dimpled bronze. Slowly the Turneresque effect rose to a climax, until the sinking sun touched the rim of the horizon, sank rapidly, and disappeared; and then, as if at the touch of a wand, the gold, the rose, the blue, the green, melted to all the shades of grey, a little breeze sprang up from nowhere, and the soft mantle of night swept in layer after layer across the sky.

Over the sands the lights of Suez now twinkled in the darkness; and then quite suddenly, as if that had been the signal, orders came to get under way again. Everyone sighed with relief; and the great ship once more vibrated with the tremor of the throttled engines. Again the searchlight sizzled in the bow, and we were slowly moving on between the half-seen banks in the darkness.

Presently the channel widened, trees appeared dimly on the right bank, verandahed houses with twinkling lights loomed up amid the trees, the Canal suddenly ended, and we were in the open sea. This was Port Tewfik, named in honour of a late Khedive. Slowly we forged ahead into the bay, till the lights of Suez streamed across the water to us. Then a launch appeared, mysterious, moth-like, from nowhere, and bore off our pilot.

A voice rose in the darkness in a singing monotone:
"By the mark—seven."

It was the quartermaster heaving the lead. A sharp
order came from the bridge:

"Let go."

There was a rattle of chains, and the great bow anchor
splashed down into the bay. The electrician shut off his
searchlight and disconnected his dynamo. We had
finished with the Canal. Someone hailed us in the darkness; and another little launch appeared moth-like in the
circle of our lights from nowhere. The gangway was
rapidly let down, for this was the agent coming aboard,
bringing our mails and the final sailing orders for the
outward voyage. Out in the bay the lights of two big
liners, homeward bound, rippled over to us. One had
her searchlight ready, preparatory to entering the Canal.
Aloft she carried the red light which showed she had
His Majesty's mails aboard. The other had a row of
four white lights at her foremast head; and with these
she was winking in Morse code to the shore. A Black
Sea tramp steamer stole past us quietly in the night. A
little tug-boat puffed away officiously with the electrician
and his gear. The Old Man came out of his cabin with
the agent, who had our homeward letters in his port-
folio. Two ghost-like figures, they said good-bye at the
gangway head in the half darkness.

Then "Pleasant voyage," came a voice half-way down
the gangway.

"Thank you," said the Old Man, leaning over the rail.
"Good-bye."

"We'll be off in five minutes now," said the Chief.
"This is the original spot—'East of Suez'—where the
Ten Commandments stop. We'll be opposite Mount
Sinai, where they were made, when you get up to-
morrow morning, Doc."

The Old Man, turning to go on the bridge, heard
the remark.

"Humph!" he said. "They cease at Dover, Doc." The Old Man is one of those who consider Heaven is a British possession and ought to be coloured red on the map. The official language there, too, is English.

.   .   .   .

Next morning we were steaming steadily between the peninsula and the Egyptian coast. The land was rugged and mountainous on either side. It teemed with legendary sites of the Mosaic pilgrimage—the Well of Moses, the place of crossing of the children of Israel, the hoary head of Sinai rising from the clouds. Looking at the inhospitable land, one did not wonder that they longed for the flesh-pots of Egypt.

After breakfast No. 1 came to my cabin. He stood rigidly in front of me, his yellow old wrinkled face like a graven image.

"What thing?" I said.

"One man makee sick. No can," he answered solemnly.

"All right. Bring him along."

It was my first Chinese patient; and he had put on his dress of ceremony for me—pigtail free and carefully braided, loose black jacket and trousers, black shoes with thick white soles. His name was Cheong-wa. Taking him down to my surgery, I found he had a ragged ulcer on his breast-bone about the size of a two-shilling piece. They had been treating this by knuckling it all over, a kind of Chinese massage. As a consequence it was very much inflamed. Under treatment, however, it was nearly well in three days, and my reputation was made. I belonged "good pidgin."

Next morning I looked at the thermometer as soon as I was awake. It registered eighty-five in my cabin. The order therefore had come to don white uniform; port-holes were unscrewed, ventilators carefully set to the wind, and from somewhere my steward unearthed a wind-chute for my after-port. On deck the awnings had been put up, and a row of deckchairs arranged close to the companion hatch. Everywhere preparations were being made for the hot weather. It felt like the middle of summer at home. Looking at the calendar, it was difficult to believe it was the first week in February.

"This is the weather we sign on for. How do you like it, Doc?" said the second mate.

"I'm beginning to feel really happy," I answered.

"You're getting the best of it," he said. "This is winter in the Red Sea. Next voyage it will be stifling here."

"Have you left a hole in the awnings for the Doc to get sunburnt through?" the Chief inquired gravely of the mate. "Nobody'll believe his yarns when he gets home, unless he's burnt a bit."

The mate smiled sleepily. Both of us felt too comfortable to reply.

Picture to yourself three long white figures, stretched in deck-chairs, heels planted high above their heads on the rail, lazily watching the horizon move slowly up and down between the bars as the ship rolled in the calm sea, too lazy to speak, too lazy almost to smoke, with no one to worry them, nothing to do, conscious that all the time, in the little island at home, people were splashing through the rain and mud, shivering over half-dead fires, struggling with one another in the mad rush for wealth, backbiting, slandering, marrying, dying—ough!

I had a copy of the *Times*. It came aboard at Port Tewfik, and was already ten days old. Politics—the attitude of Germany, Protection, Free Trade—what did it matter? Nothing. The sea somehow has a wonderful power of correcting one's mental perspective. On land the immediate environment bulks so largely that man does not feel his littleness. At sea the fallacy of the near does not operate, one is just a point in immensity, and other things fall into correct proportion.

Our climate makes for a restless energy. We have to

fight with the elements, with the soil, with one another, to make existence possible. We are aggressive in consequence by heredity; we carry our aggressive spirit abroad with us; and the non-aggressive nations succumb before us. We do not stop to think whether it is of any benefit to ourselves or others. Action for action's sake has got into our blood; we cannot help ourselves; we must be doing something. As a rule we do not recognise that this ergophilia is a disease. We even boast of it as one of our special virtues, and talk of the races who have it not as decadent.

It is only when one gets dislocated from one's environment that one appreciates the other view—the view of a man on a camel in the desert, looking at the illimitable sand, knowing that simoom may come at any moment, knowing that no effort of his will eke out the supply of water, and no device augment the endurance of the camel on which his life depends. It is natural he should be fatalistic, just as the sailor on the high seas is fatalistic. It is contact with the elemental things, the feeling of the powers of the unseen, the helplessness of individual effort, that induces it. When the mate left us to struggle with the bills of lading, I fired off these musings on the Chief.

"It's the heat," he said sympathetically. "Have another iced lager."

"Base materialist!" I answered. "It's my shout."

. . . .

Next morning, after inspection, we had our second weighing. The Old Man had gone down eight pounds; the Chief was up two; the rest were about the same. The Old Man was highly delighted. There was only a difference of ten pounds between him and the Chief.

"I'll get below him before we reach Penang," he repeated.

The Chief smiled faintly.

"He'll get tired of it presently," he said. "I've seen

him at this game before. Let's go and watch for flying
fish. Bet you a bottle of lager I see more between now
and tiffin than you do."

He did. In fact, I couldn't see them at all. A hot wind
was blowing off the Nubian desert; the sea was a grey
mass of lumpy wavelets; the fish were not flying high;
and so my unaccustomed eye could not yet make them
out.

I professed a healthy scepticism as to their presence
which exercised the Chief to much pointing. The·mate,
with twinkling eyes, professed, too, not to be able to
see them. Finally the Chief proclaimed us conspirators
in a base plot to keep him thirsty. He had his revenge
that evening. We three were sitting in the mate's cabin
playing dummy bridge, with the ports wide open. Since
dinner-time the wind had risen steadily. The mate had
just said: "I leave it to dummy," and I was looking at
my cards, when I heard a curious smacking noise. Something wet and slimy had struck the mate on the face. It
fell wriggling on the card table. The mate drew his
hand in a startled manner over his cheek.

"Well, I'm——. It's a flying fish," he said.

"It's a special intervention of Providence to demonstrate
you owe those drinks," said the Chief solemnly.

You will have guessed he was a Presbyterian Irishman
—no one else could have been capable of such a remark,
made in all seriousness. Undoubtedly the argument was
with him.

Later, when we went on deck for a cool down before
turning in, we found that quite a number had been
blown on board. The Chinamen had collected half a
bucketful, and were going to make a feast of them in the
middle watch. In appearance they were like small
herring, with the lateral fin very much elongated.

"Let's sit an hour before turning in," said the Chief.

The tropical night at sea is something to be felt rather
than described. It is dark—inky dark, and yet not with

the unfriendly dark of Northern climes, but with an air
of warm encirclingness as of someone, unseen, beloved,
bending over one. The ship is a region of dim shadows,
faintly seen, pale lights casting hazy cones of brightness,
multitudinous sounds—here, there, everywhere, indefinite,
small—blending with the all-pervading monotone of the
screw.

Far out at sea a sudden point of light appears, flickers,
and goes out. That is an Arab dhow. The captain has
seen our mast-head lights, and the long row of port-
holes, shining like dragon scales along the water-line;
and he responds by burning a "flare," to show us where
he is, so that we may not run him down in the darkness.
He never carries lights. Why should he? When his
forefathers brought the Queen of Sheba to see King
Solomon in all his glory, they carried no lights; and
what was good enough for them is good enough for him.
All round the ship a wave of phosphorescence runs from
stem to stern, composed of myriads on myriads of flying
points of flame, rushing past, countless as the sands upon
the seashore, some as large as a five-shilling piece, others
mere specks of light. They are the souls of those who
have died at sea on their way to the grave of the Prophet.
All good Mohammedans pray for their repose; and we—
why should we doubt but that it serves? On such a
night as this one can believe anything. There are times
when one's antipathy to facts amounts to positive hostility.
Such a night was this. The wind was flapping the
awnings audibly in the darkness overhead; but it was a
wind from off the desert, and one could have dressed
as Adam and yet been comfortable. I lay back too
somnolent to move. A creaking indicated that the faint
area of whiteness that represented the Chief had shifted
in his chair. Then the light of a match illuminated his
face, tanned by many years of sun and wind and sea.
Without a word he, too, sank back in his chair again.
We had got past the stage when speech was necessary.

Suddenly from overhead a bell clanged—one—two—three—four—five. There was a pause; and then from the fo'castle head the signal was repeated, and the voice of the look-out came mournfully:

"All's well. Lights burning brightly."

The Chief's chair creaked again. He had got up.

"Come on, Doc," he said. "Mustn't go to sleep here. The night dews are very heavy in spite of the awnings."

At tiffin the next day the third mate came down to report "two small islands ten points to port."

"Keep her there, Mr. Matthews," said the Old Man, reaching out for another chop.

"Yes," he said, continuing the conversation, "every man ought to get married. I was engaged fourteen times myself."

"How often?" I said in surprise.

"Fourteen times," he repeated sturdily. "Got engaged mostly after every voyage when I got home; and found out something against them next time I got back. One girl I was particularly fond of was away at a race-meeting with a man I disliked when I arrived unexpectedly home. She cried like anything when I told her she would not do for a sailor's wife. An old sailor can't be happy at sea if he thinks his wife is gallivanting about with other men ashore. I took the ring off her finger. It's thirty years ago; an' she's a widow now; but she still sends me a Christmas card every year. I remember as if it was yesterday taking that ring off her."

"What did you do with it?" said the Chief.

"Dropped it overboard—dropped them all overboard except one. Couldn't give another girl a secondhand ring—could I?"

"Certainly not. But what about the one?" I said.

"Oh! that was when I was mate of the *Cyclops*. Old Mac—you remember old Mac?" turning to the Chief. The Chief nodded.

"Well, old Mac was chief of the *Cyclops* that voyage.

I was just going to pitch the ring out of the port when he came into my cabin. 'What's that you've got?' he said. I was a bit sore at the time, and I said shortly, 'Engagement ring. Girl no good. I was just going to pitch it overboard when you came in.' 'How much did it cost?' said Mac cautiously. I told him. 'I'll give you four pounds for it,' he said. Well, I thought I might as well have the money; so I let him have it. When he'd got it he didn't know what to do with it. He was a careful old fellow, and did not like the idea of wasting it. So he married a woman it fitted; and, do you know, the marriage turned out splendidly, though it was only because he had the ring the idea ever came into his head."

Later in the day we passed close to Mocha, of coffee fame. I was on the bridge with the Old Man at the time.

"Last voyage we called here," he said, "and the little Turkish doctor presented me with some of the precious stuff. I've got a little of it left. We'll sample it after dinner."

The steward made it as the doctor had shown him last voyage. It was thick treacly stuff, very black, very strong.

"There's more Mocha drunk every year in England alone than is exported from Mocha in two years, the Consul told me. Which thing is a mystery," said the Old Man.

"If we take twice as much as is produced, where does the rest of the world get theirs from?" I said.

"That is a secret which will only be revealed at the Last Day," the Old Man answered solemnly.

"Would you like to be called as we're passing Perim about midnight?" he said, as I was leaving.

I nodded; and so at "one bell" (11.45 p.m.) the quartermaster came to call me. Though it was blowing half a gale, the wind was so hot that even in thin pyjamas one felt quite comfortable. I climbed to the flying bridge, where I found the Old Man similarly clad, standing with the Second Officer, gazing at the low-lying island, seen dimly in the moonlight, with about a dozen lights dotted over it.

The Old Man turned. "See those two lights, Doc? Well, when we get them in line we're opposite the harbour entrance. Then we'll signal."

I watched in silence the lights grow closer and closer together as we swept onwards. All was very quiet. Suddenly—so suddenly I jumped—the quartermaster started to strike "eight bells."

By now the lights had almost met. "Ready, Mr. Horner?" said the Old Man sharply.

"Yes, sir," answered the Second Officer; and the two lights fused.

"Dead on. Light up," exclaimed the Old Man; and as he spoke, Horner, standing to the starboard side of the bridge, struck a fusee, applied it rapidly to the rocket-signal fastened ready, and immediately afterwards the whole ship was flooded with a bright blue glare. Then slowly, one by one, six blue balls of flame shot up into the night, exploded, and went out. Then all was dark again.

"Watch for the answer. There it is," said the Old Man.

A glimmer had started on the highest point of the island. It grew brighter, and then suddenly burst into a red glare, flared a moment, and was gone.

"That's all," said the Old Man. "My wife will know to-morrow that we've passed Perim safely. We've been married eighteen years; and she worries still. I cable her from every port."

Every sailor is a sentimentalist when women are concerned. He looks upon them as something too fragile and precious for this rough-and-tumble world, something to be guarded and protected from anything that would ruffle their rosy-tinted views of life. He sees so little of

them, when he is on shore, that in the long night
watches, with only the stars for company, he weaves
haloes of imagination around the very name of woman
till every petticoat becomes a Venus-Madonna.

"There are no bad women," the Old Man once
remarked to me. "When you hear of one, it always
means some man's doing."

"Did I ever tell you how we came to take Perim?" he
said, as we went down to the deck below to have a look
at the charts.

"It was a very smart bit of work, and meant a lot for
England. When we took possession it was an unknown
island. It is now one of the most important coaling
stations in the world. It was in the days before the
Canal was opened; and it belonged to nobody, or Turkey
—I suppose it was Turkey; but she didn't count. Well,
at any rate, we had a very wide-awake Governor at Aden
in those days. The French were building the Canal;
and a couple of French warships, coming round the Cape,
put into Aden for coal. The Governor was very polite
to them, did everything he could to make their stay
pleasant. There was a big dinner, to which all the
officers were invited, and a dance afterwards. Nobody
asked them where they were bound; but they volunteered
the information that it was Cochin-China. The wine
flowed freely; everyone had a good time; and they did not
weigh anchor till late in the morning. But they weren't
going to Cochin-China—at least not direct. They turned
up at the supposed unoccupied island of Perim, to find,
to their surprise, a flagstaff on the highest point of the
island flying the Union Jack, and a company of British
marines calmly exercising on the shore. That's how we
got Perim."

"But how was it done?" I queried.

"Oh, a woman! One of the young French officers
confided to a girl at the dance. She told the Governor's
aide-de-camp; and so, while the French slept, fifty men

were hurriedly embarked, and got there six hours in advance."

. . . . .

In the morning the blue hills of Aden smiled at us over a sunlit sea. The wind was blowly freshly, for it was the season of the north-east monsoon. We were making for Cape Guardafui, on the Somaliland coast, running down the Gulf of Aden; and all the next day we kept on the same course—an irregular line of blue low-lying hills representing Somaliland. Towards evening, however, the point of Guardafui became visible; and at ten o'clock in the moonlight, we passed it, crouching like a huge lion, black and silent, guarding the land of Ophir beyond. I was up in the chart-room with the Old Man at the time.

"We're in the Indian Ocean now," he said, pointing to the chart pinned out before him. "Now we'll alter the course to take us to the south of Sokotra, so as to have the shelter of the land while the north-east monsoon is blowing. We're making next for Point de Galle, in Ceylon."

So for the next week the monotony of the sea fell on us. Land we sometimes saw as an indefinite blue cloud; otherwise there was nothing but the calm, everlasting smile of the Indian Ocean. At first I used to look overboard; but soon I found myself doing so less and less; and then I noticed that the others almost never thought of gazing over the side. The sailor is almost unconscious of the great world of water around him as long as everything is going on all right; just as one becomes unconscious of the furniture in one's rooms when its position is not varied. It is only when some alteration strikes the eye and penetrates to the sensorium, that one becomes alive to the presence of inanimate things. As a consequence, however, of this out-world sameness I noticed I was becoming much more sensitive to the inner life of the ship, the technical details of its fittings, the speech and actions of the crew, the curious idiosyncrasies of the Chinese firemen.

Pidgin English takes some time to learn. There are no "r's" in it. By some phonetic difficulty they become metamorphosed into "l's," and "rice" therefore is changed to "lice."

China is such a vast, unwieldy country that several languages, or at any rate dialects, exist, so that the un-educated coolies of different provinces cannot understand one another. Pidgin English, which is a corruption for "business English," is therefore used in all the old treaty ports as a lingua franca; and one of the things that amuses the traveller most in the Far East is to hear two Chinamen of different localities gravely bargaining with one another in a language that irresistibly reminds him of comic opera. Most of our men were Cantonese; but we had one who could speak only his own dialect, and hadn't even any pidgin. This man happened to get a bad finger; and so the No. 1 hauled him up before me. I tried him in my best pidgin.

No. 1 shook his head.

"Bolong dam fool," he said, pointing to the man. "No can spik English. Bolong alleesame Swatow side."

I ran a sharp bistoury through his finger, and then looked at him keenly. It must have been exquisitely painful; but the mask never moved; the dark twinkling eyes never faltered. He did not utter a sound, or make a single movement.

"All right?" I said when all was over, and the finger dressed.

"All-li," he answered firmly.

"No can go bottom-side two-thlee day," I told the No. 1.

"All-li," said No. 1.

· · · ·

The Old Man was still keen on the idea of reducing his weight; so after breakfast on the next day he had

all the officers paraded on deck, a bo'sun's chair rigged
up, and again everyone's weight was solemnly taken
down. He was lighter by five pounds; the Chief was
still the same; and so there was only five pounds now
between them.

The Chief was evidently perturbed, though he tried
not to show it.

"You'll have to knock off beer if you don't want to
be overhauled," I told him.

"It isn't worth it this hot weather," he answered.
"Besides, I know the Old Man. He won't get below
me before Penang, and, once he goes ashore there, dining
a single night will set him off again—you'll see."

We spent the morning making deck quoits out of rope,
under the directions of the mate. He produced a fid for
the Chief, and another for me—a fid is a sort of wooden
marlinspike—and showed me how to push the point
between the strands of rope and splice the ends together.
The Chief was an expert. After several failures I
managed to produce a fairly respectable-looking one. In
the meanwhile the Chief had made five others.

"That ought to be enough," he said.

We marked out the scoring board in chalk on the
deck. It is so arranged that any three areas in line make
fifteen. Ten is taken off one's score if the disc falls into
the nearest square; and ten is added on for the furthest
away. The discs must lie entirely within the square;
and it is part of the opponent's game to try to knock them
out when they are favourably placed:

	4	3	8	
10 off	9	5	1	10 on
	2	7	6	

Dahabeeyahs in the Bitter Lakes

A Station on the Suez Canal

There is a special rule about end scoring that makes the game much more exciting near the finish.

We started playing in the first "Dog," the Chief and I against the Second and Fourth Engineers. The Fourth had a marvellously accurate eye. He seemed to be able to drop his quoit anywhere he liked. They beat us hollow.

The Chief dropped down exhausted in a chair. At that moment the Old Man passed us in his pyjamas on the way to his bath, looking like a boiled hippopotamus. He always had two hot baths a day in the Tropics, declaring it was the only way to keep cool. The Chief looked at the huge bulk of his retreating figure, and smiled.

"What is it?" I said.

"I'm thinking if I keep on playing quoits the Old Man won't have the ghost of a chance of getting below me," he said.

The Chief is distinctly wily. I remembered, on thinking back, it was he who first suggested the idea of playing quoits.

I do not think a European ever gets quite accustomed to the rapidity with which day merges into night in the Tropics. At "one bell" (5.45 p.m.) the Chief and I went below to get ready for dinner. At six o'clock it was broad daylight, "four bells" had gone, and the cook was late. We both went up on deck again to watch the sun, hanging like an immense molten red globe just over the horizon. As we watched, it touched the water (we almost fancied we could hear it sizzle) and began slowly to melt into a blood-red sea. When it had sunk half-way a black something, like a dog leaping for a stick, silhouetted itself sharply against the fiery disc behind. It was a dolphin leaping for flying fish. Three minutes later all was gone; the dinner bell rang; and it was still clear daylight. At ten past six it was so dark the stewards had to switch on all the lights in the messroom. When we went on deck again for an after-dinner smoke it might have been midnight. The stars were out, though the Southern Cross had not yet risen over the horizon.

As a constellation the Cross is a disappointment at first when one sees it, in the Red Sea, after leaving Suez. But it grows on one; one gets to look out for it like an old friend; one misses it when it's gone; and hails it with delight again when it reappears, as we did steaming south beyond the Philippines.

That evening, some hours later, as on many subsequent nights, we sat, and smoked, and looked at it shining down on us, dreaming the hours away till the clang of "five bells" brought us up regretfully.

"Let's go and see what the Fourth's doing before you turn in," the Chief said; and we got up slowly, moved cautiously along the dim-lit deck, and found our way down the series of break-neck ladders to the engine-room floor, where the Fourth was walking to and fro keeping his watch, pausing to look now at this, now at that, whilst a silent greaser, oilcan in hand, crept here and there, in and out, oiling, oiling, oiling all the time.

"We've tried mechanical oilers time and again; but they're no good," said the Chief. "They're a heartbreak. Oiling requires intelligence."

The Fourth stood quietly immobile while the Chief was around. He had nothing to say except "Yes, sir," and "No, sir," to any of his questions. The Chief had never seen him, as I had, the centre of a laughing group, springing some quaint conceit or laughing retort on those around.

"Nice steady fellow," he said to me, when we had gone on deck again; and I agreed.

"Bit slow," he added; and I smiled in the darkness, having seen him imitate the Chief's gait and manner to the life that very afternoon.

Ash Wednesday is the Chinaman's New Year; and

there was a general air of holiday when we arrived at
their fo'castle on inspection. They had had extra rations
of pork served out to them, and a present of some live
ducks. Consequently every face was one large grin.

"Have got samshu?" said the Old Man.

No. 1's face clouded with regret.

"No have got samshu," he said.

Samshu is a kind of alcoholic drink beloved of the
Chinese. The Old Man was in high good-humour.

"All right. Tell Chief Steward can have beer. One
man, one pint beer. Savvy?"

No. 1 grinned widely. His eyes glistened with antici-
pation.

"I savvy. All-li," he said.

When we went up on the poop to look at the Patent
Log, a series of concerted yells came out through the
ventilators.

"They're driving away the devils we introduced when
we entered just now," said the Chief. "Polite, aren't
they! Crackers would have been better; but they haven't
got any."

Next morning at breakfast the Old Man remarked:
"We should sight Pulo Wai at ten o'clock to-night. That
means you can have your breakfast ashore in Penang two
days hence, Doc."

Then he turned to the Chief.

"I should like a chit some time this morning, Mr.
Halahan, saying how much coal you have."

"Very well, sir. I'll measure the bunkers after
inspection."

A few hours later the Chief threw himself down on
a deck-chair beside me.

"Ever heard of coal fever, Doc?"

"It's not in the College of Physicians' List," I confessed.

"Dare say! Deuced nasty thing to have, all the same.

The Old Man showed signs of it this morning when he asked for that chit. He had his reasons."

"What's the main symptom?"

"A dread of not having enough coal to bring the ship into port. The ship's company got it badly last voyage, I'm told. They had cause to. They were carrying pilgrims from Jeddah to Singapore; and the 'tween-decks had had to be kept empty. Consequently they took only what coal they absolutely needed at Port Said. The Chief, a man named Todd, said he had three days' supply when the ship was then where she is now. In the middle watch he came to the Old Man:

" 'I've miscalculated by fifty tons, sir,' he said.

"They had passed Pulo Wai by that time; and the Old Man was frantic. 'You've what?' he said.

" 'I've miscalculated by fifty tons, sir,' the Chief repeated.

" 'What the devil are we to do?' the Old Man said, marching up and down his cabin in his pyjamas in an agony.

" 'I've shut down one boiler, sir.' The Old Man stopped and stared at him.

" 'Can you make it do?' he shouted. 'If you can't, by God, you're ruined in the company. It's as far back to the coal depot in Pulo Wai as to Penang. Man, if we have to be towed in I'll never be able to hold up my head again. How the h—l did you manage it!'

"They went on. I don't envy that Chief. He came up to report that all the coal was in the stokehole; and there wasn't a sign of land in sight. The ship was swept of coal—every bit scraped together as if it had been diamonds. They crawled along at four knots.

" 'We'll have to cut up the derricks," the Old Man said with a groan.

"But they managed it—how they hardly knew. Steam ran out just as they reached their moorings. There wasn't

enough coal left to start the donkey boiler. They had
to have some sent from the shore."

"What happened to the Chief?" I said.

"Officially it was announced there was eight tons left.
Decent of the Old Man—wasn't it?"

That night we sighted Pulo Wai, an island on the
north-west point of Sumatra. The Old Man by this time
had got into the habit of sending for me when anything
interesting was about; and, standing with him and the
second mate on the bridge, we peered forward into the
night.

The second mate had the best eyes of the three.

"There it is, sir," he said suddenly.

The Old Man looked. "Yes," he said.

I confessed that I could see nothing.

"We're forty miles off. It's a five-second flare every
minute," said the Old Man. "Watch carefully over that
second ventilator on the fo'castle head to starboard.
Time, Mr. Horner?"

"Ten seconds still, sir."

Presently he snapped his watch. "Now, sir."

It came, a glow far out on the edge of the horizon;
then suddenly burst into a bright light like that of a
falling star, and as suddenly went out again.

Sixty seconds fled, and again it was repeated.

"That's all, Doc," said the Old Man. "I'll run in as
close as I can to let you see the Achin coast in the
morning."

He was as good as his word. At "seven bells," on
the way to my bath, I saw the coast rising wild, rugged,
and mountainous all along for miles behind and in front
of us, culminating inland in one great peak, the Golden
Chersonese, from which the fabled gold of Ophir is said
to have come. It is a wild and rugged land, this Achin—
a land of old romance. Once the seat of a mighty
empire, its sultans made treaty with Queen Elizabeth.
Under its great leader, Iskander Muda, it raised an

armada of five hundred sail, manned by 60,000 men, to
fight the Portuguese. It was by the aid of the Achinese
the Dutch eventually took Malacca, broke the power of
the Portuguese, and established their ascendancy in the
Malay Archipelago. That quaintly pious buccaneer, the
inimitable Dampier, sailed in a native prau from the
Nicobar Islands to Achin, after he had been marooned.
He says:

"Being now arrived at Achin again, I think it not amiss
to give the reader some short account of what observations
I made of that city and country. This kingdom is the
largest and best peopled of many small ones that are up
and down the isle of Sumatra. . . . There is one hill
more remarkable than ordinary, especially to seamen.
The English call it the Golden Mount, but whether this
name is given it by the natives, or only by the English,
I know not. 'Tis near the N.W. end of the island; and
Achin stands but five or six miles from the bottom of it.
'Tis very large at the foot, and runs up smaller towards
the head; which is raised so high as to be seen at sea
thirty or forty leagues. This was the first land that we
saw coming in our proe from the Nicobar Islands. The
rest of the land, though of a good height, was then
undiscerned by us, so that this mountain appeared like
an island in the sea; which was the reason why our Achin
Malayans took it for Pulo Way. . . . But that island, tho'
pretty high champion land, was invisible, when this
Golden Mount appeared so plain, tho' as far distant as
that island."

It was a land of much gold, and great trade, in those
days. The ubiquitous Chinaman was then, as now, the
chief trader in the Far East; and a great fair was held
in June every year, lasting two or three months. The
laws of the country were very strict. Malefactors were
severely punished—arms and legs were cut off—and they
were generally banished to Pulo Wai; so that "on Pulo
Way there are none but this sort of cattle; and tho'

they all of them want one or both hands, yet they so
order matters that they can row very well, and do many
things to admiration, whereby they are able to get a live-
lihood."

But all this is a thing of the past. The glory is departed. No longer have the sultans droves of 900 tame
elephants. The hand of the Dutch has fallen heavily
on the Achinese. For more than two hundred years they
lived at peace under the shadowy protection of England.
Sixty years ago that protection was withdrawn in return
for some barren concessions in Ashanti. England gave
up all her historic rights in the huge island of Sumatra;
and the Dutch immediately picked a quarrel—the quarrel
of Naboth. It is probable that in the same position we
should have done the same*; for truly we cannot afford
to cast reflections on the Dutch, since as land-grabbers we
are easily supreme. Besides, the Dutch share our genius
for governing and colonising, if indeed they do not excel
us.

The Dutch have taken two hundred years to spread
over Sumatra. They have been fighting the Achinese
for fifty years, and have not conquered them yet. They
have lost thousands of men through wounds and disease
in Achin, these natives proving unexpectedly difficult to
"pacify," the spirit of their ancient fame evidently sur-
viving the decay of their body politic.

Eventually, of course, they will be civilised. At present they have a very uncivilised habit of thinking the
Dutch robbers, and treating them in the way their forefathers treated malefactors in the time of Dampier. When
they capture a Dutchman they return him minus a nose
or limb; and the Dutch do not like it.

When we were going into Batavia some months later,
we passed a troopship bound for Padang, crowded with
soldiers to hurry up civilisation. Perhaps you wonder
why the Dutch are bothering about it at all. The answer

*We seem to have done it in Sarawak.

is that there are great quantities of gold and tin and oil in the interior which the Achinese will not let the financiers get at—very childish of them, and very irritating to the financiers. So more and more drafts of fine, big, boyish, Dutch soldiers are being sent out from Europe to die of fever in the swamps, in order that the financiers may get at the gold more quickly—that is to say, in order that "they may have an opportunity of opening up the resources of the country, and of bringing peace and security of life and property, under the ægis of the Hollander flag, to a country erstwhile torn with internecine strife." Substitute the Union Jack for the Dutch tricolour, and it is obvious that, if we claimed Sumatra, we would be doing exactly as the Dutch are doing now.*

* The more recent history of Java and Sumatra since the defeat of Japan, and the claims to independence of the native races in the Netherlands East Indies, will be fresh in the memory of all.

CHAPTER III

PENANG

NEXT morning someone shouted down my ventilator, "Hi, Doc! Get up! We're in sight of Penang."

It was about half-past six; and I rushed on deck as I was. This was what I had come 8,000 miles to see, and every moment lost seemed wasted. It was twenty-one days since we had touched solid ground; and my feet ached to be ashore again.

The first impression was of a wonderful green: the land seemed smothered in vegetation. It rose precipitous from the water's edge, crag upon crag of naked rock jutting out grey amongst the green, with here and there the white outlines of verandahed bungalows, perched perilously on the heights, which, half hidden in the verdure, rose higher and higher, and culminated finally in one great peak 2,700 feet above the sea.

Passing Muka Head, a promontory on the extreme north-west end of the island, we swung round a red buoy for Georgetown, running between the island and the mainland. The deep blue of the Indian Ocean had ceased; and the water was a milky white. The mainland, known as Province Wellesley, once part of the kingdom of Kedah, was a green belt of palm trees, fringing a yellow strand, stretching back to the blue hills behind.

All around us lay crazy-looking fishing praus, with batwing palm-leaf sails, brown and yellow, patched to the limit of patchiness, manned by half-naked, copper-coloured Malays. Stakes sticking out in the water in rows showed where they hung their nets.

61

All along the yellow strip of sandy shore on the Penang side, hidden amongst the green of the palm trees, the brown thatched atap-roofs of native huts drew one's eye to the houses standing on their bamboo props.

Breakfast over, I watched the panorama spread before me: Rat Island with its column and its solitary Buddhist priest, the undulating outline of Penang, the dark green of Province Wellesley, and over all the deep blue sky.

We anchored opposite the jetty in thirteen fathoms of water; and the first thing that struck us was that it had suddenly become intensely hot—we were no longer making a breeze for ourselves. The next impression was that we were being boarded by pirates. They came from every side, sampan racing sampan for which would be first to reach the lowered gangway. They tumbled on deck in heaps from every quarter. In five minutes they had penetrated to every corner of the ship—Parsees, Malays, Klings, Chinamen and Eurasians. There were money-changers with bags, clinking the large silver Straits Settlements dollar, cigar merchants selling Burma cheroots, tailors wanting to measure one for white suits, men with fruit of tropical lusciousness, boys with the inevitable picture-postcards.

Almost before the engines had stopped a series of lighters, with great bamboo masts and yards, began to arrange themselves around the ship. Scores of brown, half-naked, turbaned coolies swarmed on board, opened the hatches, and with naked feet on the levers started the steam winches running. In an almost incredibly short period after our arrival cargo was going over the side into the empty lighters, and khaki-clad Chinese tally-clerks in puggarees, standing one at each hatch, were checking the loads as they rose from the hold.

The heat was sweltering. Everyone was busy—the officers looking after the cargo, the Old Man closeted with the agent, the Chief seeing about the supply of fresh water which was being pumped from lighters into the tanks.

The Chief Steward was going ashore to order fresh provisions; so we took a sampan together. The sampan is the universal boat of the East. It varies slightly in different places; but materially it is a cross between a gondola and a punt. In Penang it is rowed with two broad sweeps, the rower, or rowers standing erect facing the direction of progress.

Our man rowed with a powerful swing against the tide, the muscles of his arms and legs rippling underneath the coppery skin like a living bronze statue, his face in deep shadow underneath his sugar-loaf palmetto hat.

He ran us neatly alongside the landing stage, crowded to overflowing with passengers coming and going, and loungers looking on. A detachment of Sikhs belonging to the Malay Guides had landed in front of us. They were forming up on the pier as we got ashore, tall, grave men, eagle-featured, bearded like the pard, very gorgeously Oriental in their uniform, towering head and shoulders over the little Malay troops alongside.

A bronzed English officer at their head uttered a sharp, quick word of command; and like a machine the whole mass moved forward up the pier, like a wedge through a lane of brown and yellow faces.

We followed in their wake. It was with difficulty I could persuade myself that I was not looking on at a theatrical performance—the cosmopolitan crowd composed of every nation in the East appeared so tricked out for effect, the vivid colouring of the Orient smote the eye so insistently. Impressions followed one another so rapidly that, when I tried to recollect them afterwards, my mind was a confused palimpsest of primary colours and grinning Celestials—for the Chinaman is everywhere, he makes up more than half the population, he apparently does nearly all the work, and he evidently has the monopoly of retail trade.

When we got to the bottom of the landing stage we saw two long rows of rickishaws, one on either side. The owners of the nearest two leapt across the road, whirled their light vehicles round, and stood grinning till we each mounted. They too were Chinamen. All the rickishaw men in the Straits Settlements are Chinese. The Malay is much too lazy to compete with them; nor has he the physical stamina.

My man was dressed in bathing drawers, a sugar-loaf hat, and a broad smile. The calves of his legs and the muscles of his back were an anatomical joy. The other man wore a loose *baju* jacket as well.

They stood holding the shafts of the rickishaws, waiting for directions where to go. I had not yet acquired any knowledge of Malay; so I shouted to the Chief Steward: "You tell them where to go. Anywhere's the same to me." He did so; and we whirled off.

Malay is the lingua franca of the Settlements. Everyone speaks it—Chinese, British, Dutch, Indian. It is the simplest language in the world to learn, and one of the most beautiful to hear spoken. The Malay has wakened up to find his land taken from him, his country invaded by every nation on earth; he has shrugged his shoulders, and gone to sleep again; but somehow or other he has imposed his language on the conquerors. When a Dutch planter from Sumatra comes over to Penang on business, if he does not know English, he talks to the English clerks in the offices in Malay; when he traffics with the wily Chinaman he does the same. The Malay is so lazy his language must be simple. If it were otherwise he wouldn't trouble to speak. There is a "Pukka Malay" used in literature, and in addressing high native dignitaries. It is studied by learned pundits, and spoken in the presence of rajahs; but that does not concern the man in the street—he uses the vernacular.

We sped along wide open streets, lined by Chinese

shops, past patient oxen dragging springless carts, past
itinerant merchants carrying their stock-in-trade in large
hemispherical baskets, slung, one on either end of a long
bamboo pole, over one shoulder, and held by the corresponding arm, whilst the unoccupied hand worked a
wooden rattle to attract the attention of possible customers, past big Sikh policemen, who gravely saluted when
we paused to look at them, past Chinese temples, dragon-
haunted, lantern-hung, along a gaily decorated road, past
an open space where little pigtailed Chinese boys were
playing football, barefooted, with the temperature at 95°
F. Other rickishaws met us, carrying pale-faced Europeans dressed in white, with pith helmets like ourselves. They all stared at us. Sometimes a passing
rickishaw would carry a portly Chinese merchant, or a
Chinese woman with death-like, white-chalked face and
henna'd lips, or little Chinese girls with tinsel crowns
and flowers in their hair—for the celebration of the Chinese New Year was not yet over.

A young man in a passing rickishaw craned round
as I sped by, shouted something, and my runner stopped.
His man turned round.

"Well, I'm jiggered!" he said.

"Me too, Henderson," I answered; and naturally so
since I had not seen him for eight years.

"What on earth brings you here?" he said.

"Ship's surgeon. And you?"

"Rubber! Perak! Hole of a place! Spend my time
gently persuading my Chinks with a revolver not to run
away to the tin-mines in too great numbers for my directors' comfort. Sick to death of it. I'm over here for a
holiday."

"It's a bit of a change from reading for the Bar," I
hazarded.

"Moral suasion for legal suasion," he said. "Always was
fond of the bar," he added sardonically.

I had been trying to remember what it was. Of course
that was it: "Too fond of the bar."

"Who's your pal?" he said.

I looked up. The Chief Steward's runner had stopped,
and turned half round. The world, after all, is a small
place; and one's faculty for astonishment quickly ex-
hausts itself. We pulled up alongside him.

"I wasn't sure if it was you when you passed; and I
looked round," said the Steward. "I was surprised,
though, to see you talking to our doctor."

Henderson had been staring at him. Then his eyes
brightened suddenly.

"Gee whiz," he said. "Why, it's Bruce." He turned to
me: "D——n it. We went through the Cuban war together, fighting for the Yanks. This bangs Banagher.
Come on, you fellows."

He gave an order in fluent Malay, and soon we were
stringing after his rickishaw along the straight white road.
Turning a corner, we sped for a short distance along a
quiet side street, and finally drew up at the porticoed
doorway of a restaurant. He led the way into a big,
cool, columned room with an open roof, and a fountain
of running water in the centre of the marble floor. There
were lots of little marble-topped tables and Indian cane
lounges around; and it was a great relief after the glaring
sunshine outside to drop limply into a chair, and listen
to the grateful splashing of the water. Already the other
two were rapidly comparing reminiscences, and retailing
subsequent experiences. The proprietor now appeared,
a smiling, soft-footed Hungarian. It was evident Henderson was *persona grata* in the house.

"My shout! What'll you fellows have?" he said. Presently the proprietor's daughter appeared, very plump,
very dark-eyed, very pale-faced, very black-haired. Again
it was evident that Henderson was very much at home.

She sat and chatted with us amiably, with a large,
good-natured coquettishness: Had we seen the decora-

tions? Weren't they fine? What! We didn't know
what they were for! Hadn't we heard the Duke of
Connaught was to be here on Monday, coming up from
Singapore? Ah, of course we had only arrived that
morning. Penang—no, it was not as gay as Singapore;
but then Penang had the Crag. The Crag was delightful
—so cool; Singapore people envied them the Crag; they
had no place where they could get cool. We must
really go and see the Crag. She talked on easily. We
were half somnolent. Her big dark eyes turned from
from one to the other eloquently. She moved her plump
hands, dead white with subcuticular duskiness, as she
talked. Once she touched Henderson's casually; and he
raised his eyes to hers. When she moved, her body fell
into voluptuous curves. Her thick round lips smiled continuously. She betrayed her native blood in the swinging
silence of her movements, in the deferential, eager way
she listened to any casual remark of ours, in her Oriental
taste in scents, in her look of perfect ease in the heat,
in the almost imperceptible oiliness of her skin, in the
deft way she managed her cigarette, in a thousand-and-
one other little ways that could not be defined.

After an interval I caught the Steward's eye.

"I must be going! I've got to see the ship's comprador, and get back," he said.

"Me too," I said.

Henderson protested. Why hurry? It wasn't every day,
etc., etc. He was very comfortable, and why shouldn't
we make an evening of it? He didn't feel inclined to
move. The daughter of the house dropped her big black
lashes over her big dark eyes, and smiled. Her fingers
under the cover of his glass pressed Henderson's for a
moment, and were gone. No! He was dashed if he'd
move! Let the rickishaw men wait. That's what they
were for. Well, if we must be going—see us again to-
morrow. No! Filled up to-morrow! Well, perhaps next
day! It wasn't every day one saw one's pals, etc., etc.

We left it at that. He ordered another drink, and lay back. I turned to the doorway. The dark-eyed daughter of the house was handing it, leaning over him, smiling down into his eyes.

We did not see him again. The world is full of Hendersons. I remembered his people—his nice old mother, his two proud sisters—and wondered what they would think if they could see Henderson, sitting soaking at the other end of the world, smiled on by the half-caste daughter of a saloon-keeper. Perhaps it was just as well they did not know. Sometimes I have idly wondered since what became of Henderson. Probably he went back to Perak to make dividends for you and the other people who dabble in rubber. Sometimes I have wondered, did the dark-eyed daughter of the saloon-keeper go with him? Perhaps not. Perhaps, after all, it never came to anything. Perhaps he died. I shouldn't wonder. People like Henderson do not last.

　　　　·　　　　·　　　　·　　　　·

We found the ship's comprador, a big greasy Bengali, having his afternoon *siesta,* and, the ship's business done, turned for the pier again. The Steward's rickishaw stopped suddenly, and I drew level.

"Say, Doc! That's a Japanese tea-house. Would you like to go in? It'll not be quite the thing; but you'll get an idea before we get there."

We entered into a stone hall. A brick staircase ran up from it, the steps washed as scrupulously clean as an operating theatre in a hospital. Three pairs of Japanese sandals lay on the lowermost steps. We mounted, and found our way into a room looking on the street. There was no glass in the windows, string bead-curtains letting in a subdued light. The room was without furniture, except for a divan, and a round table in the centre of the floor. Presently a petite figure shuffled in, smiling joyously, showing her beautiful white teeth, her little white tabi peeping below the grey kimono, her slit-like eyes

twinkling, her coal-black hair a *cheval de frise* of combs.
She brought us chairs to sit on.

"We won't get these in Japan, nor the table either," he
said.

"Coffee?"—Yes, we could have coffee.

She tripped away to get it. It came in two cups, like
those one sees in restaurants used for Bovril, one labelled
"Remember me," the other "Forget me not." There were
things with them like china medicine spoons.

"This is not in the picture," he said.

While we had our coffee she sat cross-legged on a
cushion on the divan, smoking a cigarette out of a little
Japanese pipe, and conversing with us as if she had
known us all her life.

"That's all right," he said.

I looked on as a spectator while he talked. I was
beyond my depth in the bandied Japanese expressions.
What I could make out was this:

"Belong Yokohama? No savvy Yokohama. No savvy
Kobe. No savvy Nagasaki. Savvy Penang." Apparently
she had been born in Penang.

"Make love? No savvy. No can. Number 1 fine
girl house opposite—she all right; me no good. Have got
sweetheart? No savvy," smiling all the time.

"This is not in the bill either, Doc."

It was all strange to me; but I was learning.

. . . . . .

On board the ship, when we got back it was vastly
more cool; but the noise was incessant. The simplest
manœuvre seemed to require an enormous amount of
shouting among the coolies. Everyone gave his opinion;
no one paid any attention to that of the other; but the
work went on relentlessly, for the company has its reputation to keep up of clearing cargo more quickly than
any other in the East, working, as they do, night and day
in every port. At intervals whole gangs would cease, and
squat down in circles around the curry-cooks who pre-

pared their periodic meals in various corners of the ship, beating up the fresh curries in great wooden bowls held between their prehensile toes. Afterwards they would fall to again with renewed vigour; another lighter would be filled; and, raising its great bamboo yard and latticed sail, glide quietly off in the eye of the westering sun.

These coolies are not Malays. They are locally known as Klings, and are imported from the Deccan in Southern India. The Malay would scorn to labour as they do. He has the aristocratic contempt for toil which Mohammedanism seems to breed in many races. He does not mind being a policeman; for then, with his thin rattan, he can beat any Chinaman he has a special grudge against with impunity. He likes being a soldier, swaggering in uniform, and letting off a gun occasionally. He cannot understand the rooted objection we have to his being a pirate; it is one of his lasting regrets that this pleasant method of adding to the gaiety of nations is no longer permissible. It is only within recent years it has been stopped in British waters; it still occurs sporadically in Dutch territory. The pilot who brought us into Singapore told us some things about these pirates. What he did not tell us was that his own wife had been butchered before his eyes, when he was captain of a coasting schooner, and his ship taken one moonless night, thirty years before.

"He never speaks of that," said the Old Man.

The Malay has a vast contempt for the Chinaman. In the old days when he owed him money, and the Chinaman worried him for payment, that Chinaman was removed; he joined his ancestral ghosts. We have stopped all that too, very abruptly and painfully; the Malay doesn't quite understand why. It seems so obviously the right thing to rob the infidel; the pigtail seems so specially designed to be caught hold of; and the nice wriggly kris the weapon foreordained for the work. He cannot see why we should object. Still, he does his best to bear

us no ill-will. It is obvious we do not know a good
thing when we see it. Our short-sightedness grieves
him. He is sorry for us.

The Malay is, of all things, a philosopher. He squats
in the warm sun and chews betel contentedly. He sees
the obvious foolishness of working in a country too hot
for toil, when the earth is so prolific that a fortnight's
leisurely labour will produce food for a year, and the
water so plentifully supplied with fish that an hour, in
the cool of the evening with a net, will supply luxury
for a fortnight. He looks with a contemplative pity at
the yellow man toiling in the heat of the day, and with
continual surprise at the white man for not appropriating
the fruits of the yellow man's labour, since he so obviously
has the power to do so.

. . . . .

I sat in my deck-chair watching the harbour lazily. It
was a continuous panorama of things strange, bizarrely
curious.

A huge Chinese junk, looking like a model of the
Great Harry, with enormous painted eyes on either side
of her bow to see with in the night, and a castellated struc-
ture in the stern, reminiscent of Elizabethan romance,
dropped anchor a couple of cable lengths away, and
quickly made her presence felt by the odour of rotten
fish brought to us on the land breeze. Sampans and
little steam launches shot continuously backwards and
forwards across the harbour. A long black boat under
great cone-shaped sails glided rapidly past. It looked
snakishly wicked and fast. Afterwards I grew familiar
with the type. It was a Bugis prau from Macassar, where
I saw hundreds of them; and was the kind of boat
beloved of the now extinct pirates.

Presently a big P. & O. from Singapore came across
our field of vision, with the Blue Peter flying at the
fore, dropped anchor, swung down her gangways, discharged some passengers, picked up some more from the

tender, took in a sampan-load or two of fruit, weighed anchor, and was off again.

A crowd of sampans drew away from her as she started; and the sound of bursting crackers came from several of them. They were Chinese sampans; and their owners were thereby frightening away any devils that might have managed to slip unobserved from the P. & O. to them— that kind of devil being known to be particularly malevolent.

Abaft the galley a sampan had hitched on to a lighter. It was evidently the home of a complete Chinese family, any one of whom, except the baby in arms, was capable of working the boat. The eldest daughter of the house, alone in the boat, was busy preparing a meal, apparently a feast. She had got a chicken, and, after the manner of the Chinese, had cut it up, preparatory to cooking, into innumerable small pieces, washing every portion carefully, wasting absolutely nothing—not even the head and feet. Everything finished, she placed the portions carefully on a platter, and went aft to do something. I happened to be leaning over the rail near the galley at the time. Unfortunately the Fourth Steward also appeared, at that moment, on the well-deck below. He had been cleaning up the "Glory Hole"; and, contrary to all regulations, port and ship alike, without ever looking over the side and before I could give a shout of warning, he suddenly shot a whole bucketful of filthy, greasy water over the gunwale. It caught the sampan; it caught the dish; it caught the carefully divided chicken, fair and square; and the whole collection was swept neatly into the water, where it rapidly floated away in the tide. I shouted, of course, when it was too late. With chap-fallen face the steward gazed over the side. A storm of abuse greeted him from that sampan. She cursed him, his father and mother, sisters and brothers, uncles and aunts, ancestors to the third, offspring to the fourth generation. The steward fled. She looked then as if she meant to turn the vials of her wrath on me; but a big Singapore dollar, dropped into the boat, altered the whole horizon, a chicken being worth not more than four-pence. An expansive grin spread violently across her unattractive face. She quickly let loose from the lighter; and the last I saw of her was the disappearing outline of the sampan making shorewards for another chicken.

Returning to the saloon deck, I fell into the hands of Chang Wan Loo—a tailor, very fat, very oleaginous, very obsequious, with enormous alpaca trousers, fifteen sizes too big for him. The Chief said that in spite of the cut of his trousers he was a good tailor; so I asked him if I could have three white suits made, washed, and delivered before seven o'clock the next morning. It seemed a lot; but the Chief said: "Stick to it."

"Dhobi-men (washermen), Penang side, no good. Chinanen, New Yeah, plenty samshu, plenty hocshu. Dhobi men all dlunk. Tailoh men all-li. Can makee clo. No can makee wash."

I hardened my heart.

"All right. Maskee. Can get, Singapore side plenty much more cheap."

That settled him. The clothes turned up, beautifully made, beautifully washed, next morning. I gave him an extra dollar, promptly ordered half a dozen more suits, and also wrote him a testimonial which, no doubt, has since helped to persuade vacillating new arrivals of the incomparable merit of Chang Wan Loo.

The Old Man and I had arranged overnight to ascend to the Crag Hotel on the morrow; and so the steward called me at daybreak.

"Captain says the launch will be here in half an hour, sir. I'd better pack you three suits."

"But I'm only off for the day," I said in surprise.

He grinned.

"Need 'em all, sir."

"And it's pleasure I'm out for," I groaned.

I found the Old Man struggling with the intricacies of a bow when a warning hoot told us the launch was coming.

"D——n the thing. I'll never get it right," he said, his face red with irritation.

I tried for him, but found it difficult to reverse in my mind. Then I had an inspiration.

"If I stand behind you, captain, I can tie it over your shoulders, in front of the glass."

It worked. The Old Man's face was wreathed in smiles. He got into his coat rapidly as a knock came at the door.

"Come in," he said; and the steward announced "Mr. Maurice."

There is something fascinatingly neat and trim in the spotless whiteness, and semi-military cut, of the dress of the Englishman in the Far East. Everyone looks well in it.

Maurice, to whom I took an instant liking the moment I saw his smiling bronzed face under the white helmet, looked the part to perfection.

"I wouldn't bother about carrying a watch, if I were you, Doc; and don't bring any money either. We can sign chits for anything we want," he said.

Accordingly I discarded the watch and money.

"We never carry jewellery or money about in Penang," he told me later in explanation. "You see, we're one white man to three hundred coloured. We have to keep up our personal prestige; and so we try to avoid tempting anyone to rob, or steal, from the person by having nothing valuable about us. Everyone signs chits for everything; and they are presented once a month, and paid by cheque on one's bank."

Chit signing is universal in the Far East. No one ever

thinks of paying in money. Two men will stroll into an hotel, play a game of billiards, order iced drinks and cigars, sit smoking on the verandah for an hour, and then one will call out:

"Boy! Chit!"

A silent Chinaman will appear with a chit-book on a salver.

One of them will pick it up:

"How much, boy?"

"Twoa dolla, hifty cent."

He will tear out a chit, write "I owe two dollars fifty cents. Billiards, etc.," date it, sign his name and address, and hand it to the boy, who as likely as not has never seen him before. It will turn up at his office or residence at the end of the month, be duly met, and then destroyed.

. . . . . .

The little launch, with its smartly uniformed Malay crew, ran us quickly to the pier. It was about half-past seven in the morning, and beautifully cool. We drove in a ticca-gharry along the straight wide palm-lined road, with its white bungalows far back among the trees, each peeping through a wealth of tropical vegetation. Halting at the Club to pick up Maurice's suit-case, we soon were again speeding towards the foot of the hill, passing on the way many of the gorgeously gold-lettered, marble-columned, lantern-hung bungalows of the wealthy Chinese merchants, which for the most part quite outshone in display those of the dominant race. The Old Man grunted disapproval of the sight.

"The Dutch don't let them lord it like that in Java. Chinks can only live in certain parts of the towns there. There was a wealthy Chinaman in Soerabaya who built a beautiful house for himself, and when it was finished found it was just outside the area in which a Chinaman was permitted to live. It cost him 100,000 guilders to build; and it's never been occupied. He can't live in it

himself; he can't rent it, for no Dutchman would be his
tenant; he can't sell it to a Dutchman, for it is too near
Chinatown for comfort," the Old Man said. "So there
it is derelict."

Maurice laughed.

"Our Chinamen are very loyal here. It was quite
comical during the South African War to hear pig-tailed,*
slit-eyed fellows talking of 'we Britishers—our defeats—
our successes'."

Gradually the bungalows ceased; and the country grew
more primitive. Native kampongs, with rickety, stilted,
brown thatched atap huts, appeared. Primitive open
native shops on the road-side, brown babies rolling in
the dust, little boys driving fierce-looking water-buffaloes,
were constant sights. Groves of peepul, tamarind, and
coco-nut trees, plantains, mangoes and bananas, lined the
road on either side.

We stopped eventually at the foot of the hill, opposite
a rude shelter from which came a wild rush of copper-
coloured men in sarongs, with unkempt black locks
straggling from beneath gay-coloured turbans.

These were Klings waiting to carry one's luggage up
the hill. Maurice picked out three; and we started on
foot. It was now about nine o'clock; and already it was
getting appreciably hotter. The path wound steadily upwards in sinuous, serpentine coils amongst the hills. For
the most part it lay in the shadow of the overhanging
trees. New vistas continually opened as we ascended—
glimpses of valleys dense with jungle timber, with here
and there a bungalow perched on a craggy point. The
path cut its way through masses of coarse botryoidal
sandstone, with here and there a jutting grey mass of
igneous rock outcropping. Groves of bamboo whispered
murmurously at intervals; and creeping, vivid-leaved bou-
gainvillea vines, enormously long, wound for hundreds

* Chinamen still wore the pigtail when this was first written in
1911.

of yards, interlacing amongst the njamploeng trees. It was very still, except for the sound of our footsteps, till at irregular, and ever startling, intervals the cicadas broke in with their unexpected rasping rattle.

The Old Man plodded doggedly upwards; and we followed, accommodating our speed to his, the coolies, with our baggage perched on their heads, swinging easily in the rear.

Once a pale-faced European, slung in a dooly, carried by six men, swept past us down the hill; and once a Chinese lady going to take the air, passed us upwards, carried by four men, sitting in her sedan chair with whitened cheeks, immovable as a graven image.

I watched a dark patch start on the broad back of the Old Man, and spread till his jacket, soaked in perspiration, clung to him like a glove.

"It's getting deuced hot," he said, as he stopped to mop his face, now the colour of a well-boiled lobster.

"You're taking pounds off your weight," I reminded him, by way of encouragement.

That stimulated him for another half-mile.

"I'm melting away; and you fellows haven't turned a hair," he said, at length, after an interval.

"The half-way house is round the next turn," said Maurice.

"Lord! Are we only half way?" he groaned.

The Half-way House was a nipah-thatched roof supported on corner posts. We were all glad of a rest when we reached it; and sat there while we smoked a cigarette apiece, fanning ourselves at intervals with our helmets. When Maurice suggested starting again the Old Man was very loath to move.

"If it weren't for the thought of the long iced drink at the top, I couldn't do it," he said.

"It's the bath I'm thinking of," said Maurice. "Ever had a Malay bath, Doc? No! Well, you'll enjoy it all the more then."

By this time the heat had become sweltering. The winding path seemed endless. We plodded on in silence. Even Maurice began to feel it; and it was with a sigh of relief that he said at last:

"The next turn will bring us to the top, and the hotel, Captain.*

The hotel was quite unlike anything usually associated with the name. It was more like a village of bungalows perched here and there alongside winding shady paths grouped around one big central spacious dining-hall, standing on a platform of granite which was evidently the core of the long extinct volcano that had given birth to the island.

Our room was one of a row of twenty in a long one-storied, wooden, verandahed building of sleeping apartments intended for bachelors, so arranged that the wind swept through them from the open balcony behind, which projected over a precipice with a sheer drop of several hundred feet to the jungle-clad ravines below.

Depositing our traps on the floor, the coolies were dismissed, to squat contentedly in the shade for hours till we should require them again. A solemn Chinese waiter stood like a Buddha till he should have received our orders. The Old Man dropped with a sigh of relief into a cane lounge chair which stretched invitingly in the wind-swept verandah behind.

"Boy! A long whisky-polly! Savvy?" he called out.

"I savvy," the Chinaman said solemnly; and then he glanced at us.

Maurice and I decided, however, to wait till we had had our bath.

"But where is the bath?" I said.

Maurice pointed to a trap-door in the floor, which up to then I had not noticed. "Down there, Doc. You go first."

The luxury of a bath after exertion in the tropics is

* There is now a funicular railway up to the hotel.

something to be felt rather than described. It is so ineffably soothing, and yet exhilarating. Little wonder all Eastern religions make of it a ritual.

A Malay bath is strange on first acquaintance. I went down a ladder into a little square brick room, with only a tiny opening, the size of one brick, high up on the outside wall to give light. In one corner stood a barrel, breast high, into which water trickled from a pipe. Floating in the barrel was a dipper, made of a half coco-nut shell with a handle. One stood on the brick floor, and ladled the ice-cold water over one with the dipper. From the floor the water ran into a shallow groove, and then out and down the mountain-side.

It was worth the climb, three times over, to have the exhilarating sensation of that bath, and the languorous feeling of content that followed.

Clad in fresh clean suits of white, we presently strolled comfortably round to the great verandahed smoke-room looking down on the wide vista below—a vista of miles on miles of tree-clad ravines winding to the distant toy-like town, with the blue strait beyond on which the great ships looked like tiny ants. Further still the eye swept across the jungle-fringed Province Wellesley, on the other side, and over miles of paddy fields, till on the utmost limits of vision the white cloud-capped peaks of Kedah rose blue in the shimmering haze.

Lazily we lay looking at it, wrapped in a ruminating silence. I watched the faint blue smoke of my cigar rising, while Maurice, with a collection of coloured bottles, a rattan swizzle, fresh limes, soda syphons, pounded ice, and the air of a connoisseur, concocted some nectar of the gods for our prospective delectation.

"I withdraw every word I said on the way up," said the Old Man, with a long sigh of content. "It was worth it. I've just weighed myself, and I'm four pounds lighter. Besides, going down is nothing," he added characteristically.

A Chinese waiter approached a fat German sitting in a chair not far from us.

"I vill haf vat dese gentlemen haf," he said.

Maurice looked up and smiled:

"Ours is a special recipe of our own, sir—a patent 'sling'."

The German threw up his hands in horror.

"Ach! No. I am dedodal. I vill haf gin mit soda boy."

"D——n all Dutchmen," said the Old Man in quite an audible voice.

"Thought you liked Dutchmen, Cap?" said Maurice with a smile.

"Hollanders, not Germans," said the Old Man.

"Sailors," I explained, "divide the earth into British— which includes all English-speaking people—Froggies, Dutch—which means Germans and all of that ilk—Dagos —meaning thereby Mediterranean Europeans—and Niggers—all coloured people."

Presently a great gong boomed somewhere amongst the trees.

"Tiffin," said Maurice.

The big cool dining-room was almost full when we walked along the shaded path to it. People had come from all parts of the Malay States to be present on the arrival of the Duke of Connaught; and most of them had gravitated up here. They were an interesting crowd to watch—bronzed military men with keen worn faces, and the look of pioneers, younger men not yet stamped with the die of command, in startling contrast, pale-faced officials of the civil administration, governing the country from the shelter of punkah-swept offices, and here and there a few prosperous merchants, lawyers and doctors, indistinguishable from the other civilians.

Then there were the women. One shrinks from describing Englishwomen in the Far East. I looked round the room. Some of them may have been beautiful once

—the East had finished that. Now they all looked like those elderly spinsters who live a more or less predatory life on Bloomsbury boarders—pale, thin or pastily fat, cadaverous, hollow-eyed.

The soft complexions, the graceful contour, once present in some of them, had paid a heavy toll to the moist steamy-hot climate. One cannot live in a continuous Turkish bath without showing it. The bronzed lean men, used to the open and constant physical exercise, had gained, by reason of the climate, an air of ascetic dignity—the lines on their brows did not matter. But in the women a sedentary life, the tedium of movement in garments unsuitable to the climate, the necessary separation, for years perhaps, from their children, the consequent emptiness of their lives, the eagerness, therefore, with which they clutched at any form of excitement, all were reflected in the thin sharpness of their voices and their general air of querulous discontent.

It is a sorry place for women—the Far East.

There was one woman, however, who looked a queen amongst them all. She was sitting with her husband; and none of the other women, I noticed, appeared to see her. I asked Maurice the reason.

"Native blood," he answered quietly.

It was that, probably, that had enabled her, in some mysterious way, to defy the climate by remaining fresh and young. The taint was slight, only about an eighth. In England she would have passed anywhere, but here in the East—no; she was not "pukka white," and that was an end of it—she was not "received."

It seemed to weigh lightly on her. She was smiling and chatting gaily with the group of men who gathered round her table; but one cannot tell what gall and wormwood she swallowed inwardly. No doubt when the great "muck-a-mucks" were being officially received by the Duke of Connaught on the morrow, she would be one of the uninvited. Perhaps she would feel it; probably, if she did, she would never show it. But to a woman these things mean more than mere man can ever comprehend. I saw her husband watching her with adoring eyes. Perhaps in that she found her world complete.

•   •   •   •   •   •

Once or twice during tiffin the Old Man glanced apologetically at me:

"Regimen be hanged," I said; and he looked immensely relieved.

"Captain's been reducing himself by dieting," I explained.

"These curries are delicious," said the Old Man. "Try this Gula Malacca, Doc. I remember it of old."

No wonder he did. I remember its delicate nutty flavour, and the added joy of the fresh green coco-nut milk, even unto this day. Maurice smiled at our enthusiasm.

"I admit it's almost worth standing the heat for," he said. "But at times I long, in a way you fellows can never understand, for a dish of English strawberries and cream. I'd give a month's pay for that."

That started us off; and then we talked of home and country, of green lanes and English roses, of little wayside inns and the smell of apple orchards, of London streets, restaurants in Soho, and the lights of Piccadilly Circus—and I watched Maurice's face light up, and his eyes glow, and his head rise proudly, and thought of the little people who dwell in streets, and know not England. A passing Malay waiter, lean, brown-faced, under a scarlet turban, caught his eye, and brought him back to reality.

"Stop, you fellows," he said, half joking, yet half in earnest. "I don't want to think of it any more. It'll be five long years before I can see it all again."

•   •   •   •   •   •

After tiffin the public rooms became a desert. Everyone, including ourselves, retired for the afternoon *siesta* in the wide, mosquito-netted bedrooms; and it was not till some hours of dreamless slumber had passed that our Chinese boy awakened us with tea.

We took it in long chairs on the verandah of our bedroom, gazing down over the precipitous cliffs sweeping hundreds of feet below to the tree-clad ravines lying between the lower heights, covered by forests of areca-nut trees that stretched for miles and miles to southward over the edge of the horizon.

Maurice threw up his arms with a long sigh of content.

"It's much too soon to be moving yet. Though it's cool enough here, it's a furnace below. Let's play billiards."

Everyone plays billiards in the Far East; and everyone is much better than the average player at home, for it is a game that can be played comfortably in hot climates. The tables, however, are invariably abominable, even in the best hotels, probably due to the heat warping things and the plague of ants.

Thus the afternoon was idled away till Maurice decided it was time to start down the mountain again, to get to the bottom before the rapid tropical night made progress difficult. Our Kling porters seemed never to have moved from where they had squatted outside our quarters in the morning. Every time we passed we found them in the same position, their wild eyes following us carefully for any sign that they were needed.

"Think they must be fresh from the Deccan, don't understand our ways, and so are afraid to leave where they know our baggage is," said Maurice indifferently.

At a sign they seized our traps, and we started. The descent was comparatively easy. We reached the base a few minutes after sunset. But here a complication arose. Maurice had been right in his conjecture that our Klings were new arrivals. That would not have mattered; but what did was that they did not understand

the chit system, and we had not a cent between us.
Maurice explained in Malay that they would be paid on
presenting the chit the next morning. But they did not
understand Malay; and so, gesticulating wildly, they ran
after the rickishaws when we started. Soon, however,
we left them behind.

"They'll find out all about it from the others," he said
philosophically.

Riding back in the darkness, in the cool evening air,
behind the dim figure of the runner, put the finish to a
perfect day. Everyone seemed to be out on that particular night. Strings of twinkling rickishaws, each with its
sidelight, came in and out of gateways, or passed us, each
holding dim white figures, half recognisable as the passing light shone in on them. The porticoed bungalows
were all aglow like fairy palaces in their tropical framework. The long straight stems of the coco-nut trees,
lining the road, flashed endlessly in the light as we
passed; while the land breeze murmured gently in their
feathery tops far overhead.

Presently we arrived at the International, where we
had arranged to have "makan" (dinner). The menu was
written in Malay, so the Old Man and I ate in faith.

.   .   .   .   .   .

Fancy is a curious thing. There are people one likes
at once, others one takes an immediate antipathy to—
why, one cannot explain; it is the riddle of Dr. Fell.

After dinner we forgathered with two or three friends
of Maurice's, who were dining in the hotel. One I took
a particular liking to. He was very quiet; he was a
Scotsman; and I could see he was drinking more than
was good for him; and yet I knew immediately I should
like him.

He smiled gravely at me, and hitched his chair round
to my side. We sat on the big verandah, under a whirring electric fan, in long cane basket chairs, around a
little table. Two silent barefooted Malay waiters stood

The Landing Stage, Penang

Singapore Harbour

behind us. The cigars were good, the coffee excellent; everyone felt pleasantly post-prandial.

"What do those three d——d niggers want?" said one of the men suddenly.

Everyone turned round to look. We three, as it happened, all had our backs to the open space, in front of the hotel; and on turning we saw three brown, half-naked figures standing at the foot of the steps, staring silently up at us. Immediately one of them held up a chit towards Maurice.

"Why, it's our Klings," he said in surprised vexation. "They must have followed us the whole way here. They evidently think we're trying to do them out of their pay."

"Deuced cheek of them following you here," said the man who had first noticed them.

"They don't understand," Maurice explained.

"Deuced cheek, all the same," the other replied.

Evidently the Malay policeman thought so too. The Malays hate the Klings almost as much as they do the Chinese; and our waiters had heard the muttered disapproval. Something was said to the policeman; and immediately he precipitated himself on the three figures. There was a brief violent scuffle; and then all three disappeared beyond the range of light, mixed up with the policeman, who presently reappeared smiling joyfully.

The residents took it all as a matter of course.

"Why not pay them from the hotel?" I suggested mildly.

The Old Man nodded approval; but all the residents, even the good-natured Irish doctor, negatived the suggestion.

"Ye haven't to be livin' here," he said. "We have; an' it's these poor divils have to be taught not to be botherin' us for nothin'; an' it's the Malay policeman enjoys himself teachin' them that same," he added with a grin.

The Scotsman—Guthrie—looked at me and smiled.

"You think it very high-handed?" he said.

I nodded.

"Man, if you come to think of it, our mere presence in the country is the most insufferable high-handedness. We haven't a moral leg to stand on."

"Who's talkin' about not being able to stand so early in the evening?" protested the Irish doctor. "You say you're not goin' to the Reception, Guthrie! Well, then, I'll toss Roberts, best of three, who wears your frock-coat and topper to-morrow. Haven't worn one since I went round Merrion Square, I don't want to think how many years ago, when I was lookin' for testimonials, to gull long-sufferin' lay committees, when I was up for a job."

This was a subject of vastly greater importance than any Kling's feelings. Frock-coats were scarce in Penang. No one used them. They did not suit the climate. But they would be *de rigueur* on the Duke's arrival on the morrow; there were not enough to go round; and everyone who hadn't got one was hunting round amongst his friends who had.

So the Klings were totally forgotten in the excitement of watching the throw of the dice.

"Three fives in two. I'll stand," said the doctor.

The other man rattled the dice-box and threw.

"Three sixes in one," he said calmly. "Mine, Doc."

The Irishman laughed.

"Never mind," he said. "It's lucky in love I'll be. Besides, I'll charge old Cheong Ta double fees for seeing him when I ought to be at the Reception I can't go to; for 'every little helps,' as the captain said when he threw his wife overboard to lighten the ship in a storm."

"At any rate," said Guthrie, the owner of the clothes, "we all score a dinner off the winner. You'll come, Captain, and you, Doc?"

"We sail to-morrow morning. Otherwise——" the Old Man said.

"So. Then you'll miss all the excitement. But then I forget. It's nothing to you fellows. To us it will be the main topic of conversation for months. You lucky devils living at home. You'll be back in England in two or three months. As for us, we're chained——" His voice trailed off in a sigh of regret.

"Hasn't seen his wife for three years—poor old Guthrie," Maurice explained afterwards. "Climate nearly killed her. Had to send her home. Deuced fond of each other. Rotten hard lines. Men shouldn't marry in the East."

A native bearer came hurriedly up the steps of the verandah, and delivered a note. The waiter brought it to the doctor; and he tore it open casually.

"Excuse me, you fellows," he said.

As he read the look of good-fellowship faded, his eyes grew grave, his mouth firm. I could see the professional mask falling like a drop-curtain over his whimsical countenance.

"Sorry," he said, getting up abruptly, "I'll have to leave you fellows. Got a call."

The Old Man caught my eye. We rose simultaneously.

"We should be back at our ship, too," he said.

"Don't let me break up the party," the doctor protested, hailing his rickishaw at the same time with a preoccupied air.

"No. Don't go, you fellows," Guthrie said sleepily over his cigar.

Our rickishaw men had appeared, however, as if by magic from the darkness.

"It's rather late; and we've got some things to do," said the Old Man.

Guthrie nodded somnolently, looking at us stupidly.

"Better say good-bye to Guthrie, then," said Maurice. "He's living at the hotel. I'll see you as far as the pier."

So we said good-bye and left him. The doctor had already hurried off.

One meets so many good fellows just for a day in passing. One feels one would like to know more of them; and then one's paths diverge. I have the picture in my mind, quite sharply still, of Guthrie as we left him, lying limply in a long cane chair, his thin spare figure clothed in white drill, a series of coloured glasses on a little table in front of him, two or three silent saronged brown figures hanging sedulously in the background, with a fan whirring overhead trying to create a current of air in the still tropic night, heavy with the scent of *ylang-ylang* and tuberoses all around. I can see the body of Guthrie, lying there, drinking more than is good for it, while his mind is some 8,000 miles away in a little island we call Home, wandering in fancy with the one woman in the world for him.

The East is full of Guthries, and England of grass widows. Some of them—but is it any use being cynical? Time, absence, and opportunity make culprits of most of us. For life is, after all, for the most part, a desert with unexpected oases, which most of us have an unhappy knack of missing, finding sand only, or perhaps, worse still, the mirage. Let us hope Guthrie had the better fate.

. . . . . .

Maurice joined us on the ship at breakfast. The first thing we asked was "Were our Klings paid?"

He laughed. "Oh, yes! That's all right! They found out things in the night, and came to the office this morning, with someone who had explained to them. I talked to the man who it seems is their head, and asked him how he dared send out coolies without explaining the customs to them. I put the fear of God into that chap. So it won't occur again."

"That's all right," said the Old Man.

"Of course!" said Maurice quietly. "Honesty is our

policy in the East. It's the greatest mistake possible to 'do' the nigger. That's where the Portuguese failed, where the Germans are failing to-day, and where the Japanese will lose if they don't change pretty quick."

"That's so," said the Chief. "It's a pity the Jap is such a rogue. The man I like is good old John Chinaman."

"Hear, hear," said the Old Man. "John Chinaman is dirty. He's as wily as an Armenian, and the Armenian can beat the Jew any day; he'll drive the hardest bargain possible with you; but his word is his bond, and he'll keep it even if he loses heavily by it. Yes, sir; John Chinaman is a gentleman."

And this I found was the general opinion throughout the Far East. When one dealt with a Chinaman one felt safe that the bargain would be carried out. With a Jap, on the other hand, one preferred to have one's money in advance

I went ashore with Maurice after breakfast, partly to do some shopping, partly to look up an old College friend who was in the Colonial Service there. Eventually I found him sitting as a judge in the courts. He was trying some wretched Chinamen who were accused of letting off fireworks to the public danger in Beach Street. Rather to the surprise of the prosecution, he let them off with a nominal fine. I found, then, he had seen me at the back of the court, for he presently sent round to ask me to come to his office.

"Do you know," he said later, "it was something in your eye made me let those Chinks off. I couldn't help thinking, when I saw you, of how we once started a fire in the 'Bay,' and commandeered the basket chair of a man neither of us knew to make it burn more vigorously. I thought of the delight we had when we dodged the Junior Dean, and got back safe to our rooms without detection. I thought of the elaborate plans we made to decoy the porters off when we wanted to get our fire going strong; and I simply couldn't fine those Chinks."

"It's a sort of belated conscience money," I said.

"Yes, that's about it."

When I got back to the office I found the ship's papers were not yet ready; and so while I was waiting for Maurice I cooled down under the office punkah pulled by the quaintest little cross-eyed Chinese boy, sitting with the immobile face of a Buddha, hypnotized by the monotony of his duty. All the clerks were Chinamen. They seem to be the only orientals with any head for figures. The Japanese are not trustworthy; the Malay of course is hopeless; but the Chinaman is accurate to three places of decimals. It was a curious meeting of East and West to see a Chinaman, squint-eyed, pigtailed, banging away at a Remington with the speed of a sleight-of-hand artist, his face all the while like that of a graven image.

"Ready?" said Maurice, coming out of an inner office.

"Quite ready," I answered.

We bundled into our rickishaws, and hurried to the landing stage. Steam was up when we reached the ship; and our farewells to Maurice were hurried. The Old Man, as usual, was fuming to get away. In five minutes we were off; the launch with Maurice's waving figure swept shorewards; and soon we were gliding smoothly round the great head of Muka, and slipping down the Straits of Malacca, bound for Singapore.

· · · · · ·

Penang is the gate to our Empire in the Far East. But for Penang it is probable we should never have had Singapore, or the Federated Malay States, or the British portions of Borneo. They would all in the natural course of events have become absorbed in the Dutch possessions in "Nederlands Indie," with Java, Sumatra, Borneo, Celebes, and the rest. The immense mineral wealth of the Native States, which is at present in British hands, and the great rubber industry, would have been monopolised by the Dutch. As luck would have it, we are in possession; but all of our present rights are due to the friendship of an obscure British sea-captain, Francis Light, with a foreign Malay potentate, the Sultan of Kedah.

The history of how we acquired Penang reads like a romance; and a romance, be it said, that does not reflect much credit upon England. As a nation we seem to have been the favourites of fortune; our mighty Empire has been acquired almost by haphazard; and the talking shop at Westminster, save in the fatal case of the American colonies, has been rescued time and again from egregious folly by the forethought and timely action of the younger sons, forgotten sailors, or obscure soldiers, who have helped to thrust greatness upon us, often against our will. We have thus been saddled with the burden of Empire, as it were, almost by inadvertence.

Such is the story of Penang, and the life-history of Captain Francis Light, its founder. Leaving the Navy in 1765, Light went out to India to seek his fortune in the days when India, in popular imagination, was still a land of fabulous gold from which returning nabobs came home, with enlarged livers, it is true, but also, at the same time, with untold wealth in rubies, diamonds, pearls, and golden mohurs, locked up in great teak chests, as compensation. The nabob bulked as largely in those days as the later Australian and Californian and the more recent American and South African millionaires; and Light, no doubt, had golden visions of a similar affluence when he set out for India. At Calcutta he got command of a ship trading to Lower Siam and the Malay States. Everywhere he went, however, he found the hand of the Dutch against him. Established at Malacca, they were jealously watchful of everyone encroaching on what they considered their sphere of influence. They tried to prevent the natives trading with the British by every possible device, going so far, sometimes, as to destroy crops rather than that the English should have them. Every petty excuse to harass British shipping was adopted; there were mutual recriminations and retaliations; and in consequence no love was lost between the traders of the rival nations.

In spite of the Dutch, however, Captain Light won the confidence of, and acquired much trading facilities from, the people of Kedah; he became an honoured friend of the sultan; and there is a persistent legend that the sultan gave him one of his daughters in marriage.

Penang was part of the sultan's possessions; and it was probably this friendship that suggested to Light its strategic importance as an outpost against the aggression of the Dutch, and its great value as a port of call on the way to China: for it must be remembered that at that time the future Singapore was an unknown and un-named swamp. At any rate, in 1771 he attempted to interest Warren Hastings, the Governor-General, in its acquisition; but the attempt failed. The non-success, however, of a later plan to use Achin as a base brought the idea again into prominence; and Light's friendship with the sultan smoothed the way to an agreement. We gained Penang in return for a pension of 6,000 dollars a year to the sultan, and the promise of protection against his enemies, more particularly the Siamese.

On August 11, 1786, therefore, Light hoisted the British flag, named the island Prince of Wales Island in honour of the future George IV, and the capital George-town, after George III. It is now a place of immense trade. The municipal revenue amounts to over a million dollars a year; and there is an enormous future before it, owing to the coffee, tin, and rubber industries. We have held it ever since Light's time; though at one period it was gravely suggested that it should be abandoned, and that the Andaman Islands would be better as a port of call. To the lasting disgrace of England, however, we shuffled out of part of our agreement; and when the Siamese attacked Kedah, in the reign of the succeeding sultan, we supinely allowed it to be overrun and con-quered, thus repudiating the treaty made by Light,

besmirching his memory in the eyes of the men who had
trusted in his integrity, and casting an ugly blot on the
fair fame of England. It was a typical example of the
diplomacy of the East India Company; and on a par
with its subsequent treatment of one of its greatest servants, Sir Stamford Raffles, Governor of Java and founder
of Singapore.

CHAPTER IV

ON THE WAY TO JAPAN

In an hour after leaving Penang all signs of land were gone, and we had fallen into the calm routine of sea life again.

The Chief came up from below, and threw himself into a deck-chair beside me with a grunt of satisfaction. "One bell" had gone, and the steward came up on deck with tea.

"It's fine to be at sea again," he said; and I, scarce knowing why, agreed immediately.

Thinking it over, I came to the conclusion that it was the relief from the heat, the confusion, the clash of colours, the babel of tongues, that made one appreciate the neutral tints and the calm monotony of the sea by contrast. In a day or two, we knew, we would be looking forward to making port again, talking eagerly of what we would do at Singapore; but for the present the rest of the old routine was very pleasant.

As the day waned we gradually approached the land again, a green-rimmed outline, with blue hills behind; and, in the darkness of the night that followed, the heavy odour of jungle vegetation swept over the ship in waves from the unseen shore. The sea was as glass. Not a wind stirred. Far out to starboard, over the mountains of Sumatra, the lightning flashes played continuously, without sound.

That evening, as the Chief and I sat watching them, he puffed luxuriously at his cigar, and said: "I'm enjoying this, because in three days' time we'll have turned Singapore and be threshing up the China seas in dirty, squally weather, with the temperature dropping fifteen degrees a day, till we're all shivering in heavy 'blues' again, instead of these thin white duds."

"Lucky for me, I'm running short of whites," I answered.

"Tosh! I can see you can't quite grasp it yet. You just wait," he said in an aggrieved tone.

"Sufficient unto the day," I murmured contentedly in the darkness.

. . . . . .

In the morning I was called to see the ancient city of Malacca, once the greatest port in the Far East, now a mere calling place for little coasting steamers, and native praus from the opposite Sumatran coast.

"We can't get within two miles of the place," said the Old Man. "It's full of reefs and very shallow. It used to be a great port in the old 'Company' days; but Singapore and Penang have taken all the trade—nobody goes there now."

Seen from the ship, the city appeared as a huddled line of houses with their backs towards the sea, and their backyards, so to speak, projecting out on pillars in the water, as much as sixty feet (according to the Old Man) from the shore. This peculiarity in architecture is possible because there is practically no tide in these seas; and the Chinamen, who love deep, narrow houses, have accordingly seized the opportunity to build right out into the water.

Through the city a little river winds down to the sea; and on a green hill, easily seen from the ship, there stands the ruin of the famous old Portuguese church of St. Paul, scene of the miracles of St. Francis Xavier, that wonderful pioneer missionary.

That is all that remains to commemorate the hundred and thirty years of Portuguese occupation, and the mighty exploits of the redoubtable Albuquerque, unless one includes a plentiful crop of Eurasians with high-sounding Peninsular names.

After the place was captured by the Dutch it flourished mightily; but since it passed to England the advent of steam has sounded its death-knell.

Dampier, who visited the place in 1688, when it was under the Dutch, found the Chinese, even then, in possession of the trade:

"The Chinese also are seated here, who bring the commodities of their country hither, especially tea, sugar-candy, and other sweetmeats. Some of them keep tea-houses, where for a stiver a man can have near a pint of tea [tea was in those days in England a royal luxury] and a little porringer of sugar-candy, or other sweetmeat, if he pleases. Others of these Chinese are tradespeople, and they are all in general very industrious, but withal extraordinary gamesters, and, if they can get any to play with them, all business must submit to that."

The Chinaman now is as the Chinaman then, still a gamester to his finger-tips. Our men in the fo'castle spent hours of their leisure gaming. Sometimes tragedies arise from the habit.

"It was on the voyage before last, when I was on the *Nestor,*" said the Chief. "We had a Chink crew; and on the morning after we left Singapore the quartermaster sounded 'seven bells.' There was no answer from the Chink on the look-out, though they could see him quite plainly from the bridge, standing on the fo'castle head looking out to sea. The mate got mad, and sent a quartermaster to 'wake up that darned Chink.' They couldn't waken him—he was dead. He had hanged himself by hitching his pigtail round his neck and over a stanchion. It turned out he had lost all his savings, and gambled away his earnings for the next two years; so he had concluded the best thing was to clear out. He had sounded 'six bells' quite deliberately, and then before the eyes of everyone, totally unsuspected, calmly taken his life."

Steaming into Singapore in the early morning is a memory to be marked with a white stone. It is one of the most beautiful sights of the beautiful East.

Gradually the Straits narrow, and the ship passes between the mainland, green with mangrove swamps, creeping out into the water, and island after island, jungle-clad to the uttermost limits of riotous vegetation.

The channel grows narrower and narrower, and, looking closely, one can see the venomous noses of huge siege guns peeping out on either side from the apparently innocent tree-clad islands—for this is the Gibraltar of the Far East, and England intends to hold it, if necessary, against the world.*

Suddenly one seems to have come to an *impasse*; and then the ship takes a sharp turn; there is a sound of swirling water; the trees almost touch the ship's side; and we are through into a wide bay, wharfed along one side, and lined by ships of every nation, flying every known flag, whilst on the other side island after island appears in one long sweeping chain, fading away into the opal distance on the rim of the horizon.

So many strange things strike the eye that the mind refuses to accommodate impressions with sufficient rapidity.

At one moment one catches sight of a queer native village, built entirely on posts in the water, with amphibious Malay boys playing as contentedly in the sea as English children on the village green, diving like porpoises, upsetting one another out of dug-outs not much bigger than themselves, treating the water as if it were their native element. Next some of the islands are studied, laid out as they are like tropical gardens, with the coolest of cool white bungalows scattered here and there over them. But the sailor's eye is irresistibly at-

* We did not reckon then, nor indeed even at the beginning of the second World War, that Singapore could possibly be attacked and made untenable from the land.

tracted to the other side, where miles and miles of the
Tanjong Pagar wharves accommodate ships of every build
and nation—coquettish white Dutch mailboats running to
Java, squat Germans, Japanese flying the blood-red Sun
flag, a long white American transport ship refitting for
Manila, and close to her a grim slate-coloured British
cruiser coaling with feverish haste. Blunt-nosed cable
ships lay out in the bay, and further out still those
pariahs of the ocean, two or three petroleum ships, flying
the danger flag.

There were three of our own company's ships moored
alongside when we arrived; and so, as soon as our gangway was lowered, half a dozen old shipmates of our officers invaded us. Following them came the usual nondescript crowd of native merchants, compradors, Chinese
tailors, Bengali money-changers, cheroot merchants and
performing fakirs, one so soon gets accustomed to see
on board.

"Hullo," said the Chief, "here's our old 'sew-sew'
woman." He pointed to a little wrinkled old China-
woman climbing up the gangway, carrying a big round
basket covered with oilcloth. When she got on deck,
she made straight for the Chief, bent in a profound
salaam, and said: "Sew-sew, sew-sew?"

She made a quaint picture with her uncovered head
of glistening black hair tied in a tight knot behind,
fastened with two big boxwood skewers, her blue glass
earrings, little jacket, wide alpaca trousers and bare
wrinkled yellow feet.

Producing a little stool from her basket, she sat down
in a shady corner of the deck and waited.

"But what does she want?" I said.

"Oh, she'll darn, patch, sew on buttons, anything you
like. She's a 'sew-sew' woman."

I dived below to fetch my camera; but when she saw
it she covered her face, gathered up her things, looked
the picture of misery, and prepared to leave the ship.

"Better not," said the Chief; "she thinks it is the evil eye." So I refrained.

"Belong damfool," said a fat Chinese tailor, who was standing near. "You takee me. All-light. Me likee;" and he smiled an expansive, greasy smile.

But I had no ambition to spoil a plate on a fat Chinaman in a brown puggaree.

"Have you locked up your cabin, Doc?" said the Mate in passing.

"No," I said.

"By Jove, I forgot, too," said the Chief.

He made a hasty stride to the side of the ship and looked over. It was lucky he did. Through his open port, which lay alongside the wharf, a Chinaman had inserted a long rattan with a hook on the end of it; and he was feeling about inside when we looked over. We shouted; and, dropping his rattan, he fled. Down the gangway the Chief and I pelted after him; but we'd never have caught him had not a little wiry Malay policeman, who saw him running, skilfully grabbed him by the pigtail and held on till we arrived.

The Chief was very mad. He was out for the Chinaman's blood. But when, on the policeman searching him, it was found he had not had time to fish out anything, he began to cool down again. It was intensely comical to the onlooker. There stood the Chinaman, looking immensely frightened, the fierce little turbaned Malay policeman, in his bare feet, hanging on to the Chinaman's pigtail like grim death, the rather stout, red-faced Chief, somewhat out of breath, mopping his forehead, covered with beads of perspiration, and myself, standing near, wondering why I had not had the sense to bring my camera and photograph the whole tableau.

The Chief thought rapidly, then he smiled grimly.

"Say, Jack," he said to the policeman. "You give him plenty stick. All right. Can do. You savvy—march."

The policeman's face broke into a broad grin. His eyes snapped with delight. He chuckled in guttural joy.

"I savvy," he said.

He didn't wait to have the order countermanded, for if there is one thing a Malay likes better than another it is beating a Chinaman. So he ran his prisoner off at once; and the last act of the drama we saw was the Chinaman running rapidly, with the Malay clinging to his rear, thwacking him, with immense gusto, all over the body with his malacca truncheon.

After that I locked my door and closed my portholes carefully in every port when I was not in my cabin.

We had no cargo for Singapore; and so were only stopping long enough to coal before clearing for Nagasaki, our next port of call. I had no ambition, however, to endure another coaling—Port Said had cured me of that; but so quick were they that before the Second and I were ready to go ashore they had already started; and long strings of Chinese coolies in limpet-shaped hats, carrying great wicker-work coal-baskets, each slung on a bamboo pole between two of them, were running in an endless chain up and down the improvised gangways to the bunkers.

It was quite a quarter of an hour's rickishaw's ride from the wharf to the city. On the way we passed a company of Sikhs, very fine and fierce, gorgeously Oriental, very trim and soldierly. They had been through so much ceremony during the week of the Duke of Connaught's visit that when we came on them suddenly the whole company came to the salute automatically.

"They take you for one of the 'muck-a-mucks'," I said to the Second. The Second smiled complacently before contradicting me.

. . . .

Singapore, like all Far Eastern ports, is a kaleidoscopic picture of all the nations upon earth, speaking in a babel of many tongues—pale whites for whom everyone makes way, yellow Chinamen, busy as nailers, little Jap ladies smiling in rickishaws, stately Parsees in gorgeous silks, grave Arabs clad in white, half-caste ladies, dressed as Europeans, casting languorous glances from exceedingly lustrous dark brown eyes, and over and above all, the ever-present, idle, semi-nude Malay, sunning himself in somnolent content. Tramways run all through the city. At first the Chinese rose against them and tore up the permanent way of the big devil engines several times; but now they use them more than anyone else.

Looking at the magnificent public buildings, the pala-tial hotels, the wide, beautifully kept streets, the splendid shops, the gardens and parks, the multitudinous life of the place, the miles and miles of shipping in the great Tanjong Pagar docks, it is almost impossible to realise that less than a hundred and fifty years ago the city was non-existent.

Yet it was founded by Sir Stamford Raffles as late as 1819 in what then appeared the forlorn hope of checking the dominant and domineering power restored to the Dutch in the East Indies by the recent Treaty of Vienna.

To Raffles the signing of that treaty must have been very bitter. He had seen Java flourish under his *régime*, Malacca, the traditional centre of European power in the Malay States, become British; and visions of a vast East Indian Empire, greater even than that of India itself, must have risen before his mind.

Instead came the agony of seeing everything restored to the Dutch, even islands never before claimed by them handed over in addition, and last of all, and perhaps most bitter, himself, an object of suspicion to the cautious merchants of Leadenhall Street on account of his ex-pansive views of Empire, banished out of harm's way to an honourable exile at Bencoolen, in Sumatra.

It was enough to break the spirit of any but the most strong-willed of men; and it is extraordinary that Raffles, shaken in health as he was by that time, did not give it

all up and retire, as he might in all honour have done,
to the life of honoured ease which his soul craved for.
Had he done so there would have been no Singapore.

The restoration of Malacca to the Dutch came as a
great blow to British prestige in the Far East; and the
Dutch were not long in returning to their old aggressive
ways. Claims were made of sovereign rights over Pahang
and Johore; alleged exclusive treaty rights were advanced
which would have been ruinous to British trade; all the
old obstructive tactics of the previous two hundred years
were employed with a new and startling virulence. A
determined attempt was made to drive the British for
ever out of the Malay Archipelago. The Governor of
Penang, Colonel Bannerman, wrote despairingly to the
Governor-General on the subject. He was a weak man
with no initiative, and threw up the sponge even before
any attempt to get at close quarters had been made. But
the active, impulsive mind of Raffles was not thus to be
suppressed. Finding Bannerman worse than useless,
with the tacit approval of the Governor-General, he
secretly set sail from Penang with a little fleet of four
vessels for an unknown destination. This was the almost
uninhabited island of Singapore; and here he raised the
British flag before the Dutch had even become aware
of his presence. It was the bold act of a master mind
seeing the enormous future before the port, and the vast
political power its strategic position, commanding the
Straits of Malacca, must inevitably confer on its pos-
sessors.

Almost immediately the Dutch, seeing at once the vast
importance of its possession, made claim to the sovereign
rights of the island, and demanded the withdrawal of
the British settlement; and, as might have been expected,
the wiseacres in Leadenhall and Downing Streets, looking upon the act as that of an intemperate, aggressive
person bent on embroiling us with the Dutch, sent a
despatch severely censuring Raffles, and suggesting to

the Governor-General the advisability of withdrawing all support from the scheme.

Luckily the Marquis of Hastings, then Governor-General, was annoyed by the peremptory manner in which Baron Van Der Capellan, the Governor-General of Nederlands Indie, demanded the withdrawal of the British. He knew from Raffles that the Dutch never had had a station there, and was disinclined from every point of view to admit their claim to all the unoccupied islands around the coast of the Malay Peninsula. He refused, therefore, to evacuate the port; and his position was strengthened by the fact that Raffles had been able to get a concession of the island from the Sultan of Johore, who denied the sovereign rights of Holland over any of his territory. Nevertheless it was not until after five years of constant negotiations that the Dutch claims, so persistently made, were finally repudiated, and the occupancy of the island received official sanction.

Raffles had the highest possible hopes of Singapore. He expected it would become the greatest port in the East, "a great commercial emporium and a fulcrum whence we may extend our influence politically as circumstances may hereafter require." "One free port in these seas," he stated, "must eventually destroy the spell of Dutch monopoly for ever."

History has amply justified him in his prophetic expectations. Singapore has now a population of over a quarter of a million; and as a port it is the largest in the British Empire after London, Liverpool, and Hong Kong. The trade in 1905 amounted to over six hundred million dollars; and the future is likely to be even more prosperous than the past. As Raffles anticipated, it killed the Dutch monopoly, and established the ascendancy of England in the Malay Peninsula.

Nevertheless so little was his work appreciated by the country he served so well that his last days were embittered by monetary disputes with the Company. A statue has now been erected to his memory in Westminster Abbey; and Singapore has honoured herself by raising him another. Londoners should be grateful to him, for he founded the Zoo. Like many of England's great sons, he is better appreciated now in death than he ever was in life.

.   .   .   .   .

Coming along the quays on our way back from the city, we stopped at one of our ships; and while the Second interviewed the engineroom staff, I called upon their doctor, a rawboned Scotsman of the deepest dye. He said they were going to Rangoon for rice, after leaving Japan.

"That means," said their Third Mate to me, "you'll be sent to Java, Doc. We've taken your turn; and we're the last rice ship this season."

"You may thank your lucky stars you do come after us," said the Scotsman. "We carried the last batch of eight hundred pilgrims from Mecca; and they brought typhoid on board with them, got from some dirty sacred well. They were carrying lots of the stuff home in bottles with them. It was loaded with germs. When any of them felt seedy he had a swig at his infected bottle; so I had to confiscate the whole lot and dump it overboard. We nearly had a mutiny over it; we should if they hadn't started dying. As it was, we dumped several bodies overboard every day all across the Indian Ocean. I'm thinking I earned my salary this voyage."

"I'd rather have liked the experience of pilgrims," I said.

"Wish you'd got them instead of me then," he said heavily.

Our Second appeared in the doorway just then.

"They're hooting for us from the ship, Doc. We'd better scoot."

With a hurried "See you in Japan," we fled. The Old Man, as usual, was having the fidgets to be off.

Everything was in confusion on the ship; the decks were filthy with coal-dust; the awnings had had to be taken down for the operation; and in consequence the place was like a burning fiery furnace.

"The Chief is as waxy as old nuts," said the Fourth, when we arrived on deck.

"What's up?" we both asked—the idea of the Chief being angry about anything was disturbing.

"Don't know! Some Chinese boarding-master has been up to something; and the Chief don't like it."

"What happened?" said the Second.

"Oh! I went below and found a new 'donkey-man' in charge."

" 'What thing?' I said.

" 'Belong new donkeyman, this ship,' he answered.

" 'The devil, you do,' said I; 'where's our old donkey-man?'

" 'No savvy,' he said in a sort of cheeky way.

"I thought it queer, so I shinned up, mighty quick, to the Chief; and he went along in a rage to the fo'castle and found our old donkey-man packing up.

" 'What's the matter, "Donkey"?' he said.

"Our donkey-man burst into tears.

" 'My mothah makee sick—makee die, Hong Kong side. No can stop this ship,' he said.

"It appears he had had the news that his mother was dying in Hong Kong; and as the ship was not going there this voyage, he wanted to leave."

"What did the Chief do?" I said, with interest, the donkey-man being rather a friend of mine.

"Oh, the Chief wouldn't have it. He refused to take the other donkey-man, refused to be re-supplied by any Number One Chinese crimp, and hoofed the new donkey-man ashore. The other fellow has been crying like one o'clock ever since; but he's here still."

"It seems a bit tough," I hazarded.

"Don't know," said the Second. "The Chief's pretty

wily. He knows Chinks; and if he thinks there's any hanky-panky, you can bet your boots on it he's got reasons."

I may as well give the sequel now, though it happened a week later. At first the donkey-man was inconsolable; then he got a bit better; and finally he came one day very mysteriously to the Chief when none of the other Chinamen were about.

"My mothah no makee die. No have got mothah," he said.

"What for then you makee talk. Plenty lie. Plenty cly?" said the Chief severely.

And then it all came out. It appeared that he had made enough money to get free of debt to the Chinese crimp at Singapore; and so the crimp wanted to put a new man in his place on the ship, a man who owed him money, so that he could draw his pay. Our donkey-man didn't want to leave and start getting into debt again; but all these people are in a secret society of which the crimps are the head, and their power over the men is almost absolute. If the Chief hadn't proved so obstinate, the man couldn't possibly have stayed, no matter how much he might have wished it.

·   ·   ·   ·   ·   ·

But to resume. It was an intense relief when at length we got clear of the wharf and were steaming out to sea again; for the enervating heat of Singapore, which sits boiling just above the Line, was now tempered by the breeze we were making; and so it was with feelings of satisfaction we saw the city fade in the opal distance, and heard the Old Man give the order altering our course to climb the China Sea.

Even in a few hours the difference was noticeable, for now, instead of the calm silence of the Malacca Strait, we were running through lumpy seas in the teeth of the N.E. monsoon, and a deck-chair was just a trifle chilly towards midnight.

It was on that first evening I got the Third Mate into deep disgrace. Sitting smoking in his cabin during his watch below, we noticed a German tramp making flash signals in the night, and idly began to read them. "Who the devil are you? Who the devil are you? Who the devil are you?" he kept signalling.

In a fatal moment I suggested we should Morse back, for it was evident that the signaller was gloriously drunk. The Third Mate jumped at the suggestion; and soon we had rigged an electric light in one of the ports, and by switching on and off, found we could signal perfectly. To our acknowledgment the German responded immediately, edging in towards us. We signalled away gaily, and were just in the middle of the enjoyment of saying sarcastic things and getting his enraged flashes in response, when a voice came down the ventilator:

"Captain's compliments, and will whoever is signalling without permission kindly stop."

"Oh, Lord," said the Third Mate.

"What?" I said.

"The Old Man will be as mad as a hatter. I'm done for, Doc."

That put an effectual damper on the fun.

"It was all my fault," I said. "I'll go up to the Old Man and explain."

But the Old Man wouldn't listen. He pretended he knew nothing about it, and vented his suppressed rage in bespattering the other ship.

"That d——d German has altered his course four times in the last half-hour. He must be roaring drunk on the bridge. I thought he'd run us down once—d——n him for a longshore lubber," he said.

When the Mate came off duty he explained it all to me; and it would seem, from his explanations, that we had been guilty of infringing a rule as unalterable as that of the Medes and Persians, namely, that no signals

could be sent from any ship without the express orders
of the master.

This was all vastly uncomfortable, and distressingly
annoying to me. Of course, as far as I was concerned, it
did not matter in the least; but for the Third Mate, who
was on his trial voyage, it might have far-reaching consequences; and that made it far worse for me than if I had
been liable to suffer for it myself. But the Mate couldn't
see it:

"It's not your fault, Doc. How were you to know
signalling wasn't allowed?"

"But I suggested it."

"Don't care. He knew better, and should have said
'No.' As a matter of fact, he's been in hot water several
times already this voyage.

"The Old Man is as wily as a fox. He caught him
cooking his 'positions' to make them correspond with the
Second Mate's observations; and he's been out on deck
in the middle watch at night, several times, and swears
he saw him asleep on the bridge.

"I don't think he has, myself. He's got a slovenly way
of leaning over the rail and gazing into space, instead
of walking backwards and forwards, that makes one
think him asleep. It's a lazy windjammer way he'll have
to get out of, if he wants to stay in the company."

All this was very unpleasant. I felt as if I had added
the last straw to the weight of the Third Mate's delin-
quencies, and consequently for the first time felt an un-
welcome restraint in the atmosphere of the ship, which
the increasing coldness of the weather, striking our sun-
baked bodies, and the uneasy motion, after a month of
calms, did not tend to alleviate. However, in a day or
two the Old Man simmered down, and we were all once
more a happy family.

But the weather did not improve. We were now in
heavy serge uniforms again; the decks were constantly
wet with spray; there was a dampness and clamminess

about everything; and leaks in the caulking overhead began again to show as stains on the roofs of our cabins.

The monsoon was dead in our teeth; and we were making at times barely six knots.

The fifth day out from Singapore was the worst we had. The Chief Steward reported water in the lazarette; and on inspection we found that a plate had been started in the night by the pull of the racing screw.

That made the Chief begin to fidget about his gear.

"I must go along and inspect the shaft in the tunnel," he said. "Like to come, Doc?"

"I'm on," I said; and so, donning a boiler suit, I followed him along the narrow passage, where the shaft turns unceasingly, night and day.

It was a long straight tunnel, barely four feet high, with not enough room to turn in till one had traversed its entire length. It lay twenty-five feet below water; and in its floor revolved the long, smoothly polished shaft, connecting the engines with the screw at the stern of the ship.

On the integrity of the shaft the life of the ship depends. As everyone knows, a broken shaft is one of the worst disasters that can happen to a ship at sea.

Crouching with heads bent forward, we went the length of the passage, till we came to the far end, where a little square space permitted us to stand erect. From this an iron ladder, set in a hollow cylinder, led to the poop thirty feet above. The Chief glanced back along the dim-lit tunnel.

"There was once a Second in one of our ships," he said. "For some reason or other he fell foul of one of the Chinamen. Once he struck the man. The Chink said nothing. Then the Second disappeared suddenly one day. So did the Chink. They searched the whole ship, but could not find them. It was the Chief, I think, who remembered he had told the Second to do something in the tunnel. They searched the tunnel—it was a very narrow one—and there they found them. They were both dead. The Chinaman had followed him in, crawling after him with a knife. They had fought it out in the tunnel. Nobody heard. The Chinaman's neck was broken. It wobbled loose when I pulled him out by the feet. I was Fourth then. The Second had been stabbed six times, once in the back and five times in front. How he twisted round in the space after he had been struck the first time, God only knows. I couldn't do it; and I was pretty thin then, not like now. But he just hated that Chink. I couldn't stand tunnels after that for a bit."

.   .   .   .   .   .

Towards night the weather grew wilder; a high wind rose; and bucketfuls of flying fish delighted the grinning Chinese. In the morning, however, it was almost calm again. The temperature had risen to 80° F.; portholes could be opened; and it was possible to lounge on deck again.

The Chinamen seized the opportunity to dry some of their gear; and so, walking along the main deck aft, I saw a lot of stuff spread out on the No. 5 hatch which looked like scraps of leather. On examination, however, it turned out to be bits of maggoty pigskin, which the Chinese cook told me were intended as medicine.

The cook and I were quite friendly now, owing to a curious taste of his. Like many Chinamen, he had tropical ringworm all over his chest. This he was treating with Stephens' blue-black ink; and instead of laughing when I discovered it, I suggested that I had something stronger he might use. Adding some carbolic, and mixing up sulphur ointment with the ink, I presented him with the mess. It stung him so much, and looked so nasty, that he was immensely pleased. We became friends for life.

Curiously enough, quite unexpectedly, his ringworm began to improve from that hour; and then the trouble began. They all wanted ink; and the ship's supply soon began to show signs of exhaustion owing to the unexpected demand.

.   .   .   .   .   .

We had continuous bad weather till we passed Turn about; and then in a few hours the change was remarkable. We were now in the Japanese Gulf Stream; and though the sea was still lumpy and yellow, the decks were dry, and the speed of the ship rose to twelve knots. Everyone grew suddenly cheerful; and we began to talk of what we were going to buy at Nagasaki. The next day was magnificently fine after the weather we had been having. Overhead was a blue sky, around us a white-flecked tumbling sea of blue. The air was bracing to an extraordinary degree. In spite of the cold it was wonderfully enjoyable.

We were two hundred miles from the Chinese coast; and yet we passed through a huge fleet of fishing junks, with whole Chinese families, down to little toddling infants, aboard—these junks being their only home. Although it was so cold, the men and women and children were working away almost naked.

Around the ship sea-birds sailed all day majestically. The lamp-trimmer came along as I stood gazing up at them, rifle in hand.

"It ain't worth it, sir. Them birds' skins ain't no good. Now if it wus goin' to Australia we wur, you could catch albatrosses with a fish 'ook."

"Ever heard of the 'Ancient Mariner,' Lamps?" I said.

"No, sir. What company was he in?"

"Can't just remember, Lamps. It was a long time ago."

Lamps, however, was not curious about the "Ancient Mariner."

"Albatrosses is fine, sir," he continued. "Their breasts make the greatest sort of muff. The missis 'as three or four I made 'er. An' the skin of the web makes a bully baccy-pouch. Yes. Albatrosses is fine; but these 'ere ain't worth the cartridges, sir."

So perished one of my oldest delusions about the superstitions of sailor-men—"Albatrosses is fine."

Early in the First Dog it darkened suddenly; black clouds overspread the sky; and night seemed rapidly approaching.

"There's a water-spout on the port bow, sir," said a passing quartermaster, as I was gazing idly out to starboard. I turned round quickly, and saw a dark mass looking like two cones touching by their apices, one rising from the sea, the other descending from a black mass of clouds overhead. It travelled rapidly with the wind across our bows, in a slanting manner, the sea portion, as it were, lagging behind the cloud. It was darkly smoky; and we were hoping the sun would come out and shine on it, as then it turns a beautiful yellow-white with iridescent edges; but suddenly, between us and it, a squall of rain and hail began to fall, and in the darkness beyond it disappeared.

Afterwards in the Java seas I saw many spouts, as it was then the rainy season; but this was my first, and therefore most interesting. Nowadays, when the romance of the sea has dwindled to vanishing point, no one bothers about spouts; but in the olden days, when the mariner went round-eyed from wonder to wonder and dragons and unicorns abounded, and the kingdom of Prester John was still on the map, sailors had a great dread of water-spouts, especially when, for the lack of wind, they could not get out of their course. Their device then was to fire the ship's cannon at the spout, with the idea of breaking it up; but "I did never hear that it proved to be of any benefit," says Dampier with naïve caution.

The *Sailor's Horn Book* gives an account of several ships that were swamped by spouts in a dead calm; but

Dampier's narrative, by its charm, absolutely demands quotation:

"And now being on this subject, I think it is not amiss to give you an account of an accident that happened once on the coast of Guinea some time in or about the year 1674. One Captain Records, of London, bound for the coast of Guinea, in a ship of 300 tons and 16 guns, called the *Blessing,* when he came into latitude 7 or 8 degrees North, he saw several spouts, one of which came directly towards the ship; and he, having no wind to get out of the way of the spout, made ready to receive it by furling his sails. It came on very swift, and broke a little before it reached the ship; making a great noise, and raising the sea round it, as if a great house, or some such thing, had been cast into the sea. The fury of the wind still lasted, and took the ship on the starboard bow with such violence that it snapped off the boltsprit and foremast, both at once, and blew the ship all along ready to overset it; but the ship did presently right again, and the wind, whirling round, took the ship the second time with the like fury as before, but on the contrary side and was again like to overset her the other way. The mizen-mast felt the fury of this second blast, and was snapped short off, as the fore-mast and boltsprit had been before. The main-mast and maintop-mast received no damage, for the fury of the wind (which was presently over) did not reach them. Three men were in the fore-top when the fore-mast broke, and one on the boltsprit, and fell with them into the sea, but all of them were saved. I had this relation from Mr. John Canby, who was then quartermaster and steward of her; one Abraham Wise was Chief Mate, and Leonard Jeffries Second Mate."

•   •   •   •   •   •

All day there had been an air of busy unrest about the ship. We expected to make Nagasaki on the morrow; and so all over the deck polishing, cleaning, brightening up was going on to get rid of the ravages of the foul weather we had been having, and to present a ship-shape appearance on going into port.

The engineers were overhauling the deck winches and seeing that everything worked smoothly; the boatswain was carefully testing his tackle; the stewards giving everything an extra rub up. Everyone was writing letters to catch the first mail home. Everyone was looking forward to hearing from England again. In the morning we should be in Japan.

CHAPTER V

FROM NAGASAKI TO MOJI, AND THROUGH THE
INLAND SEA TO KOBE

It has been the fashion in the past to gush about Japan. Everybody did so except the Europeans who lived there. It has also been customary for people who have been there for a fortnight to write a large book on the subject, just as half a century ago well-meaning persons, who had braved the Dublin crossing and done the Phoenix Park and Killarney, considered themselves qualified to adumbrate in ponderous tomes on the "Present State of Ireland." In the case of Japan the temptation has been so immense that, in spite of the best intentions, everyone suffering from *cacoethes scribendi* succumbs before it.

I had been hearing of nothing else since we left Singapore. The Old Man had been going there for more than thirty-five years. He remembered the two-sworded Samurai. He had seen the nation skip four centuries in twenty years; and his private opinion, publicly expressed many times at mess, was that they were a nation of cheats, and panders, and not to be compared in anything, except cleanliness, with John Chinaman. The Chief's and the Mate's conversation was for smoking-room circulation only; the Mate used always to end his yarns with—"But of course I can't now. I'm married."

The Chief Steward's conversation was mainly on china and bronze, ivory and lacquer ware. He had to know about these things, as the major part of his income was derived from commissions from London dealers.

One of the quartermasters, who had been a stevedore's ganger in Yokohama, taught me a lot of colloquial Japan-

ese, for use on shore; and so, long before we got past
Formosa, I felt already as if I were familiar with the
country.

"Nagasaki in the morning, Doc," the Old Man had
said before I turned in; and finding I could not sleep, I
had turned up the pages of *Madame Chrysanthème,* and
renewed acquaintance with that faery little butterfly Kiku
and the more shadowy outline of the "very tall friend."

The morning broke cold and raw, cloudy and with a
nipping wind. The coast looked a drear and ragged mass
of serrated peaks. This was not the Japan of fancy.

In the heaviest of overcoats, with the collar turned up
over my ears, I trudged up and down the deck.

Presently the sun came out, and the hills took on a
yellow-chrome colour, verging down to terraced green
below; whilst far in the hinterland the snow-capped peaks
shone crystalline white, untrodden by the foot of man.
Lugger-rigged junks scurried along in the choppy water,
under the protection of the shore; but other signs of life
there were none.

"When shall we be there?" I said to the Chief, looking
at this scene of desolation.

To my surprise he answered: "We're almost there now."

He was right; for presently the ship curled in, and a
little white lighthouse, bowered in feathery pines, appeared, round which we swept into smooth land-locked
waters. On either side were cone-shaped, pine-clad hills,
cut into terraces for cultivation. They looked so very
innocent that it was almost a shock to me when the
Chief pointed out fresh brown spots on the hills, and my
eyes caught the glint of artillery on either side, dominating everything—for Nagasaki is one of the greatest
ports of Japan, and is fortified like a Gibraltar.

A half-decked sampan, pushed out from the little jetty
underneath the lighthouse, was now approaching us
rapidly, rowed by four coolies standing up, each with a

Nagasaki Harbour
(Now destroyed by No. 2 atomic bomb)

Facing Page 116

A Junk in the Inland Sea

long sweep, while a fifth steered from behind with one equally long.

This was the pilot's boat; and we slowed down for it. A rope ladder was slung over the side; and the little flat-faced pilot climbed quickly on board. On we went along the channel, between high hills on either side. Our ensign flapped in the breeze behind; the flags denoting the ship's name flew from the flying bridge; the yellow "Doctor's" flag was on the fore-mast, that of the company at the main.

Passing close below a precipitous tree-clad island, the scene of a famous Christian massacre in the fifteenth century, we came suddenly upon the harbour itself, and saw the masts of many ships, like trees in a forest, anchored in the bay beyond. Presently a fussy little steam-launch, flying a red sun on a white ground, and having a large white "H" painted on its funnel, came alongside. This was the Health Officer's boat; and out of it poured no less than eleven Japanese doctors, in gold-braided uniform, looking like diminutive railway guards. Down went our anchor; and presently all the crew were lined up for inspection—Europeans to starboard, China-men to port.

Gravely the senior medical officer counted us to see if all were present, referring to the ship's papers mean-while. The others scattered round, felt pulses, looked at tongues, and prodded the Chinamen in the groins to see if they had got the plague.

It was all very grave, yet laughable. The senior officer said, "There iss one short, Mr. Mate."

"That's the engineer on duty," said the Chief. "We'll send for him, if you like. Ah, here he comes," as the Fourth appeared, hot and sweating in his boiler suit, from below.

Apparently they were satisfied; and soon, with pro-found bows, they all trooped down the gangway again, got into their launch, and fussed away.

The Chief was grumpy about it: "What the deuce they want so many for, I can't think. And this isn't the last of it. In twenty-four hours we'll be at another port; and it'll be the same all over again. If we reached a third, twelve hours later, it would be the same again. It's European ideas overdone."

"The way those fellows felt pulses showed me that half of them weren't doctors at all," I said.

"I've thought so, often," chimed in the Mate. "Half of them are service men spying on foreign shipping. The Japs are frightfully suspicious since the Russian war, even of a company like ours trading here since the Satsuma rebellion."

"How does the Jap doctor, on his native heath, impress you, Doc?" said the Chief Steward.

"You remind me, Bruce, of the New York reporters, who meet distinguished foreigners half way up the bay and ask them what they think of America," I said.

As a matter of fact, I had been unfavourably impressed, and so declined to be drawn, feeling the injustice of the prepossession; for the Jap in ill-fitting European clothes is not seen at his best. He is small and sallow, and to our eyes ugly. In his own garments he looks courtly and sphinx-like; he has a priestly air, and somehow or other manages to look taller. But in European clothes he courts comparison with Europeans, and every difference appears as a defect.

That was why I did not feel proud of my brothers of the scalpel. Immediately they had gone, down came the yellow doctor's flag; and, almost simultaneously, half a dozen sampans, that had been hovering round till the flag was lowered, hitched on. So whilst the anchor was being raised and the ship getting under way their owners climbed on board, and began to spread their wares upon the deck—Satsuma, cloisonnè, kaga, netsukes, tortoise-shell, ivory, lacquer, and all the thousand-and-one things lumped up by the sailor under the generic title "curios."

Most of the dealers seemed to be well known to the officers. They spread their wares, and squatted, bare-headed, in their kimonos, quietly beside them; nor did they pester one to buy, like the hungry Egyptian or the pertinaciously submissive Hindoo—they were much too dignified for that.

An old lady, bundled in half a dozen kimonos, clat-tered up in her high wooden pattens, and squatted aft with a basket of monkey nuts, oranges, cigarettes, tobacco, matches and other odds and ends. Soon she was doing a roaring trade with the Chinamen, chaffering in infini-tesimal fractions of a sen. I bought half a dozen boxes of matches from her, for which I paid one sen (a far-thing), and I knew I had been charged 300 per cent. more than they were worth.

Presently we anchored; and soon a regular fleet of lighters, each with its huge bamboo yards and latticed sail, gathered round, and a crowd of Japanese coolies rapidly inundated the ship.

Dressed in trunk hose, with huge cape-like haori coats covered with the heraldic lettering of their guild, they might have stepped out of the fifteenth century. All were bare-headed. Many had a fillet of lettered cloth tied round their temples to keep the sweat from running into their eyes as they worked. All wore straw sandals, whose thongs fitted in a special compartment of the sock between the great and second toe.

Soon they had the hatches off; the sound of the steam-winches became all-pervasive; and cargo was being dumped rapidly into the satellite lighters.

It was a cold raw day, with a suspicion of rain behind the hills. Nagasaki lay spread out on the slope of the mountain before us—a mass of roofs. It is always roofs one sees in a prospect of a Japanese city. The houses are never high, the constant earthquakes making it unsafe to build; and so there are no outstanding buildings, nothing to catch the eye. Everywhere it is roofs with the curious

Oriental curving at the eaves one's eye so soon gets accustomed to.

The Japanese seem incapable of rectangularity in thought or design. The outline of the country is irregular to a degree; plains are almost unknown; and the asymmetry of the landscape is reflected in the designs of the people: a vase is never quite plumb, a cup never quite round, every drawing has in it the elements of caricature, every carving the same. A sense of perspective seems foreign to the spirit of the people.

We have learnt from them the beauty of irregularity, the unexpected, the bizarre. Their minds have a twist and their art reflects it.

Westerners, brought up in the Græco-Roman cult of straight lines, and simple curves of thought, and art, and action, coming to Japan find themselves brought up short by a new, strange, different atmosphere. Everything they have been carefully trained to think correct is reversed— their entire sense of values is repudiated.

This in itself would not matter. The startling thing is to find that the Japanese line of evolution is as complete as, but quite different from, our own.

One so readily slips into an inelastic way of thinking that evolution can occur only in one direction, that the discovery of the contrary comes as a distinct mental jar— all of which is very discomposing.

I found the Chief in the Old Man's cabin.

"Going ashore, Doc?" said the Old Man.

I nodded.

"Well, we can all go together. I shall want you at the Chinese consulate. Mr. Halahan will explain. The launch will be ready in ten minutes."

It seemed that eleven of our firemen were being paid off, their time having expired; and we had to arrange to send them home to Hong Kong. My part was to inspect the new men sent to take their places, and see if they were free from plague, etc.

The Chinamen had already mustered on the deck with their belongings, some wrapped in Macassar mats of variegated straw, others in curious wooden boxes with elaborate locks, others in simple plait baskets. Every one of them, I noticed, had two or more English umbrellas, worth about eighteen-pence each—one old "trimmer" had no less than six, of which he was evidently inordinately proud. Off they went in a couple of sampans, chattering like parrots.

The Old Man, the Chief, and I followed in the launch to the *hatoba* (landing stage). There was a rickishaw-stand just outside on the Bund; and soon we three were seated and careering one behind the other along the front. The Old Man and the Chief looked immense behind the little wiry men, in limpet-shaped oilskin hats, who were pulling them along at a steady jog-trot of about six miles an hour.

The Jap rickishaw men are not to be compared with the Chinese in stamina. Their physique is poor in the extreme. In Singapore a two-seated rickishaw is common. Here the Jap cannot pull two Europeans, though he can make shift with two of his own dainty country-women with ease.

Once we had transacted our official business the Chief and I left the Old Man closeted with the agent, and started sight-seeing. We had two hours to rush round the city; and so we hailed our rickishaws and hurried away. Everything was new, everything fresh to me. The curious noise in the streets made by the wooden pattens of the pedestrians, the absence of horses, the constant passage of rickishaws with little Japanese ladies, chatting, smiling, dressed like dolls, with hair elaborately coiled and shining, absorbed my attention.

The itinerant merchants with their stock-in-trade slung in two hampers on a bamboo pole, the narrow little streets, the open shops innocent of glass, selling things of which one could not even imagine the use, fascinated me. Everywhere I noticed signs in Japanese and Russian, for Nagasaki contains a large Russian colony—officers captured and sent there during the war, who have taken up permanent abode in Japan and sent for their wives and children rather than return to Russia.

That they were none too popular we learnt to our cost, after directing our men to take us to a tea-house.

Round a corner they swung, along an alley, and finally drew up before the doorway of a verandahed wooden house. There were four ricks at the entrance, but no other sign of life.

In we went to a brick hall, where there was a row of sandals at the bottom of the brick staircase. Up this we went, still seeing no one, till we came to a room on the first floor. The floor was covered with beautiful white tatami matting, scrupulously clean. It seemed a shame to step on it with our heavy boots; but the Chief stumped on.

The walls were of wooden laths, made to slide back if necessary. One side of the room was a framework of glazed paper, acting as a window. There was no furniture except a round table, rising nine inches from the floor, with a square hole in the centre of it.

The Chief clapped his hands—it made one think somehow of the Arabian Nights—and sliding one of the wooden partitions aside, a girl glided in, bowed, and brought us cushions to sit on. Later she returned with a brazier, a square box containing lighted charcoal, which she set in the opening in the little table. Then drawing her kimono coquettishly round her, she sat down opposite us, struck lights for our cigarettes, accepted one for herself, smiling all the time.

For some reason or other she directed all her conversation to me, smiling continuously; but I could not make out a word, and finally came to the conclusion she was speaking neither Japanese nor English. The Chief also confessed his inability to make out what was said.

Then an old lady came in, wrinkled, grey, looking like the Witch of Endor, in a kimono. She stared at our muddy boots and looked quite cross. She also spoke to me. I asked for tea for myself and beer for the Chief in Japanese. Then she went away grumbling.

"Something seems to be bothering the old party," said the Chief.

"I think she doesn't like our boots," I said.

"Hang the boots," he retorted.

The little maid had followed the old lady out of the room; and presently she came back with the tea in little handle-less cups, a clear straw-coloured fluid, without sugar or milk. The Chief would have none of it. He demanded beer. The little maid looked very subdued. She had ceased to smile. She shrank off from the Chief's side to mine, as if for protection. The old lady brought the beer herself. It was *kirin,* a Japanese brand, very clear and agreeable, like light lager. She demanded two yen for it (about four shillings). The Chief was indignant. We both got up and walked out, followed by vituperations from the old hag.

The Chief's face was like a confused thunder-cloud.

"I can't make it out," he said. "I've been coming to this country for eight years now; and it's the first time I've ever been treated like this."

"I'm sure there's some mistake," I said.

My rickishaw man knew some English; and I turned to him. The old lady was holding forth on the Chief's iniquities.

"What thing?" I said.

"She say, big fat man bolong Russian," he answered.

"What?" said the Chief. "Russians, bedad. So that's it." His face began to clear.

"Here, boy, you say, 'No savvy Russian. Bolong English'."

The boy talked rapidly to the old woman. The other

boy explained to me: "She no likee Russian. Him kill two—three her son."

Gradually the old woman was made to understand; and then she was suddenly all penitent. She made us uncomfortable by her abasement, wanted us back, wanted to do all sorts of things for us, apologised in endless circumlocutions.

"Let's get," said the Chief irritably.

So after assuring her it was all right, we climbed into our rickishaws hastily, and fled. It was an unpleasant adventure.

To soothe his ruffled feelings the Chief insisted on going to an hotel. The hotels in Nagasaki are not good; and everything is very dear. A curiosity about Japanese hotels is that all the responsible people in them—managers, cashiers, head waiters, etc.—are Chinamen, for the Japanese cannot count properly, having no head for mathematics.

After the Chief had been soothed, we went the round of the shops and curio stores. The Nagasaki shops are famous for Satsuma ware—the province itself is just over the mountains—and tortoiseshell. I was beginning to enjoy myself, bargaining for stuff I did not want, when the Chief looked at his watch. Our quarrel and the soothing had taken up more time than we had thought.

"We'll have to buck. Ship sails at eight; and it's close to dinner-time now," he said.

So we had a hurried rush back to the *hatoba*, where our men, with all the *aplomb* of the old-time London cabby, tried to overcharge us 300 per cent. My Japanese came in useful then. I had a stock of expressions, which I used most effectively. Some of them I did not quite understand; but I had been told they would be useful on occasions such as these. The rickishaw men evidently came to the conclusion we were residents, and so not to be fooled like tourists. They dropped two dollars in price,

stood grinning as we got into a sampan, and with a
courteous *Sayonara* bade us good-bye.

When darkness fell we steamed out quietly in the
night amongst the islands, through the Tsushima Strait.
We were bound for Moji, the coaling station at the
entrance of the Inland Sea.

The navigation here is ticklish; and the Old Man
stayed on the bridge all night; yet in the morning he
looked as fresh as if he had just got up.

After breakfast I watched the islands as we passed,
and the snow-peaks on the mainland, alternating with
brown velvet hills. Approaching Moji, we saw the smoke
rising above the hills concealing the entrance; and then,
rounding a pine-clad promontory, we came on a little
white lighthouse with a flagstaff.

Up went the ship's flags—the yellow quarantine at the
fore, the House flag at the main, and the old British
ensign floating out behind.

The telegraph rang "half speed"; and we rounded the
corner, to see the roofs of a little village nestling in a
tiny bay on the lee side, climbing up in straggling
groups of houses to the terraced land above, with its
little temple and steep graveyard, bristling with rect-
angular tombstones, dominating all. I had a curious
feeling that I had seen it all before, and could not quite
think why, till I remembered that in my cabin lay a fan
with a picture on it, drawn in a few inimitable strokes,
which might have passed as a reproduction of the scene
before me.

Below, a steam-launch lay at anchor, flying the now
familiar blood-red sun flag of Japan. Down went the
starboard anchor, with a rattle of chains, and we were
hove-to waiting permission to proceed. Presently a sampan put off from the village and drew alongside the
launch. Then the launch started for us and soon we
were boarded by the pilot and four gold-braided medicos
—only four this time. They all disappeared into the Old

Man's cabin; and then I suddenly remembered I had forgotten to inspect the eleven new firemen we had taken
on the previous day. When therefore the Old Man sent
for me, I thought it might be necessary to throw out
a bluff about them should they ask any awkward questions. They were all smoking in the Old Man's cabin,
sitting stiffly in their chairs like ladies at an At Home
who do not know one another well.

The Old Man introduced me to the P.M.O., and I
signed a lot of papers.

"Have a cigar, Doc?" said the Old Man.

Now I knew the Old Man's cigars. There were several
grades. He kept a job lot of Burma cheroots, at a dollar
a hundred, specially for Japanese officials. They are a
little better than the English "tuppenny" advertised as
having a "rich, nutty flavour"; and it was these the
medicos were smoking.

I said, "Thank you, sir," dodged the open box, and
found a fine Havana for myself. The Old Man's eyes
twinkled.

It was all very solemn—like a funeral. The P.M.O.
alone could speak English; and his vocabulary was limi-
ted.

"Had I been to his beautiful country before?— No.—
Ah, my visit then should have been later.—The cherry-
blossom would not be fully out before I left.—Yes, oh
yes; it is very beautiful as it is.—But the cherry-blossom——"

Presently we made a movement to the deck, where
the crew were lined up; but the examination was merely
perfunctory. We were not landing—merely calling for
coal—so it did not matter.

The Old Man and I bowed them off the ship; down
came the yellow flag; up came the anchor; and we
steamed between the hills into the Shimonoseki Straits.

The mountains ran up high on either side, pine-clad,
snow-capped, in the distance. Sleepy little villages met

one's eye at every turn.   Once we had to make a detour to pass a sunken steamer.

Gradually the scenery became less sylvan—a railway track appeared along one shore, and on it American engines were hauling train-loads of coal wagons.   Then came huge cement works, with great tall factory chimneys, huddled houses underneath, and a general air of murkiness suggestive of the Potteries.

Soon a perfect forest of masts appeared; and we passed junks of every known rig; tramp steamers, English, American, German, Jap, and Chinese, one of the Canadian Pacific "Empress" boats, looking like a queen amongst the squat merchantmen, and then the trim grey outline of a Japanese cruiser, anchored in the bay.   The cruiser dipped to us as we passed; and, at a signal from the Old Man on the bridge, we dipped in response to the compliment.

Finally we reached our moorings, and dropped anchor in the centre of the strait, between Moji, smoky with coal-dust and factories, a parvenu of twenty years, and Shimonoseki on the opposite side, an ancient historic city, with memories of a thousand years behind it.

Shimonoseki looks down upon Moji.   Moji pretends it does not care, and grows larger, wealthier, and more ugly yearly.   It was the discovery of coal that made Moji spring suddenly from an insignificant village to a position of rivalry with Shimonoseki; and it was largely for coaling purposes we were there.

An hour after we had anchored one would hardly have recognized the ship, for the curio-dealer was everywhere, and the spick-and-span, comparative loneliness of the decks was confused by a multiplicity of exotic objects and figures.

In one corner three separate Japanese families had forgathered, started a charcoal fire, and were cooking their mid-day meal.   It was "Chow" time; and while the men squatted the women moved about, helping them to tea

out of ampulla-like jars, and ladling boiled rice out of
firkins. The babies all the while, lolling with nodding
heads, slept peacefully, strapped on their mothers' backs.
Most of the women were grimy, and had their heads tied
up in handkerchiefs to protect their hair, for they were
present to assist in coaling the ship.

Japan is a country of striking surprises. One goes
there with visions of dainty porcelain-like little ladies;
one's first intimate contact with them is when one sees
coarse harridans doing the work of navvies loading coal
at Moji.

The process of coaling is exceedingly ingenious. All
the coal is carried by hand from the lighters to the
bunkers in little round wooden baskets holding perhaps
twenty pounds. Nevertheless the number of people
working, and the rapidity with which it is done, makes
Moji one of the quickest coaling ports in the world. The
method is quite different from that at Port Said or Singapore. From the ship's side a bamboo scaffolding is erected
down to the lighters, so arranged that a number of
planks, making a staircase, can be laid on it. On each
step stands a coolie; and the baskets are passed up in a
living chain from the lighters, step by step, to the ship.

At the top the baskets are received by the women, who
slide them along a plank, topple their contents into the
bunkers, and then throw the empty baskets back again
into the lighters.

.   .   .   .   .   .

They were busy at it when we came up from tiffin;
and I took the opportunity of snapshotting one fat old
lady with a baby on her back while the sun was out for
a moment. She saw me in the act, and immediately
demanded a *comshaw*. *Comshaw* in the Far East is as
baksheesh in Egypt. There is always a *comshaw* in every
transaction. If you buy anything you demand *comshaw*.
The rick man who takes you to a curio-store receives a
small *comshaw* from the proprietor. When one pays a

bill one expects a small *comshaw* for doing it. It is all *comshaw* in the Far East.

I gave the old lady a cigarette as a *comshaw*. This she accepted with a smile, immediately going over to the Chief, who was sitting on the hatch-coaming, for a match. Then with a contented air she recommenced the monotonous task of passing, passing, passing baskets again. And all the while the baby slept serenely on her back.

· · · · · ·

At tiffin the Old Man had been laying down the law about curios.

"The only thing worth buying here, Doc, is a sort of carved wooden tray. They used to bring them on board; but I haven't seen one for years now."

"I'll try to find some when I go ashore at Shimonoseki this afternoon," I said.

"Don't let them do you in the price," he said.

"They're pretty sure to," chuckled the Chief. "But he'll probably not be able to find the things, if they're so scarce."

Of course that determined me to do my best to find them; and so when I landed at the Shimonoseki *hatoba* I decided to hunt about on foot, on the chance of finding what I wanted, and let the rickishaw-man follow after me.

A coolie hurrying past with a huge bale of rice nearly ran me down. He tacked sideways, hissed, and went on. I was astonished, even the Japanese labourers being credited with fine manners.

All the shops, in the little two-storied wooden houses that lined one of the main streets, had open fronts; and the merchants sat cross-legged in them behind their goods, smoking the little Japanese pipe, drinking tea with their families, playing some game like draughts, attending to a stray customer, or totting up their accounts with the aid of the abacus, a square frame with coloured balls on wires, like that used in schools to teach children to count.

Walking along one seemed, as it were, admitted into the whole family life of the community. I stopped opposite one shop where five chests of green tea, of varying degrees of fineness, stood exposed. An old lady sat on the raised floor behind. When I looked at her she hissed just like the coolie, and then bowed. I moved hurriedly away. This was getting distressing. I remembered stories of a sudden hatred of foreigners since the Russian war, re-membered that Shimonoseki was the scene of the firing on the Allied fleets, and that a coolie had attempted to assassinate Li Hung Chang in Shimonoseki after the sign-ing of the Chinese treaty. Perhaps Shimonoseki was anti-foreign? My first experience in Nagasaki had been un-fortunate. I began to feel uncomfortably alone. The com-pany's office was a little further along the street; and I went in to get some general directions as to what one should look at. When I told the clerk, who had been to lunch with us on the ship, of my experiences with the coolie and the old woman, he laughed uproariously.

"Thanks awfully, Doc."

"What?" I said.

"It's the best joke I've heard for a month. Why, man, it's a sign of courtesy to a superior to suck in one's breath like that."

"Well, I'm jiggered!" was all I could say in response.

Certainly things were topsy-turvy in this country. I saw a house being built. The first thing put up was the roof. The carpenters who were sawing wood below had saws broader at the tip than the handle, exactly the opposite to ours, and sawed towards themselves, instead of away, as we do. The magazines I saw in the book-shops started with a coloured frontispiece on the back of the last page; the letterpress worked also from the last towards the first; the type read from right to left, ver-tically downwards; and all the footnotes were at the top of the page.

I wandered aimlessly about the streets, watching the

life of the common people. Everything was strange, everything interesting. The streets were narrow and without footpaths. A covered runnel, which was flushed out every day, ran along both sides, close to the houses. Men with bundles of twigs tied in a besom swept the streets. Little boys and girls trotted along on their high pattens, coming back from school, with their books tucked up in the sleeves of their little kimonos. Life seemed very intimate, owing to the constant visions of the interiors one got through the open fronts of the houses. In one shop a barber was shaving the head of a little boy of about six months. His mother held him in her lap, a quaint figure of fun in his little garments, whilst the barber shaved the top of his crown, leaving a fringe around like a priest's tonsure, the baby all the time looking out on the world with round, unthinking eyes, rolling its head about in the purposeless manner of infancy.

Policemen, little men in yachting-caps and swords, swaggered about keeping law and order. Up and down the streets itinerant hawkers moved with their stock-in-trade slung on a bamboo pole, working a rattle with the unengaged hand to call attention to their wares.

At every street corner, almost, stood a man with a stand on which a charcoal brazier heated a little boiler, the steam of which escaping made a high hissing note. This was an itinerant pipe-mender. Every now and then a curious figure passed, a man with a kind of flageolet, who paused, played a few melancholy sweet notes, and then moved on again. When two or three had passed me I discovered that each was blind; but at the time I could not make out their occupation. Afterwards I learnt they were masseurs—massage is always done by the blind in Japan, and the flute note was their call to those who might require their services. Once or twice I came across houses belonging to the more important people. One particularly struck me. It was surrounded by a court-

yard, and had a most elaborately carved dragon gateway, gazing through which I noted that on the wide
shallow steps of the verandah six open Chinese umbrellas
were spread, betokening the number of visitors within.

While I was looking at them a company of Japanese
cavalry on rough little Manchurian ponies passed. Climbing up a long flight of steps to the parallel street above,
I was gazing, pipe in mouth, at the Torii at the entrance
to a Shinto temple, when three small schoolboys passed
me. They stopped, looked at me, and grinned from ear
to ear. It was evidently my pipe that amused them;
and, smiling back, I let them look at it. The oldest of
the three returned it with a solemn elaborate bow; and
then they all laughed again, and ran clattering off on
their wooden pattens. Everyone seemed to be smiling
that day, except a solitary priest who stood like a sentinel
at the temple gates.

A pathway led from the temple to a little graveyard
beyond; and a young girl, washing clothes, had appro-
priated the two sides to hang them out to dry. Several
garments had fallen on the path, blown down by the
wind; and so I walked carefully to avoid them. Seeing
this, she smiled, and called out something to someone
in the house behind. This brought out the old grand-
mother, holding in her arms a chubby little infant. The
old lady bowed to me like a queen; and I felt like a
mountebank bowing back in response.

Beyond the graveyard the path led down by steps to
the street below; and along it two geisha girls, looking
like Solomon in all his glory, were picking their steps
with dainty feet.

A man turned to stare after them; but apparently they
were totally unconscious of his admiration, for they
walked on steadily, without a sign of recognition till they
came to the corner. Then one of them looked back; but
by this time the man had gone.

Coming along the street on the opposite side, a coolie,

carrying a pile of flour-bags, had placed them in a heap on the ground to rest. A little toddling infant found them there, and immediately proceeded, with much joy, to roll in them, covering himself completely with flour-dust. When I arrived the mother had just become aware of what was happening, and had rushed to the child, taken him in her arms, and started reviling the chuckling coolie. The child was taking absolutely no notice of the mother, but instead was crowing joyously at the coolie —a ragged, barelegged person with an exceedingly humorous face, who was snapping his fingers for the child's amusement, making weird grimaces, and all the while carrying on a wordy warfare with the mother. His retorts must have been immensely amusing, for all the onlookers were kinking with laughter, and the mother looked very discomposed. At length, finding the contest too hot for her, carrying the infant upside down, she fled incontinently, followed by a volley of laughter from the onlooking crowd.

By this time I had begun to get a general idea of the topography, for I had discovered that most of the streets lay parallel with one another on the side of the mountain, and were connected at intervals by cross flights of stone steps.

All the time I was wandering aimlessly, looking at odd-looking temples, queer signs, or anything strange in the shops, I was thinking about my wooden trays, watching for them and never finding them; and so it was quite an unexpected delight when, turning into what appeared a *cul-de-sac,* I came upon a woodcarver, squatting on the dais of his open workshop with his tools around him, and caught him in the act of making the very things I wanted. He could speak no English; but he was most polite. He motioned me with an arm-wave to ransack his stock-in-trade of carved things, while he went on steadily at his work. When he saw I had lit on what I wanted he stopped, got up, and came over. I had

selected a nest of five, carved with a design of a temple
in some thirty masterly strokes.

I asked him how much he wanted for them; and he
took out coins, laid them in order, and showed me what
he required.

It seemed so ridiculously little I paid it on the spot.
He looked so dignified, and was so evidently an artist
to his finger-tips that it seemed like a disparagement of
his work attempting to chaffer.

I called my rick-man and placed them in the *kuruma;*
and then, feeling I had done what I came out for, let
myself luxuriate, trundling aimlessly around the city at
the *kurumaya's* fancy.

In one of the streets we passed a detachment of in-
fantry, the men walking hand in hand like schoolchild-
ren. Further on, swinging round a corner, we nearly ran
into a curious procession. It was some sort of religious
service. There were kimonoed women with samisens and
biwas playing, and a man in a semi-military uniform
talking to the people. They had a flag. I recognised
that. It was our old friend the Salvation Army flag. I
regret to say I laughed. It was all so unexpectedly incongruous. Yet anyone who knows Japan, and what the
Salvation Army has done for the women of Japan, feels
that its work can certainly not be laughed at.

I had brought my camera ashore with me, and taken
several snapshots as I went around the city. Now I
fetched it from the rickishaw to snap the Army meeting.
It was the last plate I had.

Immediately I found myself in trouble. More troops
were passing at the time. A Japanese officer looked at
me, saw what I was doing, and before I knew what was
happening I was under arrest. I looked around, and
every face was hostile. Even the rickishaw man glared
at me stonily.

The officer pointed to my camera. A soldier stretched
out his hand towards it; but I held on. The officer

waved him back, and then in peremptory tones, though I could not understand a word he said, gave me to understand I was to march straight ahead.

Apparently I was being taken to gaol.

For the life of me, I could not make out what was the matter; and that made me all the more uncomfortable. But I evidently had to march, and that pretty quickly. We went along the street, two men in front, two behind me, a crowd following, and my rickishaw man, who hadn't been paid, in the rear.

Turning a corner, I recognised the shop where the old lady had hissed at me, and knew the agent's office was near. I was lucky. The identical clerk who had laughed at me was coming out of the office. I beckoned him with my hand; and he came quickly forward. The officer evidently knew him, and allowed him to speak to me.

"What on earth's the row?" he said.

"Dashed if I know."

He saw the camera in my hand, and immediately said, "You haven't been fool enough to be taking photos, have you?"

"Yes. Why not?"

"Oh, Lord! Man, this place is fortified no end. They're as suspicious as old maids; and no one is allowed, under any pretext, to take photos near fortified places."

"I've been snapping all over the place," I said in despair. "I suppose they'll smash my camera, and give the company no end of trouble clearing me."

"It's the devil of a mess. I'll do my best to explain; but, dash it all, there's a big notice on the *hatoba* against it," he said.

"Very likely. Never saw it, though."

He turned to the officer and explained volubly, but apparently with very little effect.

"I'm afraid it's not much good," he said.

I was beginning to think things might be becoming serious, when a Japanese gentleman, who was passing, and had had to get out of his rickishaw on account of the crowd, stared at me, smiled suddenly, came forward, and held out his hand.

I had not the faintest idea who he was; but he knew me, pronounced my name, and was evidently a friend. I shook hands with him as if he had been my long-lost brother. The officer evidently knew him also; he saluted gravely. The agent's clerk knew him; and seized the opportunity of asking us all into the office. In a few minutes the whole complexion of things was altered. They talked away about it in the office; and all the time I was puzzling my brain trying to make out my unknown friend's identity.

Presently they announced their solution. He had been talking away the officer's suspicions; and they had mutually agreed that my camera was to be taken, the plates developed, any not approved of destroyed, and the rest returned to me on the morrow.

"We sail this evening," I said. "Can't I have them then?"

But to this the officer could not agree. The agent, however, promised to send the camera on to Kobe, if we sailed before it arrived; and so it was settled.

We went down again into the street. My rickishaw man, now all smiles, pushed forward through the crowd, which quickly dispersed; and my friend's man did the same.

"I haven't seen you since the old days at King's years ago. Whatever brings you here?" he said.

And then I remembered a little Japanese student, whom no one took much notice of, working away laboriously at a dissection of the middle ear, to whom I had one day, in a good-natured moment, given a demonstration on some point he did not quite understand. Afterwards he had got into the habit of coming to me in a difficulty; and I had always done my best to explain. I had forgotten all about him; but now it all came back.

The agent's clerk said, "You're lucky to have got out of it so well, Doc."

I thought so too, myself, and said so as I thanked him for his help.

"But what's my friend's name? I'm ashamed to say I don't know it."

"You make me laugh," he said. "Why, it's Dr. Tomatoda, the Principal Medical Officer in charge of troops here."

"Right. I've got it now; thanks."

I went to thank him and say good-bye before directing my man to take me to the *hatoba*; but he was not to be shaken off so lightly.

He had got it into his head that I would have a poor impression of the Japanese after my experience, and was most apologetic for the bother I had had. He insisted, therefore, that I should go back with him to his own home and drink tea with him; he would have no denial.

So we were soon stringing out, his rickishaw man in front; and in a few minutes we arrived in front of a Japanese house of the better sort. A perfect little flower of a maid came running out into the piazza, and pulled off our boots. His were elastic-sided. Previously I had noticed that most Japanese in European costume wore elastic-sided boots, and had wondered why, for somehow in England one associates them with the Nonconformist conscience. Watching her struggling to unlace mine, I soon saw their convenience in a country like Japan. I tried to assist; but she would not let me. Eventually, however, between us we got them off; and I followed my host through a sliding screen he had pushed aside into the house, feeling very queer indeed going to pay a formal call in stockinged feet. We came into a room quite bare of furniture, covered with tatami matting fitting in squares. It was empty.

"My father would have nothing European in the home," he said.

"And a good thing, too," I answered quickly.

"You think so really?" he said in surprise.

"I'm sure of it," I answered sincerely.

I was pleased he did not ask me why; because I should have had to explain that the Japanese, though they have such exquisite taste in everything pertaining to their own methods of living and furnishing, when they begin to copy European models seem to lose all their good taste, and manage to imitate the very worst traits of the models, missing the best completely. As a consequence houses built and furnished in Japan on European lines are inimitable examples of how not to do it.

Pushing aside a leaf of the partition, we came into a room at the back of the house looking on to a garden, with a little pond, a bridge over it and a quaint little shrine beyond placed on the ridge of a miniature mountain, green with very small but exceedingly old-looking, gnarled matsu trees.

Turning my eyes back to the room, I saw that in a recess a gaily painted scroll hung down, and at its base was a vase with a single sprig of cherry-blossom. A few bright-coloured cushions lay on the matted floor. There was no other furniture.

Presently two girls, in red-trimmed, modified kimonos, with their hair in pigtails, came into the room. They were his sisters; and the costume, I afterwards understood, was that prescribed for high-school girls.

They bowed profoundly to their brother and me, and then ambled round in their little white *tabi* (one-toed socks), finding cushions for us to sit on, smiling all the time, and waiting on us hand and foot.

They were introduced to me as "My sisters, Hana and Kiku," very graceful, clear-eyed little girls, very dimpled and smiling. They looked exactly like skilfully made dolls.

"They will want to speak English with you very much.

They learn it at school. Will you be graciously pleased?" he said gravely.

I was "graciously pleased." I felt somehow as if I were acting in a Gilbertian opera, and took it all quite seriously.

Once or twice I felt like protesting, remembering they were ladies, whilst they were looking after my comfort, bringing the *tabakabon*—a brazier for smoking—lighting my cigarette for me, drawing screens to shut off the draught from me. Afterwards I was glad I did not, as it is counted the height of rudeness for any Japanese lady to delegate to servants any small personal attentions necessary to the comfort of her male relations and their honoured guests.

The little maid I had first seen brought in tea. It was served by Hana in the usual tiny cups without handles, and was the usual straw-coloured fluid I was now beginning to like.

Presently their tongues loosened; and they plied me with questions. I wish I could repeat the quaintness of their English. They asked me many things—often the most awkward things—with the most innocent, round inquiring eyes.

I think they must have been catechising me for over an hour. Time flew rapidly, and it was with regret I tore myself away from their fascinating little presences. But the day was flying, and I had been warned to be back at the ship before dinner. I made as ceremonious an exit as I could, feeling boorishly awkward beside these polished bowing little ladies.

Dr. Tomatoda insisted on seeing me to the *hatoba*, got me a sampan, instructed the man where to take me, and reiterated warmly his invitation to look him up again when the ship came back after leaving Yokohama. With a pleasant feeling that my afternoon had been well spent. I climbed up the gangway to the deck above, carrying my precious wooden trays under my arm.

On the way to the ship I began to fear I had been done over the price, remembering I had made no bargain. So when I got on deck I stealthily hid them under my coat, and slunk down to my cabin to get rid of them.

Coaling was still going on; and, coming on deck again, I was hailed by the Chief.

"D'ye remember about those trays?" he said. "Well, funny thing, just after you had gone a dealer brought some on board. I bought one, a beauty, and was going to get one for you too; but I thought I'd wait, though I didn't think you'd be able to find any ashore."

"I got some," I said.

"You did, did you? Hope they haven't diddled you, Doc."

"Let's see yours," I said hastily, to change the subject.

Nothing loath, he took me below. It certainly was a beauty—the same size as the largest of mine, and with the same design on it.

He was immensely pleased. He had paid one-third of what had been asked.

"How much?" I said. He told me.

"They can't diddle me," he said. "I've been coming too long to the country for that."

I am afraid I laughed in his face. It was partly the relief of it; for I had paid just one and a half the price of his one for my five. When I told him he refused to believe me; but on my affirming again positively, he said, finally, with a crestfallen air, "Well, I'm jiggered! I'll never give you advice about prices again, Doc."

And he never did. On the contrary, he came to me. I had established my reputation as a bargainer. The thought of it makes me laugh still.

At one bell, just before dinner, a little Jap came up the gangway. I had got out of mufti, and was standing in uniform at the companion hatch. He made a bee-line for me, drew himself up, saluted, and then said in an explosive voice: "I am the post-office."

It was evidently a sentence he had learnt off by heart; he had probably been repeating it all the way out in the sampan; and now he shot it rapidly at me before he should forget.

At the same time he thrust a long blue document at me. I looked at it, found it was a telegram for the captain, and so directed the "post-office" to his cabin.

Its receipt evidently put the Old Man in a bad temper. All the way up from Singapore he had been talking of a great friend of his, a Captain Outram, one of the pilots of the Inland Sea. At Nagasaki he had wired for him to take the ship through the narrows to Kobe; and this wire in reply was to say he could not come.

The Inland Sea is rather a difficult piece of navigation, and all ships have to carry pilots according to Japanese Government regulations. Most of the pilots are European, but an increasing number of Japanese qualify for the posts yearly, and in a decade will have supplanted the foreigners altogether; for as the older pilots die out they are replaced by natives, the Japanese wishing to keep the pilotage of their own waters in their own hands.

After dinner, however, another wire came, saying that if we did not start before 10 a.m. Outram could get to us in time to take us through.

"I'll wait," said the Old Man. "He's the only pilot I care to have on my ship."

"We won't have finished coaling before six in the morning," said the Chief.

"That's all right, then," said the Old Man.

Finding we were not to start that night, I had some thoughts of going ashore again, but the Old Man dissuaded me.

"Certainly, Doc, you can go if you like. But if you take my advice you won't. It's very risky. There's a nine-knot current in these Straits, and a doctor was drowned here a few voyages ago coming back in a sampan."

It was a cold raw night; there were no sampans about; nobody else wanted to go ashore; and the Old Man's lugubrious yarn daunted me. Afterwards I found it was the same tale at every port. Apparently doctors were in the habit of getting drowned at ports, always the port we were in at the time. The Mate said it was more or less true. Doctors were clumsy coming aboard in bad weather in the dark; they could not manage with the sailor's sure-footedness; sampan-men will never make the slightest effort to save a drowning man, because they have a superstition that thereby they acquire all the sins he has committed; and so several doctors actually had been drowned close to their ships.

"But of course what the Old Man wants, though he is too clever to say so, is to have you handy in case of an accident. Accidents don't happen much at sea, where the doctor is always available; they happen in ports, the only place where cargo is being handled, and usually occur when the one man who knows how to tackle them is ashore sight-seeing. That's why the Old Man spins cuffers at you."

"The Old Man's as wily as a fox," said the Chief. "He has to be to keep his end up."

"He's euchred the Doc all right this time," said the Second. "Never mind, Doc. We want a fourth at bridge. Come along. . . ."

· · · · · · ·

After breakfast next morning there were two people discomposed on the ship. One was the Old Man—it was nine o'clock, and no Captain Outram had arrived. I was the other—no camera and no plates had appeared. I had kept my adventure with the camera to myself and asked the agent to do likewise, knowing I should be the object of ponderous jokes all the rest of the voyage should it leak out. So I did not care to appear to be watching for anything; yet I could not help continually squinting toward the Shimonoseki side. The Blue Peter was flying at the fore; the coal was all in; the scaffolding and lighters gone; the curio dealers were packing up their wares, the bo'sun and his men beginning to clear the decks of the accumulated coal-dust; steam was up, and everything was in the uneasy state of imminent departure. Still there was nothing from the shore. At last, mindful of the watched kettle proverb, I decided not to look any more; and it was then when I had gone below to see a China-man, and the Old Man had ambled for'ard to look at something in the fo'castle, that the white launch ran alongside, put our pilot aboard, and with him my pre-cious camera and two plates—two out of a dozen. Appa-rently I had been photographing all the places I ought not; but I was so relieved to see my Kodak again that even the loss of ten plates seemed trivial in comparison.

In a few minutes all was bustle. The telegraph rang sharply; up came the anchor; and the sound of churning water caused a stampede amongst the curio-men. Down the gangway they scuttled to their dragging sampans, cast off, and were soon dancing specks behind.

The shore slipped past us like a panorama. In through a narrow neck we steamed, between cliffs honeycombed with guns; and in a moment we were in the Inland Sea beyond. An upturned Jap steamer, lying on a sandbank a total loss, showed how careful one had to be in this treacherous channel, and made me appreciate why the Old Man had been so keen to wait for his friend Captain Outram.

.   .   .   .

The Inland Sea is an immense stretch of water be-tween the middle and the two lower islands (Kyushu and Shikoku), and 200 miles long, studded with hun-dreds of little islands, through which one's vessel winds a devious way, past people and villages forgotten through the ages.

It is nevertheless one of the most frequented waterways in the world; and as we steamed through at full speed

we passed every style of craft afloat, from the mediæval
junk to square and fore-and-aft rigged sailing ships of
the latest type, from little tin-pot tramp steamers to the
lordliest of all ships seen in Eastern waters—the beautiful
"Empress" boats of the C.P.R.

In the summer the islands are said to be of the most
entrancing tropical loveliness; but as we saw them then,
bare and wind-swept, with snow-clad mountain-peaks
sinking into a pearly haze behind, they looked more
like the Outer Hebrides than anything I had ever seen
elsewhere; and as the little Gaelic quartermaster said to
me in a voice of pride: "They're naw in it, sir, wie the
Kyles o' Bute."

. . . . . .

After tiffin I came across Captain Outram strutting
about the deck. We were now in open waters; and he
had taken the opportunity to leave the bridge for a spell.

"No," he said in the course of conversation, "I have
no use for the Japanese. Lived with them twenty years,
and like them less each year. There's an old saying
about Japan that what it lacks are:

> 'Men of honour,
> Women of virtue,
> Birds that sing,
> Flowers that smell.'

The man that said that must have been a sailor, for he's
all wrong about the last two. But the first part's right.
It makes me sick to hear the 'P. & O.-ist' talking frothy
nonsense about advancement, culture, civilisation—the
mission of Japan. It's all tommy rot. The reason Europe
respects Japan is because she has learnt all the latest
scientific ways of killing, and can hold her own at the
game. Between ourselves, the Japanese hold us all in
contempt as barbarians. They use us because they want
to learn certain useful things from us; and as soon as

they've mastered it they throw us aside. 'Japan for the Japanese' is the cry now; and people like us, who have had them in leading-strings, have got to quit. They've learnt all we can teach them. The Jap is an Oriental to the core, and don't you forget it."

"Ever been in Korea, Doc?" he added.

"No," I answered.

"Well, perhaps your ship will call there on the way home. If it does, you'll see how a brave, cultured people, without the military spirit, get treated by the Japs when they have a free hand. It's the Oriental at his worst."

He was snapping the triggers of a breech-loader as he spoke. His eyes twinkled.

"There's a 60 per cent. *ad valorem* duty on this; but I don't think it's going to be asked for, eh, Cap?"

"Oh, no. It's your gun, and of course you take it ashore with you," the Old Man said solemnly. "The Doc's a good shot," he added parenthetically.

"So. Well, if you'd care to come, Doc, we're going duck-shooting in Osaka Bay the day after to-morrow."

"I'll come if you'll lend me the tools," I said emphatically.

"That'll be all right. We've got loads."

.   .   .   .   .   .

"The most difficult bit of navigation in the Inland Sea is about midnight," said the Old Man at dinner. "We pass through the narrows then. It's about a cable length across. Like to be called, Doc?"

"Please," I said.

So at "one bell" they called me. It was pitch-dark, so dark that even the water was barely visible. Away in front, a point on the starboard bow, a light glimmered low down, growing steadily larger and brighter as we approached. The water, formerly quiet, seemed now to have acquired a running sound, which grew momentarily more and more intense. One could feel that the ship was moving at tremendous speed in the unseen current.

Sound echoed cavernously from the precipitous cliffs that
were narrowing around us, unseen in the darkness.

Suddenly a hoarse order came from the bridge; and,
with a swirl, the great ship half turned in her course,
throwing me bodily against the rail.

Another light appeared. Again the order echoed in
the cavernous night; again we canted; and now a third
light flashed in evidence. Then came a slackening; the
sound of waters died; the darkness grew less intense; and
the faint glimmer of open water appeared. We were
through.

On the bridge the quartermaster struck "eight bells."
Ere the brazen sound had died it was repeated from the
fo'castle head. Then the voice of the look-out came clear
and melancholy through the night:

"A-a-all's well. Lights burning brightly."

A dim figure leant over the bridge rail.

"You there, Doc?"

"Yes."

"Come up, and look at the chart."

CHAPTER VI

KOBE, YOKOHAMA, TOKYO.   GOOD-BYE TO JAPAN

In the morning we arrived at Kobe, one of the greatest of the Treaty Ports.

A martello tower and a white quarantine ship marked the outer boundaries of the harbour. Here we were boarded by the doctors—two of them this time; and I noticed that the nearer we got to Yokohama the better-looking they were, and the better-fitting their uniforms.

Once the yellow flag came down we made all speed to our anchorage, a line of big white buoys about a mile from the shore. One of our company's ships was just leaving harbour; and two others had the Blue Peter flying, indicating they were due to start within twenty-four hours.

It was late in the afternoon before any of us could arrange to get ashore; but time did not hang heavily on our hands, as the curio-men were everywhere, spreading their wares all over the ship, and squatting with Oriental calm beside them ready to bargain with anyone. They asked, of course, enormous prices at starting, prices such as one would have to pay in London, but evidently only as a method of commencing business. They expected to be offered one-sixth; and then the real bargaining began.

At one's offer they would throw up their hands in impotent protest, and repeat their first price. At this point one shrugged one's shoulders and left. Then they would call one back, protesting at the absurdity of one's offer, smiling, or looking gravely hurt at the disparagement suggested by the would-be buyer's price. A fresh offer, twenty-five per cent. less, would be made; and this one parried by again repeating the previous offer.

147

With a sad look the curio-man now washed his hands of one.

Half an hour later he would say, when one happened to come round his way, "How much you give?"

And then one began to increase one's offer. The stewards, quartermasters, and A.B.'s were bargaining off and on all day. They had little or no opportunity of getting ashore, and so all their purchasing had to be done on the ship. Most of the things they bought were resold to the Liverpool shops at a profit of 100 per cent.; and a considerable part of their income was thus derived. Consequently they were experts at bargaining, sometimes taking two or three days haggling over something special.

The dealers knew them, of course, and also the futility of attempting to overreach them. So they were able to make on the average much better bargains, for small things, than the officers, who had neither the time nor the patience for this interminable chaffering.

The Second Steward said to me, "If you see anything you fancy, sir, tell me, and I'll get it for you a good deal cheaper than you can."

In the afternoon the Chief and I, our pockets stuffed with rolls of paper money, hailed a sampan to take us to the *hatoba*.

A cloud of *kurumayas* (rick-men) pounced on us as we landed. We picked out two, and told them to follow us till we wanted them. Then we strolled leisurely along the streets.

Kobe, like every Japanese port, is the oddest mixture of periods. Mediæval houses stand overshadowed by tall telegraph poles; open-fronted shops with beautiful bronzes, china jars and vases, lacquers and enamels, stand next to glass-fronted ones filled with European rubbish of the 6½d. bazaar type; bare-legged peasants clad in garments of rice straw rub shoulders with policemen dressed like *gendarmes*; dainty little women garbed like

The Great Buddha at Kamakura

Facing Page 148

Soerabaya, the Javanese Sadoe

butterflies, solemn robed Buddhist priests, ordinary citizens, bare-headed, kimono-clad, and men dressed in "complete-suit-one-guinea" European slops mingled in the kaleidoscopic crowd.

There are two sights Europeans go to see in Kobe: one is the so-called Temple of the Moon (Tanjoji), and the other is the Nunobiki Falls. The temple is beyond the falls, further up the mountain; and the Chief suggested we should see them both that afternoon.

So we mounted our rickishaws; and away our men rattled at a long swinging trot, past hotels, temples, over a railway line, through street after street of wooden houses one or two storeys high, till at last we came to the halting place, at the foot of the hills.

Here we got out, rickishaws being no longer of any use, and started to climb. All the way, however, the Chief's athletic fervour had been evaporating. He was not at all so enthusiastic about the climb, when we were at the bottom of the hill, as he had been when proposing it; and he now suggested we should do the waterfall, and leave the temple till another day.

Perhaps it was the natural cooling after ardour, perhaps the thought of the two hours' climb, that made him suggest the shorter journey only. Or perhaps it was the pretty face of Sono-San, the little tea-house girl, standing bowing in the doorway of the *chaya* opposite and saying with a quaintly piquant accent, "Peese come inside," that made him disinclined to move.

At any rate he looked at her, and then at me.

"Let's go in. We've lots of time," he said. "I feel thirsty."

So it is not surprising that in a few minutes we found ourselves squatting on cushions, warming our hands over the charcoal *hibachi* (brazier), chatting with our hostess and the almond-eyed little lady who had first enticed us in, drinking the inevitable straw-coloured tea, and watching the dexterous way the little ladies handled their cigarettes, smiling at us with their slanting eyes the while.

So much has been written about the Japanese woman that the subject is almost worn threadbare. She has been praised extravagantly; she has been as vehemently abused. She has been acted in opera, sung about in musical comedy, portrayed in every form of decorative art. One cannot get away from her—her presence is so all-pervasive in her own country. Every time one buys a fan or a piece of china she is there. Her presence sends a ray of sunshine into every street; her costume insistently catches the eye. It is impossible to avoid her. As a rule one doesn't try to; for the Japanese woman is the greatest thing in Japan. Her beauty is of a difference —it grows on one day by day; and the longer one stays in the country the more one admires it. Men who have lived there tell me that it slowly permeates till one wakes up suddenly to find some day that the high aquiline Caucasian type has become distasteful when by chance one meets an unknown fellow-countrywoman in the streets of a Japanese city.

She is so dainty, so fine-lined, so small, so very gorgeous in her dress, so very artificial in her headgear bristling with pins; her smile is so ever-ready, her temper so equable, it is difficult to believe she can be really alive, could ever look cross, or be untidy.

She is inimitable, the apotheosis of Japanese civilisation. There is nothing in Europe at all like her. But there are rumours that she is being spoiled by Western ideas, freed from the thraldom of "The Greater Learning for Women." It is stated that girls educated in the missionary schools can be readily distinguished by their awkward gestures, and want of graciousness, from those trained under the old *régime*. If that be so, the schools have a lot to answer for. At present the Japanese woman is perfect. It seems an unnecessary risk to try to paint the lily.

We climbed up to the lower waterfall in the cool of
the afternoon. At the inevitable tea-house at the top the
ancient lady who acted as hostess greeted the Chief as
an old friend, and talked the queerest of slang English
to him. One of the *musumés* sang an English song for
our edification. Wonderful to relate, it was no less than
"Ta-ra-ra-boom-de-ay," and sounded like a dim echo
through the centuries. There was one of the tea-house
girls particularly pretty, who after our arrival kept persistently in the background. When we entered she had
looked up quickly at us for a moment and then returned to
her occupation again. Apparently she was trying to tie
knots in a strip of white paper with her thumb and little
finger—a somewhat difficult feat. The little *musumé*
looking after our particular wants saw my eyes following
her, and pouted.

"She no your girl. What for you look?"

"I want to know what thing. What for she tie paper
so?"

Hari laughed, and then explained: "You no savvy that.
She bolong sick. Have got Inglee-ish man lover no
come."

"What for he no come?"

"No savvy. His ship come. He no come."

"What for she tie knot, so?"

Hari twirled her long taper fingers in imitation of the
other and laughed.

"She tie knot so—bring lover back."

Afterward I had it all explained to me. It was a charm
to bring back an absent lover. The knot tied in the
prescribed way was taken to the shrine of the Love God,
in the Temple of Kwannon, Goddess of the Unhappy,
and placed before the image by the forlorn maiden. A
prayer was then said, a small offering made, and the
influence of the incantation patiently awaited. Should
it be successful, the maiden then presented a gaudy

picture, purporting to be that of the object of her affections, to the Temple, and all was well.

"I don't believe for a moment that any Japanese woman ever falls in love with a white man," said the Chief on the way down. "Our features seem hideous to them. These girls smile at us for the sake of trade; but they're really saving the money for some shock-headed, cadaverous little Jap round the corner, who is their ideal of manly beauty."

"You think so?" I said thoughtfully.

"Sure of it," he answered, "Can you imagine an Englishwoman ever falling in love with a Jap? You know you can't," he added triumphantly. "Well, then, reverse the picture."

I had told him of the girl above; and I said, "So you think this girl——"

"Tommy rot," he answered positively. "Hari was bluffing you, and your head is full of 'The Geisha.'"

Our *kurumayas* gave us a wide-grinned welcome when we got to the bottom again; and soon we were bowling along the little narrow streets once more. Turning a corner, we came on the following notice in English: "Satsuma factory. Visitors are respectably invited to inspecte the factory." We laughed, though we could not have made anything like as good a sentence in Japanese.

A very obsequious proprietor took us round. He explained that the china itself was made in the province of Satsuma by a secret process known only there to a few, but it was painted in Kobe, Yokohama, etc., as they had better artists in those cities. That is largely true; but nevertheless the figures painted in Nagasaki and other southern ports, though not so perfect in outline, are much more grotesquely diabolical, and so appear more in keeping with the character of the china.

We watched the process from the first outline in black, drawn with a fine brush made of rats' whiskers, to the completely finished picture. Each colour put on has to be baked separately; and so it requires some ten or twelve bakings to perfect the design.

The work was wonderful to watch, marvellously, intricately minute, like everything else produced by these remarkable people. Most of the delicate tracery seemed to be done by boys from designs by one of the older men. A fine bowl was shown us by the guide-proprietor. It would have held about a pint of water, and was an intricate mass of fine gold and black lines. He gave me a magnifying-glass to hold over the bowl; and then I discovered the lines were in reality delicately drawn butterflies. There were twenty-two thousand on the bowl, he informed us, and every one of them fitted accurately in a mosaic so complete that not a pin-point of the underlying basis could be seen.

We found it difficult to tear ourselves away, but night was falling. Our men outside had each lit a coloured paper lantern, which was attached to his rickishaw; and all the other ricks we passed were similarly illuminated. Pedestrians on foot had servants walking before them carrying lanterns on the end of long flexible bamboos; all the shop fronts had rows of lanterns along the cornice; and the entire effect was that of a Fancy Fair.

At the Oriental Hotel, where we stopped for dinner, we seemed to have suddenly shifted back again 15,000 miles to England; for there a party of four, a typical English family, were sitting in evening dress, going quietly through the menu—a menu that might have graced any restaurant in the environs of Piccadilly Circus. The manager, too, to keep up the illusion, was a German. The only foreign note was the waiters.

The menu card, I noticed, was printed with the dishes numbered 1 to 12; and I could not understand why till I heard a voice say: "Boy, bring me No. 5," and then I understood. The waiters could not understand French, but they knew the numbers of the dishes in English.

Most of these boys learn their English at the missionary schools; they attend these assiduously till they think they have learnt enough English to act as waiters; then they promptly leave.

It was a black night, with only a few stars shining, when we left the hotel. A cold raw wind was blowing. We bundled hastily into our waiting rickishaws, and told the men to take us to the *hatoba*.

Hailing a sampan, we got in.

"Don't say a word," said the Chief. "They'll take us to our ship without our saying which it is."

The two oarsmen stood up to the long sweeps, and pushed out into the darkness. A few faint lights, more than a mile away, showed where the ships lay at anchor.

"That's ours," I said quietly to the Chief.

"Wrong," he said. "You let the sampan-men alone."

I did after that, though I was quite certain we were going all out of our course. They ran us, straight as a dart, to the gangway.

"Wonderful, aren't they?" said the Chief.

.   .   .   .   .   .

It was on the following evening, at the Club, that Captain Outram suggested to the Old Man, after a game of billiards, that we should have a Japanese dinner. There was a man present who lived "native" in the interior six months in the year. No one knew anything about him except that he was exceedingly quiet, always seemed to have plenty of money, and said he was a commercial traveller. He was popularly supposed to be an international spy. Certainly he could talk English, French, German, Russian, and Japanese with equal facility. The English ladies in Kobe looked askance at him—he had a Japanese wife, some people said several wives.

For some reason or other he seemed inclined to talk to me; and when Captain Outram said, "Would you like to have a Japanese dinner, Doc?" he chimed in quietly, "Yes, do. It's an experience, Doc."

"By Jove, the very thing. You're just the man we want, Thompson. You know all about these things. Will you come too?"

Thompson hesitated for just a fraction of a second, and then said: "Thanks, Captain; I think I will. I know the very *yadoya* you want."

We tailed off in our rickishaws, after him, out into the night, till, turning up a narrow alley in a back street, he stopped at an open doorway. Into a narrow hall we trooped, to be greeted by a bowing, grey-kimonoed host.

A little maid rapidly removed our boots; and we walked upstairs, on stockinged feet, to the usual Japanese room, devoid of furniture, the floor covered with the usual tatami matting.

Cushions were brought; and we started to make ourselves comfortable. The Old Man, however, was so stout that he could not get his legs under him comfortably; so they brought a little table piled with cushions, and this he used as a chair.

We left the ordering of the dinner to Thompson, and he sent for, and had a long conversation with, the cook who was to serve us.

Presently a maid brought in a *hibachi*, filled with red-hot charcoal, and set it in the centre of the circle. A round table, about a foot high, with a square hole in the centre, was fitted over the *hibachi*, and now the cook reappeared. She carried an affair like a frying-pan greased with fat; and attendants brought her the raw materials for the feast, which she proceeded to cook in front of us. Huge bowls of rice with chop-sticks were placed at intervals around the table, opposite each of us. The rice formed the basis of the dinner; and course after course was added by the cook to act as a stimulus to eat more. The Old Man and I made very poor hands at manipulating the chop-sticks till Thompson showed us just how, and then we found it not so impossible to raise things to our lips.

I had no idea what I was eating; some of the things were cooked; others appeared to be made up of raw fish; everything was cut up very fine; most of it was decidedly savoury. I could see that Thompson was enjoying himself immensely.

In front of each of us was placed an ampulla of hot *saké*, with little drinking cups, and a bowl of clear water. The taste for *saké* is said to be an acquired one. It is easily acquired. To me it tastes like whey with a suspicion of sherry in it. It is inclined to be rather heady. Thompson got through his supply rapidly; and fresh jars kept arriving for him—also for me. A particularly charming little attendant had been deputed to look after me (we each had one, our host, on account of his position, two), and she kept filling up my *saké* cup whenever it showed any signs of emptying. I watched the face of Thompson, opposite me, grow larger and hazier, feeling more and more comfortable; bright lights flashed in front of my eyes at times; voices came somewhat muffled. It began to dawn on me that I was having too much *saké*!

Then there was an interruption. Three little painted women sidled into the room, each carrying a wooden box like a long plain gun-case. These were the geisha. They bowed to the floor, and said: "*Kombanwa.*" Two of them produced samisens (Japanese guitars) from their cases, and squatted before us. Thompson smiled at the third, dipped his *saké* cup in the water-bowl, and presented it to the geisha. This is the recognised form of salutation to a favourite, like bouquets to a prima donna. The geisha raised it to her forehead; the waiting maid filled it with hot *saké*; she put it to her lips, and then returned it to Thompson.

After that she rose to her feet, and with a fan in her

hand went through the celebrated butterfly dance, the
other two accompanying her on their samisens, singing
all the time in the peculiar high screechy note so characteristic of Oriental music. The dancing was all done
with the body; there was practically no movement of the
feet. Her movements were wonderfully graceful; one
felt one ought to appreciate the marvellous skill more.

Thompson's face was a study of delight. He had
reached the stage in which to him it was exquisite. We
others found it only interesting. When she had finished
she dropped on her knees, and touched the matting with
her forehead, before us.

It was in the early morning when we finally separated,
the Old Man and I to the *hatoba*, where a launch awaited
us, the other two to their homes. As we left the door-
step in our rickishaws, the proprietor, the geisha, and
the waiting-maids, all assembled, bowed to us profusely;
and the host called out the customary salutation to a
departing guest: "*Sayonara. Mata dozo irasshai.*" (Farewell! So must we part! Be pleased to come again.)

. . . . . .

Horner, the Second Mate, had been sticking to the
ship very closely since we had arrived at Kobe. Once
or twice I had idly wondered why. On our first excur-
sion ashore the Chief had asked him to accompany us;
but he had shuffled out of it; and we had not asked him
since. As a companion he was very quiet. If anyone
had asked me I should have said he was not a man of
much imagination, for he was very Saxon in his type,
very steady, very reliable, an excellent officer. Sometimes in his watch below he would sit and talk to me,
usually of his Devonshire home. His ideal was to make
enough money to retire and keep a yacht near Plymouth.
We were rather friends.

On the morning of our fourth day in port he came
into my cabin, looking somewhat embarrassed. We
talked casually for some time about things of no im-

portance; and I could see all the time he wanted to ask me something. I waited patiently, letting him work up to it. Finally he blurted out, " Going ashore to-day, Doc?"

"Not till evening, I think. The Old Man and I are going with a party of Americans duck-shooting in Osaka Bay," I said.

"What time will you be back?" he said. "I want you to go ashore with me, Doc, rather badly."

There was evidently something on his mind he wanted to tell me very much. I promised to go ashore with him after dark.

"I don't want the Chief to know," he explained diffidently.

I successfully concealed my surprise, and said, "That's all right, old chap. You and I will go ashore, and that's all about it."

We got back before nightfall, the shooting launch, strung with dead duck, looking like a poultry shop. The Americans had arranged a big dinner and a geisha performance for the night. They pressed us to go. The Old Man was unable, owing to official business, as we were sailing on the morrow. I had more difficulty in framing a plausible excuse; but I, too, declined. The Second Engineer wanted me to go ashore with him. Again I had to invent difficulties; so finally it was with a feeling like that of conspirators the Second Mate and I at length stole away together in a sampan in the dark.

"Read that," said Horner, thrusting a note into my hand.

By the dim light of the sampan lamp I made it out. It was a very artless, simple little note. At the time it made me feel choky. I wish now I had transcribed it, for I can only give it from memory.

"I look see your ship come Kobe side five-six month. Two day your ship come—my heart is very glad. I think

you come look see little Ponta. You no come. Red-faced
man, your ship, come *chaya* (that was the Chief), thin
man come (that was meant for me), you no come. What
for you no come? My heart is very sad. I think you
no love me any more."

I handed it back to him in silence.

"You saw her?" he said.

I nodded.

There was a silence. Suddenly he blurted out, "I'm
a d——d fool. I like her so much that it hurts like hell
to have a note like that. I didn't know she cared so
much. I swore I wouldn't go ashore this trip. I wanted
to break it off. It's been going on every voyage now for
the last fifteen months. Don't laugh, Doc."

"I'm not laughing."

"Sorry. I know you're not. I've got the jumps, Doc.
It's getting worse every voyage. The first time it was
all right. We were a week in Kobe; and I used to go
up and see her every night. I thought she was a nice
little thing. When we left I felt sort of lonely. I was
on one of the Pacific boats that trip. We were back from
Vancouver about six weeks later; and we stopped a
night here. I thought I'd toddle up and see her. She
was frightfully glad to see me; and I felt flattered. You
know what these girls are. I thought it was rather a
score for me, her remembering. Well, I didn't see her
again for four months. I had been shifted to another
ship; and the Second Engineer was shifted too. The
first night here I couldn't get ashore. The Second went;
and she recognised him. She inquired for me. I was
pretty badly in love with her by now; and I felt—oh, you
know just how, when he told me she had been asking
for me. I was funky of her forgetting now. There was
a fat German making eyes at her, the Second said; and
of course she had to be civil to him. I wanted to punch
that German. That was the voyage before last. I'm
getting worse every time. I can't get her out of my head

now. I've thought of asking the company to give me a
shore billet here, and then buying her off the beastly old
ruffian, Ogawa, who employs her. It makes me sick to
think of her there, with every American tourist or bloated
German making love to her, and her having to put up
with it. She wants me to buy her. You think I'm a
d——d fool, don't you?"

"How much could you buy out her indentures for?"
I asked, evading the question.

"She told me the old devil paid her father 200 yen for
a three-years' agreement. I could get her for 300."

This was serious. It was evident he had been making
careful inquiries.

"I'm absolutely miserable about it," he added dismally.

Of course he hadn't got the money. A sailor never
has any money; and even if he had had, and bought her,
it would have meant exile in a foreign land and the end
of his career to have settled down with her. He was on
the roster for promotion to First Mate. In ten years' time
he might be looking forward to a captaincy. The thing
from the standpoint of the world was ridiculous. But I
was not the world, and had no intention of playing the
part of Mr. Worldly Wiseman.

At the foot of the hills we got out.

"The waterfall place is shut at night," he said. "She'll
be in the Lotus-Leaf now."

The house was dark; the *amado* closed when we
arrived; but a number of rickishaws round the dim-lit
door, and the tinkle of the samisen within, told that
something was going on.

Ogawa, the proprietor, a little wizened ruffian in a
grey kimono, received us obsequiously; but at our request
shook his head regretfully.

"No. The most beautiful Ponta could not be seen.
She was entertaining four honourable gentlemen with
the music."

He said it with a cunning smile, watching us all the time.

He knew Horner, of course; and probably thought he might attempt to pay her father's debts, and so take her away from the tea-shop.

At the same time he wanted to have any money we were spending; and so did not wish to turn us from his door. Moreover, if he made difficulties, and we were not content with other entertainers, he probably thought that a little delay would make us offer a better price for the music.

"I must see her," said Horner. "Tell the honourable four to clear out."

Ogawa was pathetically helpless in his gestures. The honourable four had specially asked for the most beautiful Ponta. How could he offend his most honourable guests?

Horner was inarticulate with rage. I watched the man shrewdly, and thought he was lying; so I nudged Horner to be quiet, and explained that we were very sorry. We had hoped to spend the evening in his honourable house; we had wanted two beautiful maidens with samisens to entertain us; but—well, we sailed in the morning, and must go elsewhere for our last evening.

Horner made a movement forward. I held him back.

"It's all right, man; he's bluffing for more money," I said in a quick aside.

Ogawa suggested then that perhaps the honourable gentlemen might care to see some of the others. There were several of the most beautiful——

I turned away resolutely, catching Horner by the arm. We walked a yard or two.

"I can't, Doc," said Horner miserably; "I feel that I want to wring the old ruffian's neck. I must go back. I must see her."

I began to fear he was getting out of hand; but just then the little man came running after us. The honour-

able four, it seemed, had just asked for their bill; they
would be going soon; and if the honourable gentlemen
would deign to wait a little in his miserable house——

We had not long to wait. A little maid brought in the
glowing *hibachi* and a pile of cushions. We squatted,
warming our hands over the charcoal flame, each lighting
a cigarette. Horner was irritable with suspense. The
tinkle of the music still came to us through the thin
paper partition. Then a shutter moved, and she came
listlessly in, followed by another, whom I recognised as
Hari, carrying a samisen.

In a moment she uttered a queer little gulping cry;
her little white *tabi* flashed across the matting; there was
an iridescent flash of garments; and she was in his arms.
I turned my head away and stared at Hari, who was
watching with eager eyes. I could hear him murmuring
"Sweetheart—sweetheart—sweetheart," and her sobbing
quietly, and murmuring softly inarticulate words of en-
dearment in response.

I kept staring still at Hari.

Presently a voice said, half confusedly, "Sorry, Doc.
You can look round now, if you like. She won't mind."

Hari smiled at me.

"You give me cigarette?" she said coaxingly; and the
tension was over.

Soon three of us were squatting on our cushions around
the *hibachi*; the fourth was Horner, and he lay full
length on the matting, looking up into Ponta's face, his
head resting on her knees. We talked—how we talked.
They laughed—how they laughed. Hari played the
samisen and sang. Ponta smiled down on him, and
rumpled his hair tenderly with her fingers. It was very
fine, golden, and curly—a constant wonder to her. It
dawned on me for the first time that Horner was very
good-looking. Half an hour before I had thought him a
fool. Now I found myself beginning to envy him.

"Why the deuce don't you make love to Hari?" he said contentedly.

"She say she likee you ver-much," said Ponta encouragingly.

.   .   .   .   .   .

They brought us rice and chicken in bowls, with chopsticks. The two little women shrieked with laughter at our attempts to use the sticks. They brought us hot *saké* in little silver ampullæ; and we exchanged cups of ceremony. I could feel a gentle languor stealing over me. With very little persuasion I should have fallen asleep; and it was therefore with an effort I looked at my watch. It was past midnight.

"We'd better be going," I said.

Ponta looked up quickly; then she pressed his head more down on her lap without a word.

"We're going to stop the night," he said. Then more quickly added, "I can't go, old chap. Oh, d——n. Don't leave me."

"We sail at nine o'clock," I reminded him, feeling like a brute.

"I don't want to think of it. Stay with me, like a good fellow. We'll clear out at six. I may never see her again."

Of course it was all wrong. We were only putting off the evil hour. I knew it would be just as bad in the morning, and I said so. The more I talked the more obstinate he became; and all the while her fingers played with his hair. She never said a word. The Japanese woman is trained to conceal her emotions. I knew all the time it was useless arguing with him. I only did it because I felt I must. I knew also that I dare not leave him alone in the state of mind he was in at the moment; and so I agreed at last to stay the night with him, if the *yadoya* could accommodate us, feeling that if I left him he would probably fail to rejoin the ship at all. The proprietor was called, and said we could have a room. That settled it.

They brought us each a big kimono, some rugs, and a little wooden Japanese pillow. That was our bedroom furniture. We discarded the pillows, and substituted two or three cushions. With these we knew we would be quite comfortable, sleeping on the tatami matting. Six months previously I could not possibly have slept thus; but a period of nights on deck during the hot weather in the Indian Ocean had taught me how to be comfortable without a mattress. Hari promised to call us at five-thirty, and soon I was half asleep; but in my somnolent state I could still hear the quiet, insistent talking of the Mate in the room I had left; and when I finally fell asleep his couch was still unoccupied.

· · · · · ·

It was a very cross Second Mate who gave directions aft when we were moving out from Kobe in the morning, Yokohama bound. The A.B.'s could not make out what had come over his usually sunny temper.

"I'm sick of life," he said to me, in passing. I could only look sympathetic.

A sister ship of ours, the *Dardanus*, flying the Nippon Yusen Kaisha flag, on commission, was due to sail an hour after us. She was a faster boat than ours; and as we steamed past her they chaffed us from the deck, wanting to know if we had any messages for Yokohama. Nothing annoys a sailor more than that; and we retorted to the best of our ability. I am certain, therefore, that the Old Man and the Chief pushed the ship a bit, for it was some hours later before we sighted her smoke astern.

Do what we could, however, she was rapidly overhauling us, until, quite unexpectedly, Nature came to our relief. We were in the narrows, just before leaving the Inland Sea to shoot out into the Pacific, when suddenly, without any warning, we ran into a fog bank.

Then the hooter went furiously; and we could hear the answering hoot of the *Dardanus* astern.

We circled in the fog for perhaps a quarter of an hour, till suddenly again it lifted, and we saw the lighthouse on the port quarter. The Old Man knew then exactly where we were; full steam ahead was ordered; and we shot out into the Pacific.

But the *Dardanus* was not so lucky. She lay enveloped for hours, and consequently was still ten miles astern late that same evening. It was, therefore, not till well on in the night that she passed us far out to starboard.

The coast was very indistinct as we steamed along it in the early morning. The volcano on Vries Island was not visible; and sacred Fujiyama, the most beautiful mountain in Japan, lay enveloped in mists out of sight.

As we approached Yokohama we saw the *Dardanus* lying at anchor, to pass the quarantine; and so she got in barely an hour in front of us.

Yokohama harbour is one of the finest in the Far East. There is a huge breakwater, outside of which lie those lepers of the sea the tankers, and inside a multitude of ships of every nation. No one is allowed to smoke on board the tankers; and they are never admitted near other shipping. Only the week before there had been an accident. A lighter had had its tanks filled with petroleum from one of them, and was sailing into harbour, when the wife of the *sendo* (Japanese captain of the lighter) dropped a lighted match in her little cabin aft. The explosion that followed blew lighter and crew into eternity. Luckily it happened outside the breakwater.

We were all looking forward to our letters from home, as we had missed them at Kobe; and so it was with much disappointment we found that all our mails had been lost in the wreck of the *Dakota*, the huge American mail-

boat that had run ashore two days previously. The
Chief talked as if it had been done especially to spite
him. As it was, he was the only one to receive anything.
It was an empty, delicately scented, mauve-coloured
envelope, posted in London, and written in an unknown
female hand. To this day he has never been able to
discover whom it was from. We said it was a romance
nipped in the bud. He asserted it was probably a bill.
The Chief is a confirmed bachelor.

The usual inundation of curio-dealers followed our
anchoring; but in addition a number of rickishaw men
boarded the ship and presented their cards. The advent
of trams in Yokohama had cut seriously into their earnings, and there is a great struggle between them, therefore, for custom. As with taxis at home, there is a regular
tariff; but, like the old London cabby, they try to get as
much more as possible; and many are the wrangles one
has, if one objects to extortion.

I hired a man for the day, paid him 1 yen 50 sen (three
shillings), and had him waiting at the *hatoba* whenever
I wanted him. Any day I was not ashore I paid him just
the same; and I found the system excellent and the man
absolutely reliable. He was always there, no matter what
time I wanted him, night or day.

The Mate had been instructed by his wife to buy her
enough silk to make a dress. The colour she said was
to be heliotrope; and he was very much afraid he'd get
the wrong shade. Accordingly he got the Chief and
myself to fortify him in his search, and we all went together to one of the big silk shops, so that by our combined wisdom we might lessen the chance of error.

Before we could even state what we wanted we were
served with tea. This, it appeared, was the custom of
the house. Afterwards they were all attention to our
needs. It was with regret that we found we could not
get what we wanted. We were bowed out as politely as
if we had bought the complete stock. In the Benton-

Dori we found what, after much vacillation, appeared to
be the thing. It turned out afterwards that our combined
wisdom had been completely wrong. The mate's wife
refused to wear the stuff. She was "that kind of a
woman," the Chief said; but I have an uneasy suspicion
she may have been right.

.   .   .   .

Everyone who has ever been in Yokohama talks about
the Bluffs and Mississippi Bay. It is the European
quarter of Yokohama; and here one finds the exiles, the
people who have taught the Japanese the modern way,
and who are now being discarded by their precocious
pupils, to their no small discomfort and annoyance.
They talk of ingratitude, sharp practices, cheeseparing
economies; abuse the country, the climate, the morals,
arts, everything except the courage of the people.

The houses of these exiles strike the very latest note
in early Victorian furniture, probably because most of
the stuff has been made in Japan from faulty European
models, for the European furniture made in Japan is
unspeakably bad, just as the European architecture of
the Government buildings is of the poorest workhouse
pattern.

The houses on the Bluffs are very jerry built. There is
nearly always a pathetic attempt to have everything
about them as ultra-English, as little Japanese, as possible
—English flowers and fruits in the garden, English
pictures on the walls, heavy English china ornaments on
the mantel-shelves, even Britannia metal teapots.

It is easy to laugh at it all; but six months' residence
brings understanding; for the people—the only people—
who appreciate England are those who have had to live
out of it. There are no Little Englanders amongst her
sons abroad.

It was St. Patrick's Night; and they were giving an
Irish concert at the Bluffs. The concert-hall might have
been the school-room of the parish church in any village

in the Midlands—a little oblong building, with rows of
hard American pitch-pine seats, and a raised platform
at one end, on which stood a harmonium.

The dresses of the ladies were just enough behind the
fashion to strengthen the impression of the country
village.

They played duets; they sang, mostly from Moore's
Irish Melodies, as it was an Irish concert. None of them
sang very well; but it was very pleasant. One young
fellow recited. He was the funny man. The medical
missionary's daughter said to me, "You will enjoy him.
He's just too killing."

He thought so, too, himself. They all liked him.
They laughed uproariously at his jokes, jokes with
whiskers on them, and screamed at his comic recitations
—recitations of the *Bell's Elocutionist* type. They
thought he was immense. I laughed with the rest, not
wishing to appear *blasé* or uninterested, and feeling just
a little ashamed of my secret reactions. They had been
kind enough to send me a special invitation when they
heard I was an Irishman. To me the whole performance
was very pathetic.

Then the end came. Everyone stood up; the men
threw back their shoulders; the women drew themselves
erect; every cheek was flushed; every eye glistened. They
were singing "God Save the King."

It was not two hurried bars by a foreign orchestra
whilst everyone is scurrying to get on their wraps and out
before the crush. No. They stood up to it and sang it—
sang it as if they meant it. One has to go outside
England to hear "God Save the King" sung properly.

Then they separated; and the light outside, shining
on the yellow faces of the rickishaw men, reminded them
of what, for the time being, they had forgotten—that
they were 15,000 miles from home.

.   .   .   .

Every day we were in Yokohama was to be our last.

We were being sent to Saigon; we were going to Manila; we were positively being sent to Shanghai. It was a different tale with the Old Man every morning at breakfast. The Mate snorted, "We're going to Java, Doc. You see if I'm not right."

I wanted to go up country to Nikko, to see what are probably the most wonderfully beautiful temples in the world. But we were under orders for twenty-four hours' notice; and I could not go. I haunted temples, went to see the great bronze Buddha at Kamakura, planned to go to the hot baths of Myanoshita. One morning the surgeon of the *Dardanus* and I decided to go to Tokyo. At the railway station all the clerks in the booking offices were girls, most of whom spoke excellent English. There was a restaurant, with an excellent menu, which we sampled. The menu-card was printed in Japanese and English. The railway carriages were of the corridor type, like those of the Underground in London. We ran smoothly across the great plain of Tokyo, through a country which was a mass of cherry-blossom.

At the Shimbashi station in Tokyo we went to the jinrickishaw office, paid a fee, and so hired a rickishaw man each for the day. Had we known it there were electric cars all through the city. In spite of that, however, Tokyo is still very Japanese. It is an immense city of some millions of inhabitants; and when once one gets out of the great main streets one sees that it is as Japanese as Shimonoseki.

We lunched at the Imperial, the most magnificent hotel in the Far East. A party of very smart Japanese officers of the Imperial Guard, in full-dress uniform, were lunching in the restaurant, and were a source of much interest to the American tourists, who were flooding the place.

After lunch we started doing temples. One gets rather too many temples in Japan. Many of them are little more than glorified huts; but the temples in Shiba, con-

taining the graves of six of the Tokugawa Shoguns with
their wonderful gold lacquer, and the imposing rows of
votive lanterns, should be missed by no one who wishes
to see what Japanese art at its very best can do.   There
is an air of solemn grandeur and immemorial calm about
them that wraps one round as with a mantle while the
guide walks reverently from tomb to tomb, talking of
the bygone splendours of these Tycoon Emperors.   Instinctively one's voice lowers in the presence of the
mighty dead; and, like Agag, one treads delicately
around the dust of these buried Cæsars.*

The same feeling follows one when one is viewing
what the public is permitted to see of the Imperial
Palace.   The priest-like seclusion of the Mikado is a
thing of the past; but the tradition of the Son of Heaven
is difficult to eradicate; and old-fashioned Japanese still
reluctantly regret the presence of his statue exposed to
the gaze of every passer-by in the Imperial Museum,
considering it as a sacrilege almost that anyone should be
permitted to look even on the counterfeit representation
of the Emperor.

But that the old order changeth nothing could have
proved more eloquently than the first sight we saw after
leaving the palace.   It was some thirty Russian cannon
captured in Manchuria, and arranged in one of the
public parks, opposite the War Office, an ugly red-brick
building, looking like a block of artisans' flats.

At a tea-house, the Soyoken, run on European lines,
we were much interested in watching a number of
Japanese students, under the guidance of an elderly man,
sitting on chairs and trying to handle spoons, knives, and
forks in European style, solemnly watching and imitating
their leader all the while, like a gymnasium class following the movements of the instructor.

It must have been extremely uncomfortable for them;

*Since these lines were written this beautiful temple, alas, has
been destroyed by one of those disastrous fires so frequent in Tokyo.

but they went through it solemnly as a duty. It was a part of their education, for the secret of their marvellous success is that they study even the minutest details. We caught them surreptitiously watching us. My companion inadvertently started balancing his spoon on the edge of his cup; and we smiled furtively when we saw four of them imitate him. But, all the same, the thing impressed us. These were the men of the New Japan; and they were being trained to hold their own with ease amongst Europeans.

Outside, in a little grove not far off, was a bronze statue of the Great Buddha (Daibutsu), and close to the statue a huge bronze bell, with an intensely sweet, low note. Once or twice the bell boomed softly as we sat at ease. Finally we moved over to have a look. A little old withered woman had just arrived before the bell, which was swung so that its base hung about three feet above the ground. The bell itself was about fifteen feet high, and six or seven feet in diameter at the mouth. Instead of a metal clapper it had a bamboo pole, with a drumstick head at one end, hanging suspended by the middle. The old woman seized the pole and swung it against the side of the bell, once, twice, thrice, and again we heard the low, sweet sound ring out softly in the still afternoon air. Then slowly she turned to the face of the inscrutable Buddha, and, dropping on her knees, offered up a prayer. That was the Old Japan, the Japan of the Samurai and the Forty-seven Ronins, whose tombs we had been gazing at in the morning. It was a charming Old Japan, hopelessly picturesque, impossible to sustain. The marvel is that it lasted as long as it did. We felt privileged to have seen even a little of the last of it.

.   .   .   .

The next day we got our final orders. We were going to Java. The Mate had been right after all; and this was to be our last day in Yokohama.

"Have you ever seen massage after the Japanese manner?" said the Chief. I confessed I had not.

"It's as good as a Turkish bath," he said enthusiastically. "I tell you what, Doc. We'll walk over the Bluffs to Honmoku, through the rice-fields, go to a tea-house I know, and have the old blind masseur in."

It was a beautiful spring afternoon, and we were in a pleasant glow when at length we reached the little village by the sea. The tea-houses were on the sea-shore; and little landing stages ran out from them into the water, so that one could walk straight off the balcony and plunge into the Pacific. It was too early in the year, however, for bathing; and so after a smoke, and the inevitable tea, we surrendered ourselves to the masseur. All masseurs in Japan are blind men, as their hands are wonderfully supple, on account of their greater delicacy of touch. In Europe massage is always done in the direction of the venous flow; but, as one might expect, in Japan they do the exact reverse: I am puzzled to this day to know which is right. At any rate, when we got out of the masseur's hands we both had a feeling of intense exhilaration, so much so that we decided to walk the whole way back.

It was dark and the way was winding, a mere track amongst the paddy-fields. We wandered off into a bamboo grove, and wandered out again; dogs barked at us in the night. We still pushed on. The rice-fields on either side were bare of vegetation; the path was a mere track in the darkness; not a soul passed; not a sign of habitation was anywhere.

At last we saw a light in the distance, far off to the left; and stumbling across found that we had left the path completely. Except for the light in one corner the house was in total darkness. Stumbling over the threshold of the verandah, my foot struck something soft; and I should have fallen had not an arm thrown up, un-

A Street Scene, Java

Native Women Bathing

expectedly and rather discomposingly, from below steadied me. It was the body of a man sleeping out in the verandah I had almost fallen over. Without a word he rose, threw open a door, and we found we had run across one of the smaller *yadoyas* frequented by the poorer merchant class.

We were very tired and hungry; they had no European food; there was only one steel fork, and one pewter spoon in the house; but nevertheless we managed to make a very satisfactory meal from rice and hard-boiled eggs, the Chief using the spoon and I the fork.

Afterwards the proprietor put us on the right track again, and with a polite "*Sayonara*" bade us farewell.

We tramped on steadily in the night. *Chavas* and lights were now quite frequent; and soon we saw the dim outline of a wall and the gateway of a European house.

"We've got to the Bluffs at last," said the Chief with a grunt of satisfaction.

The tinkle of a rickishaw bell came to us in the night. Then one *kurumaya* appeared from round the corner with the lantern of his rickishaw lit; and he was quickly followed by another. We each got into one, and called out "*Hatoba.*" Then the men started.

Going down from the Bluffs to the Bund there is a very long, steep hill.

"Hold tight," shouted the Chief from the rickishaw in front. Our men had started slowly; but gradually they gained momentum; and soon we were flying down the incline at breakneck pace. Their feet seemed barely to touch the ground. I felt as though my last hour had come. Suddenly we came to a sharp turn; and the men swerved quickly, leaping sideways in the air, swinging the light cars round by their weight. Down they came on their feet again, and continued their breakneck run. It was like bob-sleighing without the snow. A feeling of exhilaration came over us; unconsciously I found myself shouting encouragement. Down we swept, past brightly lighted shops, past hurrying pedestrians, till at last, panting and exhausted, the men slowed up on the crowded level highway of the Bund.

When we got back to the ship all was confusion. We sailed for Soerabaya, in Java, on the morrow, and some of the cargo was not yet in. A huge arc-light hung over the ship; and the winches were working furiously; but as I had nothing to do with cargo I turned in, and in spite of the thunderous noises soon was fast asleep.

Some time in the early morning, however, they finished; and then the stillness woke me up.

. . . .

It was a beautiful clear day when we said farewell; and the beloved Fujiyama shone inland like a great pink down-turned fan, rosy in the dawn, a picture of absolute loveliness, as we streamed out slowly through the breakwater, past the forts and the four great Japanese cruisers, dipping their flags ceremoniously to us as we crossed their beam.

That night before turning in I was going to put some plates in my camera, but laziness suggested there would be nothing to photograph till we got into the Inland Sea again. Next morning I repented bitterly. The steward wakened me at "seven bells" (7.30 a.m.). It was a bright clear morning; and I turned round luxuriously for another short snooze before getting up. I was just dropping off again when a voice came down my ventilator, "Doc! Get up quick! There's a whale harpooned in sight!"

I was up like a flash, instinctively seizing the camera, only then to remember with a pang it was unloaded. Everybody was on deck with glasses.

"She's gone down," said the Mate.

"She'll be up in a minute," said the Chief.

What I saw was a small Japanese steam trawler, which

we were rapidly overhauling, on the port bow. A man stood sharply silhouetted on her fo'castle head; and a harpoon line stretched from him for about three hundred yards into the water in front. All steam had been shut off from the trawler; the whale had dived and was hauling her along in her course. When we were almost abeam there was a ripple in the water in front; and then a cloud of vapour rose for about six feet above the sea. It was not the stream of water depicted in the books, merely a cloud of vapour, and it was the whale blowing.

Then a broad brown back, like an arc of a great circle, appeared for a moment, only to disappear again, but not before we heard a sharp report, and knew that the man on the fo'castle head had fired another explosive bullet from his harpoon gun into the quivering mass. This second dive was a short one. Probably the shot had hit a vital part. The water close to the trawler became tinged with blood; and the great mass came slowly up to the surface like an overturned ship. By this time we had passed the trawler; and soon we had left her far behind, a mere speck on the ocean. No one on board, not even the Old Man, had ever seen such a sight before. I was bitterly sorry my slackness had prevented my photographing it; and as the next best thing I asked the Mate to let me have the bearings of the scene from the official log. Here they are:

"33° 27' N.

"135° 36' E. Off Edsu Saki in the Kii Channel, West from Siwo Misaki light, eight miles."

.   .   .   .

We were going back through the Inland Sea to coal at Moji, and were due at Kobe about four o'clock that afternoon. All the time we had been in Yokohama we had had some twenty-five coolies from Kobe on board, painting and caulking the ship. The decks had all been caulked, the holds painted red and the outside of the ship black; so we were now very spick-and-span for Java. The coolies were to be landed at Kobe again; and we were stopping for that and to pick up the pilot.

Horner looked at me at tiffin, and I knew his thought.

"Any chance of stopping the night?" I said.

"Not an earthly," he answered gloomily.

We passed the spot where we had been caught in the fog, on the way up to Yokohama, about one o'clock. It was one of the exits from the Inland Sea. There were forts on either side, and just room to circle a ship comfortably clear of the reefs. It was a nasty spot.

The Old Man was expecting Captain Outram's wife and two daughters to travel with us as far as Shimonoseki, while the captain was piloting the ship through the Inland Sea; so when we reached our moorings at Kobe we signalled for them to come aboard. Meanwhile the coolies hastily gathered their gear together, and began to load themselves into two leaky sampans. A high sea was running, and the sampans, weighed down almost to the gunwale, made it look like a risky journey for them; but they took it quite cheerfully, fastening the bamboo scaffolding they had used in their work around the boats to act as floats; and eventually they got ashore quite comfortably.

In the roads we saw one of our ships; and another was just coming into harbour outward bound. The quarantine boat came running out towards us; but on our signalling that we were only landing coolies and waiting for the pilot, they sheered off again.

The Old Man paced restlessly about the bridge.

"Outram's a long time coming. I hope nothing's wrong," he said.

"The pilot boat's putting out from the *hatoba*, sir," said Horner.

The Old Man swung his glasses on the approaching boat; and presently he swore. It was obvious the pilot was not Captain Outram, and no ladies were with him.

Instead we got a bibulous-looking, very pleasant gentleman; and I could see from the Old Man's looks he had absolutely no confidence in him.

At dinner he had more whisky than was good for him; and I saw the Old Man watching him with gloomy eyes. From the chart-room afterwards he sent for more whisky. Then the Old Man came to me.

"Look here, Doc! I don't trust this chap a bit! I'm darned if I'll let him run my ship ashore in the narrows! I want you to go up and see him, and tell me if you think it's wise to let him have any more whisky. If you think he's not fit now, I'll take her through myself."

Accordingly I went up and found him half asleep. He was very charming when I commenced talking to him; but he was soon in a very different frame of mind when I told him I must stop his allowance if he wished to take the ship through. He swore he had never heard of such a thing being done in all the years of his pilotage; said he had taken hundreds of ships through, including C.P.R.'s and P. & O.'s; and told me I was acting entirely without precedent. I told him I had no admiration for precedents, but a very great one for the company I represented. Then the Old Man came up, chimed in, and told him brusquely he could get as drunk as a fiddler once we were through the narrows; but, curiously enough, this annoyed him more than anything I had said. He became very dignified all at once; issued his orders with military precision to the quartermaster; and made me feel I had no *locus standi* on the bridge. The trouble was he was undoubtedly a gentleman; and I felt sorry we had had to touch him on the raw as we did. He probably knew his weakness as well as, or better than, we did, and was consequently all the more sensitive on the point.

Nothing happened, however. The Old Man spent the whole night on the bridge along with him, ready to take the ordering out of his hands if necessary. We got safely to Moji on the following afternoon; and he departed, shaking the dust of the ship from off his feet, still sore at our lack of confidence.

The Old Man saw him off in grim silence, and then delivered himself to me on the whole duty of a sailor thus:

"A man undertaking any responsibility has no right to drink when he's on duty," he said sententiously. "I don't care a tinker's curse what he does off; but while he's on, 'Shipshape and Bristol fashion'—that's my style."

We started coaling immediately, for the orders were to make all speed for Java; and so we soon had a repetition of the pandemonium of the previous occasion, the same staircase of bamboo scaffolding from the lighters to the ship, the same grimy coolies slinging their oval baskets, the same repulsive women, with babies on their backs, tipping the baskets into the bunkers.

Darkness came, but the work went on unceasingly; huge flares lit the barges, and half illuminated the grimy yellow, semi-nude bodies of the sweating coolies.

There was no escape from the continual din; the atmosphere was impregnated with coal-dust; and lighters were lying three deep on both sides of the ship, creaking and groaning as they bumped against one another in the strong tide in the semi-darkness. I wanted to go ashore out of it all; but none of the officers could come. The tide was running strongly towards Shimonoseki, and it would be very difficult to get back. Besides, there were no sampans about. Still, after dinner I made up my mind to attempt it, though dolefully dissuaded by the Old Man; and so I climbed perilously down the scaffolding on to one of the lighters, crossed over the others in the half-darkness, and shouted for a sampan.

There was only one; it was an open boat, manned by a boy; and he was disinclined to take me, as he belonged to Moji, and the tide running towards Shimonoseki would give him a heavy pull against it when he turned for home.

The magic of a dollar persuaded him, however; and we were soon racing, almost without an effort, in the fierce current running towards the Shimonoseki shore.

In a few minutes the din of the ship subsided. It was a clear, cloudless night. The stars glittered multitudinous on the dimpling waters. We passed some tree-clad islands in the half gloom, and soon were in the main channel. The lights of Moji under the beetling hills subsided to pin-points, and those of Shimonoseki began to shine in rippling streaks across the water. We passed close under the bows of a German coaling; and the sound of music floated to us from the lighted fo'castle. Someone was singing "Der Wacht am Rhein." We swung in the half darkness under shadowy junks, worked round anchored luggers, till finally the boy ran the sampan cleverly ashore, stern first, along the slope of the landing stage. I paid him, and then watched till he disappeared in the gloom, rowing strongly against the tide.

The city was very much awake; people were moving about everywhere, lighting themselves with huge paper lanterns. A *kurumaya* turned his rickishaw when he saw me, and waited. I tried to make him understand I wanted to go to Dr. Tomatoda's, but found it impossible as I had forgotten the address. Finally I made for the English Club, and raised one of the agent's clerks.

He said he was bored to death and wild for a night out, so we rapidly made our programme. A short ride brought us past a theatre with great flaring lights outside, such as one sees at a country fair. There were huge pictures illustrative of the play, very gory and exciting. Enormous long flags hung down like streamers from the roof, covered with ideographic writing. Turning up a quiet alley, not far distant from the theatre, we alighted at a *yadoya* and, after removing our boots, went upstairs. We wanted to go to the theatre; and Wilson arranged that we should have two geisha to accompany us. Presently the little women arrived, with their inevitable wooden cases.

We hurried through the dinner that followed, and to which we invited them, as we wanted to get to the theatre as soon as possible. Not even the delicacies provided, such as rice cakes, raw fish, daikon, etc., could restrain the eagerness of the girls. They, too, wanted to be off, giving us to understand that a particularly famous actor was performing, and everybody was crazy about him. So, after some ceremonial *saké*-drinking, we put our boots on loosely and followed the maids the short distance to the theatre on foot. There was a great crowd in the street; and instead of taking our arms in the crush, European style, the gorgeous little ladies held on to our hands, after the quaint Japanese fashion. At the entrance our boots came off again; and one of the maids took them back to the *yadoya*, leaving us sandals in exchange. Our box had been previously obtained while we were at the *yadoya*, for the doorkeeper handed a slab of wood, covered with letters, to one of the geisha. There was a hole in the slab, and a string was passed through the hole. This was our ticket.

Our box was part of the theatre floor, about six feet square, surrounded by a moulding about four inches high. It was covered by matting, over which was a red rug. Several cushions and a *hibachi* had been brought from the *yadoya* for our use.

Our party consisted of six people—the two geisha, ourselves, and two maids behind to attend to our wants. There was a sloping pit, on which everyone squatted, and a gallery, with side boxes, above. The stage was elevated above the pit; but there were no footlights, a row of hanging oil-lamps serving instead.

On our right, facing the stage, sat a boy with a pair of wooden clappers, which he banged every now and again when anything interesting was happening. Behind

him, in a cage-like side box, was a kind of orchestra; and
above this, in a similar cage, sat a woman with a samisen,
and a man who every now and again burst into a rapid
explanatory recitative before anything began to happen—
acting, as it were, the part of the Greek chorus.

On the left of the stage, as seen from the front, there
was a pier-like prolongation, extending out into the
auditorium, intended for the use of the hero, enabling
him to appear unexpectedly at any thrilling moment on
the stage.

The play was of the interminable variety. It had been
going on for some days, and all that day.

We gathered, at the time of our entry, that a woman
in distress had been captured by robber barons, and,
when we arrived, the hero was busy delivering her, in
spite of all sorts of witchcraft tricks. The costumes worn
by the characters were of the most gorgeous. They were
replicas of the old-time costumes of the country, and were
intensely interesting to us on that account.

The hero was dressed as a Samurai, with top-knot, a
long flowing brocaded garment, and two swords. When
we entered he was having a wordy fight with the chief
of the robber barons. They wrestled. Then they drew
their swords, and fought. As the swords clashed each
stroke was accentuated by the boy with the clappers
making a loud bang on the board before him.

The hero slew the robber baron and carried his dead
body off. Then he lay down nonchalantly to sleep at
the door of a temple in the background; and as he slept
he dreamt strange dreams, for as he dreamed a little
black-robed boy appeared with a mystic scroll on the
end of a fishing-rod. This he dangled over the sleeper's
head till, half awake, he grasped it. By a stage con-
vention the black-robed boy was supposed to be invisible;
and so the hero was now in possession of a mysterious
scroll from nowhere which was a talisman against all

spells. When he awakened he found the scroll in his hand; and after searching vainly for any signs of a donor he fastened it to his temple. This ended the act.

As soon as the curtain fell a lot of little boys immediately rushed up and put their heads below it to see the scenery shifted. They were able to do this, of course, quite easily, as there was no orchestra or footlights to separate them from the stage.

In the interval the audience smoked, had food brought to them, and partook of tea in little parties. Our little geisha drew out mirrors and combs from somewhere, and inspected their elaborate headgear. They were noted belles, and probably had lovers in the audience of whom they were demurely conscious all the time. Everybody talked at once. The people in the box behind us had their whole tea-making outfit brought in by two attendants. During the interval the lady rescued previously, or perhaps it was another lady, was again apparently captured, for on the curtain rising she was found in the hands of a set of villainous-looking ruffians. Their chief made certain propositions to her, which the woman (marvellously acted by a boy) refused indignantly, whereupon she was beaten with long flexible sticks to the accompaniment of the clapper. Still refusing, she was tied to a tree, beaten again, and a fire lit under her. The smoke rose, choking her, and still she refused.

Suddenly along the narrow pier rushed the hero. He appeared on the stage like a bolt from the blue, fell upon the robbers, and rescued the lady. There was a great noise of clapping; and the curtain fell over the resuscitation of the fainting lady.

In the next scene the curtain rose showing a huge man of most ferocious mien (a mask) sitting on a dais facing the audience. He was supposed to be a wicked *daimyo*; and he was clad in the most gorgeous robes that ever Satsuma artist pictured on a vase. He posed immense like a god before the people; and the little geisha drew their breath inwards as they gazed on him.

In to him was brought the husband of the lady who had been rescued in the previous act. (Apparently they were a most unfortunate family.) The *daimyo* looked at him ponderously, and made a slow, malignant speech of triumph. Then the prisoner taunted him with cowardice, said he hid behind his myrmidons, employed others to do the work he was afraid to attempt himself, and challenged him to mortal combat.

With fierce rage the giant *daimyo* answered him, accepted the challenge, and told them to unbind the prisoner and furnish him with a sword. Then they began to fight, the smaller man with his sword against the giant with a huge club. It was a good full-blooded fight; and they went at it as if they meant it. It was well worth seeing. The smaller man slowly began to get the worst of it; he was visibly failing; his blows came more feebly; the audience held their breath in suspense. Suddenly the giant made a mighty sweep with his club, as if to finish the business. The other wearily ducked; the great club swung narrowly past his head; and the *daimyo* stumbled forward. Like a flash the other had him; the sword flew out straight; and the great mass of a man tumbled, doubled up on the stage. It was an immense piece of stage management. The audience rose to it. Slowly the *daimyo* raised himself to a sitting posture. Apparently he was not mortally injured; but he was defeated, and he knew it. The only thing left was to commit hara-kiri; and this he deliberately set about doing in front of the audience. Everything was ready for the ceremony; the *daimyo* bowed his head; and then the supernatural came to his rescue.

A demon goddess appeared, and with a wave of her wand dropped the conqueror unconscious at her feet. Thus the *daimyo* was saved for further wickedness. A crowd of robbers came in; and the unconscious captive

was bound and strapped to a couch. Then the wicked
daimyo, restored to his power, climbed up above the
captive, who had now recovered, and told him slowly
with minute detail, exactly how he was going to proceed
to disembowel him. This was obviously the hero's
chance. He appeared just in the nick of time; another
fierce fight took place; the *daimyo* was slain; and the
captive rescued. But all was not yet well. They had
reckoned without the demon goddess. With wild, venge-
ful eyes she now appeared again, armed with a long
spear; and once more under her magic spell the erstwhile captive fell unconscious. But not so the hero. The
talisman he had so mysteriously acquired protected him.
He drew it from his temple, where it was fastened, and
pointed it at her. Immediately she was shorn of her
demoniacal power, and the captive was raised again.

But though her magic power was gone, the malignancy
of her hate and her physical power remained unabated.
Fiercely she stabbed at the hero with her huge, long
spear; and skilfully he parried the unexpected attack.
Again there was a fight; and again right triumphed. The
curtain dropped on this scene for the night. It was
twelve o'clock; and the play would be continued on the
morrow at noon.

Rapidly the theatre cleared; and we went out with the
others, donned our sandals, and walked awkwardly the
thirty yards back to the *yadoya,* the little women tripping
daintily at our sides. We had entertained them; and
now they felt it incumbent on them to entertain us in
exchange; so they sang and danced for us, smoked many
cigarettes, laughed, chatted in broken English, pretended
to teach us Japanese, and ever kept filling up our *sake*
cups. Night is their time for entertaining. Probably
they sleep most of the day. Entertaining is their occupation; and they have been trained up to it from early
infancy. To the Japanese they are of course much more
interesting than to us, because they can appreciate their

singing and dancing, the witty tales they tell, and the poems they have been carefully trained to declaim from the Japanese classics. Their beauty, too, is of the extreme Japanese type—intensely oval faces, very much slanted eyes, very willowy figures. It takes the European eye some years to appreciate such points. Wilson confessed he had not been long enough in the East to do so yet.

By two o'clock I knew the tide would be turned; and by that time I also came to the conclusion I had had quite enough *saké* for a man who had to climb up an intricate mass of scaffolding to get to his ship.

The bill was sent for, and came in a roll of paper eighteen inches long. We paid it and went below to get our boots. Then after a ceremonious farewell we sallied out into the night. There wasn't a rickishaw in sight; the streets were absolutely deserted From another *yadoya* a little down the street the sound of music floated out to us. It was someone playing the biwa.

We stood on the steps of the *yadoya,* the landlord having retired inside to look after the comfort of some of his other guests.

"It's a beautiful night," said Wilson. "I'll walk to the *hatoba* with you."

Suddenly I felt a soft little hand grasping each of mine, saw two little figures, one on either side, and heard a voice saying, "We come see you *hatoba.*"

It was the two geisha, who, having finished so early, had taken it into their heads to come and see us off in this quaintly friendly way.

So hand in hand we all four walked through the quiet streets, like children coming home from school, in the starlight to the *hatoba;* and there they insisted on bargaining for me at the sampan office. It was a good thing for me they did. The official in charge was as wax under the magic of their smiles. I had a half-decked sampan, under which I could lie comfortably sheltered from the wind, and two sturdy boatmen to take me to the ship. Looking back, I saw them standing, two quaint little figures, one on either side of Wilson, in the starlight, and heard them calling, *"Sayonara—sayonara—sayonara—"*

CHAPTER VII

ON THE WAY TO JAVA

SUCH was my good-bye to Japan; and for the next week I ruminated on what I had seen, wishing to have a mental stock-taking before new scenes and fresh peoples dimmed the sharpness of memory's retina.

Preconceived impressions, I found, had been destroyed or modified, new and discomposing ones added, unexpected sidelights thrown upon events and people, curious defects and equally unanticipated virtues laid bare before me.

I had looked at things, at first, with the European eye; now I tried to see with those of the Oriental, to judge by standards different from my own, to think not of what was lacking, but of what had been accomplished; and the general impression arising from it all, I was forced to admit, was one of respect for the efficiency of the nation, and more particularly its rulers. Of its moral code, judging from European standards, I was in doubt.

In China religion and philosophy have ingrained in the people a contempt for the military spirit; and as a consequence the Chinaman has little patriotism. Theoretically he is therefore on a higher ethical plane than ourselves; but practically, as a consequence, his country has been parcelled out into spheres of influence by foreigners, such as English, French, German, and other barbarians, who have not yet reached his high standard of ethical perfection. He is a brave man; but nevertheless he allows himself to be dictated to by nations whom, if he cared to exert his enormous inherent power, he could crush like flies. He has been taught to look upon soldiers

187

as in the same category as robbers and highwaymen; and his army in consequence is a thing of laughter. It is obviously therefore not the ambition of any Chinaman to be known as a great military leader, when such celebrity would carry with it the opprobrium we attach to Morgan the Buccaneer; and so all the intelligence of the country has been diverted to the arts of peace. That is why China has produced such wonderful literature, such consummate art treasures, such capable merchants. The intellectual shrewdness of the merchant class quickly jumped to the knowledge that in business honesty is the only policy; and that is why huge transactions are still confidently entered into, between the great shipping firms of Europe and Chinamen, without a single paper being signed between them.*

On the other hand, the cult of the Samurai was until recently all-powerful in Japan; and the spirit of loyalty and obedience to the death permeated the very life of the nation, showing itself to the present day in an almost fanatical patriotism. The soldier has always been the great hero of Japanese folklore; tales of fighting and dauntless death in the performance of set duties are innumerably portrayed on their objects of art. The soldier spirit has been responsible for the awakening of the country; and the same spirit brought it through triumphant in its grim struggle with the Colossus of the North.

The merchant in Japan, on the contrary, until quite recently, was classed below the peasant and artisan, very little above the *eta* or pariahs. Japan had no intercourse with foreign nations, by command of the Emperor, from the fifteenth century till late in the nineteenth; and her merchants were mere hucksters in consequence, unworthy of the name of traders. Their commercial morality was, as might have been expected, on a par with their low social status. They were looked upon as outcasts, and it

---

* These views written over thirty years ago are, of course, no longer as valid as they were. The new era in China has materially altered the national outlook.

was a degradation for anyone of a higher status to descend to their level; so although the interdict against foreign trade has been removed, factories and great industries have been spreading all over the country, and a new class of merchant has gradually been arising, yet old prejudices are hard to kill, and it is still considered lowering for one of the old Samurai class to devote the energies he might be applying for the benefit of his country to the mere sordid pleasure of heaping up a fortune in business for himself and his family. Nevertheless a new class of merchant is slowly being formed, men of integrity and wealth, whose word is their bond; but they are not as yet, I regret to say, anything like enough to leaven the whole lump; and the European dealing with the Japanese still finds himself constantly being cheated unless he effectually safeguards himself. It is not surprising, therefore, that the sailor, judging the people from the merchants he comes in contact with, calls them a nation of cheats and scoundrels.*

. . .

The first day at sea was comparatively calm; but once outside the shelter of the land we found ourselves in trouble, as we were practically empty, running in water-ballast, and the sea appeared to know it. Spray dashed continuously over everything, leaving a clammy steaminess even in our cabins. Every minute a jarring shiver shook the ship; it was the screw racing as it lifted clear of the water. Everyone was in the dumps, for we were supposed to be steaming against time. To get to Soerabaya on the date appointed we should have been doing fourteen knots. Instead we were barely doing nine.

"When we get there," grumbled the Mate, "after all the extra waste of coal, we'll find they don't really want us for some days more, and that we might have done it at our leisure. I said we were going to Java, and nobody

* These opinions, unpopular at the time they were written, when the Japanese were our allies, have since been proved almost too favourable.

believed me. Now I say all this rush is unnecessary, and
you'll find I'm right again."

The horizon was blurred; accurate observations were
impossible; and we were more or less depending on dead
reckoning. At night the Old Man took a star observa-
tion, and found we were 40° E., so the course had to be
altered to keep us clear of the Luchu Islands. Everybody
said this weather could not last for more than another
twelve hours, but nobody believed it.

The next day the gale was still blowing; and in addition rain-storms continually swept over us. The Mate
said rain usually meant that the wind was going to shift.
Nevertheless everyone was very gloomy. They began to
think there was a Jonah on the ship—perhaps someone
had left Japan without paying his debts. A parson had
come aboard at Yokohama, and that always brought bad
luck. Finally they remembered we had had bad weather
in the Mediterranean, and an unusually rough time in
the China Seas outward bound. The conviction therefore gradually grew on them that I was the Jonah. They
joked about it, of course; but there was always a faint
substratum of belief under their joking which they could
scarcely conceal—all of which made for a vague discomfort.

The Old Man had been on the bridge all day, worrying to catch a sight of Torishima, an island in the
Luchu tail; but the rain obscured everything, and, when
we found from the patent log that we should have passed
it, we stood out west to clear.

Late at night, however, we sighted Kumishima, the
sister isle, seven miles on the port beam; and then, to our
relief, Torishima light itself came in sight seventeen miles
astern—we had passed it unobserved in the moonlight.
"That's all right," said the Old Man. Half an hour later,
with a snort of relief, he turned in, for the sea was clear
of everything now till we sighted the eastern shore of
Luzon, in the Philippines.

The Mate had been right about the shift in the wind. Next day it was comparatively calm; and everyone forgot about the Jonah.

When we left Japan it had been wintry weather; the temperature had been about 42° F.; and we had been wrapped to the eyes in heavy serges. Since leaving Moji, however, it had been rising 10° a day, and now stood at over 70° F. in my cabin. Heavy serges therefore had to be discarded and the thinnest of blue substituted.

A note of cheerfulness had spread all over the ship; the decks were dry and white; the awnings had been put up again; and a row of deck-chairs stood once more outside the companion-hatch. The sea had calmed down; and only an occasional roll reminded us of the weather we had been having.

The ship was full of canaries, bought in Moji, cages and all, for about a yen. The Mate had one, the Chief two; several of the engineers had them also; and there were at least a dozen in the fo'castle. Now when the weather had cleared, and the sun had come out again, everyone brought his particular pets on deck, and they all began to sing at once. They sang all day; they sang against one another; the ship was a floating cage of melody.

"Thank goodness, it won't last," said Horner, who was only beginning to recover his spirits. "Most of them will be sold to the Dutchmen in Java. They're worth 30s. to £2 there; and it's a regular trade with our crews."

The next day was Sunday; and so all the men, except the quartermasters on duty, sprawled about the fore and after deck smoking and sorting their gear, emptying the contents of their sea-chests on the sunny hatches to dry. The bo'sun too was very busy. We were going into the most oppressively hot part of the tropics; and so all the seamen were coming to him to have their hair cropped to the scalp, for the bo'sun was the hairdresser of the ship.

Lazily we watched the victims as one by one he sat them on a stool in front of him in a shady corner below the fo'castle head and ran the clippers over their heads till each had acquired the recognised convict crop.

At Moji we had shipped five Chinese tally-clerks, whose duties were to take a note of every bale of cargo as it was being dumped into the holds. Chinamen are employed for this work, as it is necessary to stand all day in the sun while the cargo is being stowed, and white men are found unable to bear the strain of it for more than a few hours at a time.

Since leaving Moji these new members of our crew had been invisible; but on this glorious afternoon they now appeared for the first time, and soon were squatting contentedly on the No. 1 hatch for'ard. As a class they are very intelligent. They are mostly recruited from Singapore, and are very proud of their British citizenship.

It was a perfect afternoon, seductively warm. The Chief and I lay at full length beneath the awning, with our feet on the top bar of the rail, gazing dreamily out over a sea of ultramarine. Far away to starboard the sky, a hazy snow-flecked blue, melted to a pearly-grey as it touched the horizon, which rose and fell to the eye with the slow, monotonous, regular roll of the ship. The sea around was flecked with little wavelets; and ever and anon up from it, with a hurrying rush, would dash a flying fish, glistening silver-white in the sunshine as he scurried along a few feet above the water in his rapid flight of fifty yards or so till, exhausted, he dropped with a splash into his element again.

The whole world seemed to be at peace. It was difficult to believe that three days before we had been shivering wet in a sea of troubled waters.

I made a casual remark to the Chief. There was no answer, and, looking round, I found he was asleep.

Then the Old Man came out of his cabin, red-faced

and very burly, clad in gorgeous pyjamas of batik cloth, his feet in Chinese slippers, and a bath towel in his hand.

He spoke to me in passing; and the Chief wakening quietly looked up. He smiled faintly at the figure the Old Man cut, and drew out his pipe.

Presently sounds as of a grampus blowing told us the Old Man was having his afternoon bath.

"It's not a bad plan," said the Chief reflectively.

Next day the order came to don whites; and we all appeared snow-clad immaculate at breakfast. We had been a week at sea with never a sign of a ship or sight of land since we skirted the Luchus, so it was quite an event when after the moon had risen in the second "dog," just as we got up from dinner, the sound of "two bells" came from the fo'castle head.

"Land on the starboard bow! That should be the Philippines!" said the Mate.

We all trooped up on deck; and there, faint on the rim of the horizon, we could just make out the shadowy signs of land.

Most of the officers had been several times in Manila; and they described in graphic terms, as we leant over the rail looking at the shadowy coast, their impressions of the raw American civilisation which had been so suddenly grafted on Spanish immemorial calm—the strident notes of the fog-siren that had replaced the tinkle of the guitar. Most of them, I noticed, preferred the guitar.

All the next morning we were racing along the coast of Mindanao, a mass of serrated, blue-grey mountain-peaks against a sky capped by golden cumuli, with vast forests of dark green pine running down the mountain-sides to the sea, and here and there the smoke of a great forest fire rising in the tremulous haze.

Flying catamarans manned by coppery Filipinos once

or twice came close; but we had not time to stop to buy
their fish.

We had logged 330 miles in the last twenty-four hours;
and the Old Man was so pleased that he permitted himself to chaff the Chief, saying he'd have to slow down
for fear the bottom plates should get heated by the speed
we were making.

The temperature was 90° F. in the shade; but all the
morning the cool breeze, blowing off the shore, kept us
quite comfortable. At noon, however, we had passed
Mindanao and sighted Sarangani (5° 19' N., 125° 19'
E.); we were clear away from the land; and now the starboard side felt like an oven, and the heat-waves could
almost be seen beating through the awnings as a big
dragon-fly from the land spread his iridescent wings and
preened himself on the rail before me.

I left him to enjoy himself and moved my chair to
port. A huge shark, with his triangular fin sticking up,
passed us in the opposite direction. Had we been a
sailing ship he would have hovered round for days, bat-
tening on the garbage thrown overboard, always hopeful
of a human mouthful as a tit-bit, till perchance some
day, tempted by a lump of bacon on a hook, he was
landed, fifteen feet of vicious life, on the deck.

Now and again, as I lay watching, a dolphin would
raise his nose out of the water just behind a scurrying
flying fish, which had taken to the air to avoid him;
whilst further out a line of splashing white-flecked spots
indicated a school of bonito jumping.

Everybody on the ship was busy—the Old Man over
his accounts, the Mate superintending the painting opera-
tions which were to bring us ship-shape and Bristol
fashion, shining like a baby after its morning bath, into
port. There we should have ladies aboard; and everything must be as fresh as the whitest of white paint, the
purest of enamel, and the most persistent holystoning
could get it. Down in the bunkers the engineers were

hurrying the sweating Chinamen to clear the coal out of the deep-tank, so that it could be washed and made ready to receive its share of the cargo of copra, sugar, spices, tobacco, and gums we would be bringing home to Europe.

Next day we were in a sea of glass. Not a ripple dimmed the mirror of the water. Over the vast circle of the horizon there lay a halcyon calm, only the long white line, stretching to apparent infinity behind, marking our course through the stillness. Now and again startled flying fish would rise in the calm morning, leaving little whip-lash tracks as they sank again. A solitary boatswain bird hovered around with his great wings and marlin-spike tail outspread; and now and again a group of bonito would shoot up dark against the skyline, falling back with a splash into the water again.

But every now and then a change would come over the water. Little round patches, running into one another, would form, and the clear smoothness be dimmed by a thousand dimples.

"Watching the cat's-paws, Doc?" said the Mate's voice at my elbow. "If we were in a wind-jammer you'd be anxious to see more of them. One might wallow for days in a sea like this, and never make a mile."

All morning they had been painting steadily; but just before noon, when there were yards and yards of fresh wet paint, to the consternation of the Mate the sky suddenly darkened, and almost before we could reach shelter the rain came down in torrents, sluicing along the decks, gurgling out of the scuppers, beating through the awnings, catching the Chief unawares and soaking him through.

We had all been in immaculate whites for some days; and this painting had been a sore trial to us, for every time we forgot we were sure to mark their snowy innocence with black or green or red—never by any chance white. The Chief said it was a special intervention of

Providence, this rain, to punish the Mate for what we had suffered.

In the afternoon I had an interview with the No. 1 Chinaman. It was about the opium in the Chinese fo'castle. The Dutch have very stringent regulations about opium. It is a Government monopoly; and, should an inspector discover any aboard, the ship would be heavily fined and the Chinaman responsible get two or three months in chains.

We talked it over; and he promised to put all he could find under my care till we got clear of land. But of course I did not get it all. They brought me a tin of treacly stuff, holding about four ounces, and swore that was all they had.

I had to be content with that. I had done my best; they knew the risks, and would have to take precautions accordingly.

On the next day, at seven o'clock in the morning, we crossed the Line, myself and the deck-boy being the only two on board who had not already made the acquaintance of Father Neptune. The boy, I heard, had a rough time of it in the fo'castle, having to go through the traditional handling; but, for me, as I threatened to doctor all the food in the saloon if they played any tricks, I was permitted, as a great concession, to sign a chit for the liquid refreshment of all and several who cared to call for it throughout the morning.

The Old Man was cutting corners in his hurry, contrary to the company's regulations; and as this part of the world is not very accurately charted, he began to feel a little nervous when we came so close to the southern coast of Borneo that we could see trees and houses distinctly through the glasses.

Accordingly we made more over towards the other side; and so all the afternoon the coast of Celebes lay outspread before us. Early in the second "dog," just before sundown, two bottle-nosed whales came alongside the

ship, blowing and chasing each other quite regardless of
our presence—a sign that we were in very unfrequented
waters.

It was the next day I saw my first coral island. At a
distance it looked like a fleet of fishing praus; but as we
came nearer the feathery tops of the palm trees could
be made out, then the coral reef with its pearly beach
of sand, finally a red-roofed house half buried in the dark
green of the coco-nut plantation, a spire, what looked like
a windmill, and that was all. It lay basking in the sunlight, a forgotten pearl of the ocean. Apparently it had
not even a name—the chart represented it as a dot. Probably some lonely Dutchman, or half-caste, ruled it with
his dusky wife, going with his supply of copra in sailing
praus twice in the year to Macassar, having a gay old
time there for a week, and then returning for another
six months to sit on the verandah of his red-roofed house,
and watch enviously, or pityingly, the smoke of an occasional ship like ours, passing from the hurry of the great
world to the hurry of the great world without a thought
for him.

CHAPTER VIII

JAVA: AT SOERABAYA

It was early on an Easter Sunday morning that we first sighted the high coast of Java, piled peak on peak into the blue; and all that day we were running along it, in a sunlit sea, at a temperature of 90° F. in the shade.

To starboard the low-lying coast of the great island of Madura ran in a continuous blue irregular line on the edge of the horizon. To port the mountain cones of Java, great shimmering peaks of azure, towered high above the sea in the early morning, till they were hidden by the midday haze. Cloud-capped during the day, they glow an angry red at night, indicative of the smouldering fires underneath, ready to break out at any moment and startle the world with a vast inundation similar to that of Krakatoa—for Krakatoa is but one of the fifty-six active or extinct volcanoes present in this great belt of igneous subterranean life.

All around, the sea was dotted with the triangular black-and-white striped sails of native fishing praus; while every now and then we would pass a great lumbering Dutchman under full sail, square yards rotund to the favouring wind. Close to us a trading prau, gorgeously carved, piled high with rice in great straw bundles, was making for Macassar, with her two huge triangular sails bowed like cones by the wind, her narrow thin hull steadied by two long bamboo outriggers, touching the water, one on either side.

Around us schools of porpoises rolled oilily in the summer sea; and pieces of driftwood, each with its crew of black and white sea birds, were carried rapidly in the current towards the Straits of Macassar.

Under the guidance of the pilot we progressed slowly, as we drew nearer and nearer to our destination, through a fleet of fishing praus at anchor, with nets thrown out buoyed by pieces of bamboo. The tree-clad Madura coast came closer and closer; the crenated red-tiled roofs of low white pillared houses could now be made out, and the clear outlines of two great white Dutch cruisers at anchor near the shore.

More and more ships appeared—Dutch, English, Norwegian, two of our own company's boats, a long white cable-ship with its stunted cut-off bow, and the usual petroleum boats, far out, flying the danger flag.

Slowly we swung round to the Java side, towards a line of stakes projecting from the shallow water. The sea-breeze had dropped; and a sweet, heavy, clinging odour came wafted from the mangrove-tangled shore. Sweeping past a clean-cut artificial opening, leading to a dock inside of which we saw a man-o'-war almost concealed by the overpowering vegetation, a little further round we spied a park with a band-stand, and the white glimmer of women's dresses amongst the tamarinds.

As we slowly forged ahead sampans came hurrying towards us, all very gaily painted with green and red arabesques. They were considerably different from the sampans we had been used to in Japan. Most of them had a crew of two; one man rowed in the bow with a short paddle having a heavy cross-handle at the top; the other steered in the stern with a similar blade. They all had the typical Malay triangular sail set on a long bamboo spar, with a short mast stepped for'ard; and most of them boasted a square awning amidships. With long boat-hooks they tried to catch on to the sides of the ship; but we were too high for them; and with gestures of despair they swept rapidly astern in the tide. One man, however, was more fortunate. By a lucky accident he caught his boat-hook in the open after-port of my cabin, and once he had got his purchase, hung on like grim death. Someone threw him a rope, and this he also grasped, letting go with the boat-hook. We were now opposite the entrance to a canal running up to the city of Soerabaya itself. It was crowded with praus, lighters, and sampans; and overlooking it were the landing stage and the low, rib-tiled, red-roofed, whitewashed building of the Custom-house.

Down went the anchor; and we were moored within a few hundred yards of our sister ships in the company's service, about half a mile from the shore.

Soon after a launch ran alongside; and we were boarded by a huge Dutchman, very fat, very red, very perspiring, clad in spotless whites and a big straw hat, representing the port authorities and the Nederlands Government. After him, at a respectful distance, came a crowd of Malays, turbaned, saronged, very brown, bare-footed or in Arab sandals—boatmen, barbers, tailors, dhobi-men, cigar-sellers, batik merchants, jewellers, money-changers, pearl merchants, boot-makers, kris-sellers, fruit-hawkers— any and every kind of merchant one could possibly want, and some one did not want.

That evening at dinner there was much talk of Java fever, and the risk on sitting on deck after sundown. "There's no risk at all, if you don't sit out on deck after nine o'clock," said the Old Man. "I got it once; but it was my own fault. It was at this very port of Soerabaya, too. I was mate of the old *Menelaus* at the time; and our Old Man had gone ashore, leaving me in charge. We had a Dutch crew; and somehow or other they all managed to get on a tremendous blind in the fo'castle. That, of course, was none of my business—a certain amount of liberty must be given sailors in port; but when the Chink steward came along and told me they were fighting with knives—a dirty Dago trick I didn't expect— I had to interfere. I knocked down the first man I saw with a knife in his hand, and was just going to tackle another when the man I had floored jabbed me in the

leg as he lay. I kicked him on the jaw to make him
stop, broke his 'zig' something—('zygoma,' I murmured).
Yes, that's it. I was pretty warm after the tussle; and
so, instead of going below, after binding up my leg on
deck, I sat down in my chair partly to cool, partly to let
them see I had my eye on them, in case—— There was
a lot of mist rising from the water; but I didn't bother
about that. Ten days after I was down with the fever;
and I can tell you I don't want it again."

Having delivered himself of this harangue, the Old
Man had a sampan hailed for him and went ashore.

"It's all right for the Old Man to talk of turning in
at nine o'clock," said the Chief, as we sat comfortably in
the cool darkness later, gazing at the winking sampan
lights moving erratically over the phosphorescent water;
"but he's gone ashore to the Club, and hasn't got to sit in
a stifling cabin all evening till he feels sleepy. Blow
the fever!"

So, in defiance of the Old Man's warnings, we sat up
till our usual five bells.

All the cabins were fitted with mosquito-nets; and
everyone talked of the nuisance of having to sleep under
them. As we were half a mile from the shore, however,
and the mosquito cannot fly more than two hundred
yards, I thought we must be fairly safe, and determined
to do without mine. I had forgotten, of course, that there
might be mosquitoes hidden in the lighters around us.
No one luckily had faith enough to imitate my example
except the Chief Steward, who had forgotten to have
one made for his berth in Yokohama, and so could
scarcely be considered a convert. In the morning I found
I was all right; but on the Steward appearing his face
was a caricature of blotches, both eyes were almost closed,
there were painful red nodules on his forehead and on
the back of his neck. It was difficult not to laugh. Under treatment, however, he rapidly got well; but I could
not see how I myself had managed to escape, till I dis-

covered what looked like a number of flea-bites, and
found I had been bitten in several places apparently
without producing any effect. I determined, therefore, to
try again the second night, and found, as I had hoped,
that I was unaffected. As it is denied that Java fever is
conveyed by mosquitoes, I decided therefore to discard
nets all the rest of the time I was in the East.*

To understand the situation of the Javanese ports one
must remember that the backbone of the island is a
ridge of mountainous peaks close to the southern shore,
and that towards the north, where we were, the country
sweeps in one great plain towards the sea. On the
south anchorage is deep right up to the land, whereas
on the north there is shallow water for a considerable
distance from the shore; and so, as all the cities are
inland, to be clear of the miasma, canals have had to
be made from the coast up to them, probably originally
dredged from some convenient creek. Soerabaya is such
a port. It lies about two or three miles from the coast;
and a typical Dutch canal, starting opposite our anchorage, ends in a great basin in the centre of the city.
There is also a steam-tram running parallel to the canal
from the town, and ending at the Custom-house opposite the anchorage.

. . .

I had engaged my own especial boatman. He said
his name was Jimi, and so I called him by it. He was
a most picturesque, smiling little rascal, in a brilliant red
kain-keppla turban above his brown face, loose white
baju jacket, short khaki trousers, a sarong looped round
the waist, bare brown legs, and prehensile toes. His
knowledge of English was primitive; but he seemed to
know instinctively what one wanted. He was always
smiling, always alert, nothing was a trouble to him. He

* This, of course, was an error on my part. Java fever we now
know is malaria.

took possession of me with the most perfect ease of manner.

On his left little finger he wore the Hadji ring, with its clear inset round pebble.

"Bolong my brother," he explained. "He Haj— me no can. No have got money. Perhaps allri, byem-bye."

He rowed me ashore in his sampan, where I lay, a white figure in the centre under the awning, my sun-helmet pulled over my eyes. Jimi, and his brown understudy behind him, sat, on little fixed seats in the bow, facing me. At every second stroke they stood up to take a longer sweep; and so we progressed with great speed towards the beach, passing *en route* a huge ferry prau coming over from the Madura side with numerous Malay passengers, and a great load of tropical fruits, a perfect feast of colour—pisangs, nangkas, durians, papayas, pine-apples, luscious green and yellow oranges, that made one thirsty even to think of.

The creek was crowded with praus waiting for the tide to work their way up to Soerabaya. Some of them were wonderfully beautiful with their great carved bow-sprits, their sterns sculped and painted in beautiful geo-metrical arabesques, and the scalloped lines of gilding on the stem, above the lozenge-shaped red and white and black painted belt on the sides, and the great staring black eyes with wide white rims painted, one on either bow, so that the spirit of the ship might see to guide her safely in the night.

Jimi ran us through a tangled mass of sampans to the long flight of stone steps at the landing stage, everyone making way obsequiously for the white man.

The half-caste Custom-house official gave me all the necessary information about the way to get to the town, and the fares by tram and carriage. He talked as to an equal, for the Dutch have solved the problem of the Eurasian in quite a simple way. They do not despise and degrade him, as we Britishers do, on account of his black blood. No; they say he has Dutch blood, therefore he is a Dutchman. He is accordingly treated as such; his Malay mother is ignored; and he can marry a white girl out from Amsterdam without any outcry. Consequently he is a man, and not a vicious pariah.

There are no rickishaws in Java. I found I could either take the tram to Soerabaya, or hire a one or two-horsed *sadoe,* or a carriage. The *sadoe* is a two-wheeled spring cart with an awning. It is drawn by one or more little Timor or sandal-wood ponies; the driver sits in front, and the fare crouched up balancing him, sits behind. It is a most uncomfortable conveyance; and after my first experience I, for the future, always preferred to use a carriage.

The road to Soerabaya is an open book, with living illustrations, of the life and habits of the people; for the Javanese has solved the problem of existence by living practically out of doors. There is no need of thick walls, and a complicated system of heating to keep out the cold in a country where the temperature practically never falls below 85° F.; and consequently the home of the Javanese is not a fortress against the elements, but a cool retreat where, sheltered from the sun, in his hours of ease he may chew the betel of happiness in somnolent content; for, like his brethren in the lower planes of evolutionary life, the fowls of the air and the beasts of the field, sun, wind, and rain are but adjuncts to his physical needs, not enemies of his body. He is the primitive man, Antæus-like, deriving his strength from the touch of the warm, brown, kindly earth, his mother.

It was a little after sunrise when I started from the landing stage; and the activities of the day were just commencing. The men had already had their morning swim in the canal; and the sun was now brightening to a livelier green the tamarinds on the further bank. Little boys and girls, like glistening bronze fauns, were splashing and calling to one another in the warm water; and

A *Street* *in* *Macassar*

A Seller of Durians

women with the slim bodies and wonderful carriage of the East, wearing great turquoise earrings, their softly rounded shoulders bared to the sun, fresh from the water, were coiling their glistening coal-black hair in pyramids above their shapely heads, putting in jessamine, rose, or tandjong flowers on either side behind their ears with slender, long, brown fingers.

Occasionally a barge would come lumbering down; and from the penthouse aft the denizens at their morning meal would call out softly modulated greetings to their acquaintances on the banks. All along the road, which ran parallel to the canal, under the shelter of the tall waringen trees, little native *worongs* (restaurants) now appeared: for the Javanese almost always breakfast out of doors, the midday meal being the only usual one taken at home. There are many varieties of the *worong;* the more ambitious have an atap-covered roof resting upon four corner posts, with rough wooden seats under cover; but the commonest variety, because most portable, is that consisting of two wooden boxes, one containing food, the other a brazier and crockery. These two cases, swung on a bamboo pole, can be carried by their proprietor anywhere he may think custom is likely.

That morning they all seemed to be doing a roaring trade; and having tasted the fare on several occasions later, I can testify to its appetising nature—hot steaming coffee flavoured with areng-sugar, beautifully cooked rice with an appetiser of dried fish, pink and yellow *Koee-koee* (cakes), trembling pink jellies, and syrupy "limonade."

Around each, as we ambled slowly along, was a laughing, talking group of light-hearted, careless customers, clad in loose jacket and sarong which are so eminently suitable to the climate, and which the comfort-loving Dutchwomen have adopted and wear throughout the greater part of the day, instead of the tight-fitting, unsuitable European clothes so irksomely borne by the memsahib of British India. That is why the Dutchwoman can live ten—fifteen—twenty years in good health in Java without ever going home, to the great saving of her own body, her children's health, and her husband's pocket.

Presently the steam-tram puffed noisily past, going towards the harbour, and having three compartments, one for white men, one for Chinese, and one for natives. As we approached the city the canal banks became more and more animated, and the sweating coolies, hurrying with huge bales of sugar wrapped in matting from go-down to lighter, more frequent.

The road, like all Dutch roads, was wide, smooth, and straight, lined on either side by tall tamarind, kanari, and waringen trees, casting a grateful shade along the route, and making driving a pleasure. The Dutch have made these wonderful roads all through Java, mostly, it must be admitted, by means of forced labour in the old monopoly days. Everywhere one goes, however, one finds them perfect.

Along this road we trotted, passing every kind of life —staid Chinamen in pigtails with paper umbrellas, *Para-naks* (half-caste Chinese) in a nondescript mixture of Javanese and Chinese dress, big rollicking sailors from the Dutch men-o'-war out on the spree, and Malays innumerable in every stage of dress and undress. At length we came to the centre of the city, where the canal expands into a great central basin, and there two hours later I picked up the Chief at the company's office, as arranged.

The Chinese are the merchants of Java—they have nearly ousted the Dutch from retail trade. Export trade, curiously enough, is largely in the hands of a number of Scottish firms who established themselves under the Raffles *régime* during the English occupation in Napoleon's time, and have remained, constantly recruited from Edinburgh and Aberdeen, ever since. The Dutch, on the other hand, do the governing, run the plantations, and any remaining trade left over by the Scots and the Chinese.

We turned into a Chinese shop where almost everything conceivable was sold, a huge emporium filled with European goods. The centre of the ground floor was laid out as a bier-hall; and galleries filled with goods ran in tiers above. It was very cool and refreshing to sit comfortably there after the glare outside. White-clad Dutchmen with red faces dropped in for an iced lager; fat, white-robed Dutch ladies came shopping; little Dutch girls, with long pigtails, came with governesses and elder sisters to buy toys; and the bland Chinamen and *Paranak* shop-hands attended to all their wants.

The proprietor was a Singapore Chinaman; so when we paid our bill in English gold he came across to speak to us. He said he was a Britisher. Afterwards I discovered he was almost a millionaire, and kept two steamers carrying goods to and from Hong Kong. Yet the Dutch treated him just as they would the lowest coolie. He was not allowed to live outside the Chinese quarter, had no civic rights, was taxed exorbitantly, was not permitted to buy any land, and could not even cut off his pigtail without permission of the law-courts.

The natives hate the Chinese, just as the European hated the Jew in the Middle Ages, for the Chinaman is the money-lender and the tax-collector of the East.

The Dutch dislike them because most of the trade of the country is in their hands, and they are indispensable. They have never been trusted since they joined the natives in the rebellion of 1720, when 20,000 of them were slaughtered by the Dutch. After that they were debarred from all monopolies and revenue-farming, and restricted to their present position. In 1837 an Act of Exclusion was passed, but found impossible to uphold, as all the trade of the island was in their hands, and the Dutch discovered they could not do without their Chinese compradors. Consequently all that they can do is

tax the Chinaman unmercifully, treat him as a dog, and
make things generally uncomfortable. As long, however,
as the Chinaman is making money he is quite willing to
put up with it; for, after all, his life and property are
safer here than in the Celestial Empire.[*]

Turning out of the Chinaman's shop, we stumbled
into the Arab quarter. It might have been a corner of
Baghdad, for there was the *mesigit* (mosque), and issuing
from it came a number of white-robed figures, sedately
slow, chatting with dignified stateliness as they walked
along, seemingly as if they had just issued from the pages
of the *Arabian Nights*.

Yet another street was given over to what Anglo-
Indians call "Bombay shops," full of Indian bazaar stuff,
and Japanese curios of an inferior kind at a price that
would have been extortionate even in London.

But it was the native streets—the street of the carpenters, that of the workers in bamboo, rattan, and metal,
the street of the mat-makers, that of the curry cooks, etc.
—we found so interesting. Everywhere, as is the immemorial custom of the East, those of a trade have their
shops and workrooms close together in one street.

Particularly interesting were the *pasars* (markets),
where every kind of vegetable and fruit could be bought.
Piled up in masses, they were a medley of colours that
made one ache to be an artist.

For tiffin someone had directed us to the Hôtel des
Indes; and here we found a cool delicious hour could be
spent toying with a menu splashed in places by its
Oriental origin. It was printed in French, of course—
no self-respecting proprietor could have had it otherwise
—but the beef was buffalo beef, the courses had queer
flavours not associated in one's mind with the same dish
at home, and the fruit—one is not accustomed to be
offered a pyramid of pineapples, pisangs, rambutans,
and dukus as part of the dessert of a two-franc lunch.

[*] It must be remembered that this was written in 1911.

After tiffin we wandered round the *pasars*, picking up any queer things we fancied. The Chief wanted a sarong (loin-cloth) for use during the extremely hot weather; and we wandered into several booths in the *pasars* looking for one with a design sufficiently striking. Many of these native designs are exceedingly bizarre; some of them are very intricate, and take a long time to stamp out by hand, after the native fashion. Collecting sarongs has become a craze with the wealthy Dutch ladies; and as much as a hundred gulden has been paid for a very fine specimen. But we were not looking for anything so grand—we wanted them for use—and eventually got what suited our purses in the stall of a *Paranak* in one of the *pasars*.

The Chinaman wrapped mine up in a piece of newspaper, fastened at one end by a cactus thorn. Looking at the paper, I found it was a page of a *Daily Mail* of the year before, filled with dim echoes of forgotten things in the little island that here seemed so far away. The whole episode appeared somehow unreal when one came to think about it; but when I showed the wrapping to the Chief he only grinned cheerfully.

"That's nothing," he said. "These sarongs are all made in Manchester. All the cheap ones are. But look at this international complication. I've just bought these. They're Swedish matches, printed in English, with the figure of an Arab woman on the cover, sold by a Chinaman, in a Malay bazaar, to an Irishman, working for an English company, in a Dutch colony. The Tower of Babel can't be far off. Eh, what!"

Close beside us a Javanese woman, with her baby slung in a *selendang* over one hip, was bargaining in infinitesimal fractions of a cent for a box of powdered chalk with which to whiten her forehead, and another of yellow *boreh* ointment for her arms. We left her still haggling, and, re-entering our carriage, drove on by

the side of one of the many canals that give these Javanese towns such a curiously exotic Dutch look.

There is no mock modesty about the Javanese. They
were bathing, washing clothes, washing utensils, and
drawing water for domestic purposes all from the same
source. The Dutch, since they have brought the Soerabaya water supply down from the mountains, and thus
whitened the unenviable reputation of the port for cholera, have forbidden the use of canal water for drinking
purposes; but the Eastern mind is very tenacious of
custom; and the native still dies from the polluted water
philosophically, and freshens his fruit for market from
the same source.

"That's where our dhobi-men wash our clothes so
clean and white," said the Chief, nodding sagely. "Nice,
isn't it?"

It was Easter Monday and a general holiday amongst
the Dutch. The Javanese, of course, are always holidaying; and we saw them everywhere, lying contentedly in
the sun, chewing betel, and expectorating the sanious
saliva derived therefrom from between their blackened
teeth.

Betel-chewing is as prevalent in the Malay Archipelago
as cigarette-smoking in Europe; and I cannot do better
than transcribe Dampier's description of it—written in
1686—as it is as accurate to-day as when it was first
penned:—

"This fruit (the betel) is bigger than a nutmeg, and is
much like it, but rounder. It is used all over the East
Indies. Their way is to cut it in four pieces, and wrap
one of them up in an arek-leaf, which they spread with
a soft paste made of lime or plaster, and then chew it
together. Every man in these parts carries his lime-box
by his side, and dipping his finger into it, spreads his
betel and arek-leaf with it. The betel-nut is most esteemed when it is young, and before it grows hard, and

then they cut it only in two pieces with the green husk or shell on it. It is then exceedingly juicy, and therefore makes them spit much. It tastes rough in the mouth, and dyes the lips red, and makes the teeth black, but it preserves them, and cleanseth the gums. It is also accounted very wholesome for the stomach; but sometimes it will cause great giddiness in the head of those that are not used to chew it. But this is the effect of the old nut, for the young nuts will not do it. I speak of my own experience."

That this constant use of a powerful drug seems to produce no apparent pathological effects is very surprising. That it does not, is, however, to my mind doubtful. In the analogous tobacco habit amongst civilised people every physician knows that, though the vast majority escape any injury, there are by no means infrequent cases of people particularly susceptible to the poison of nicotine, with all its grave sequelæ. Similarly, I have no doubt, that symptoms of betel-poisoning in a certain number of cases would, if carefully sought for, be found.

Perhaps *lâtah* is a result of betel-poisoning. It certainly is an exceedingly curious mental condition, almost confined to the Malay, and co-extensive with the betel-chewing habit.

To anyone who has never seen *lâtah* before, the gesticulations of the unfortunate sufferers appear at first either funny, or insultingly offensive, until explained away; for a person suffering from *lâtah* will, if suddenly startled, fall into the hypnotic state and imitate the gestures of anyone in sight—e.g. a decrepit old lady, startled by a bicycle bell, will violently imitate the pedalling of the passing cyclist with her ancient limbs till she falls down exhausted. That they make these movements entirely against their will is evident when one considers the well-known torture the little Malay boys perpetrate, when they have an opportunity, on a known *lâtah*. When he is warming his hands over a brazier the boy will suddenly and noisily drop something behind him. This is quite enough to startle him into the *lâtah* state; and then, standing in front of him, the boy will make movements of his hands as if to pick up the red-hot embers. These movements the unfortunate *lâtah* finds himself compelled to imitate time after time; and so he thrusts his hands into the hot embers, keeping level in movements with his tormentor, till his fingers are badly burnt or someone rescues him, soundly cuffing the young rascal's ears.

It is probably in the *lâtah* state that Malays run *amok;* and then they are as dangerous as a mad dog, and as little responsible for themselves. It is an idea of mine that constant betel-chewing is the predisposing factor producing a condition of nervous instability that so easily might degenerate into *lâtah.* But it is an idea only. No one, as far as I can discover, has suggested it, or attempted experimentally to prove it.[1]

But to return to the Chief. We ambled along the wide roads in a carriage almost as wide, built evidently for the matronly proportions of two Dutch ladies of chaperon age, very roomy and very comfortable. The Javanese driver took us to the European quarter; and there I made my first acquaintance with the beautiful Dutch colonial houses, built like Grecian temples, with

[1] The subject of *lâtah* is one of great interest to those interested in Malay psychology. Popular accounts of this peculiar affection will be found in Swettenham's "Malay Sketches," Clifford's 'Studies in Brown Humanity," and an article by H. A. O'Brien in the *Asiatic Journal* for 1883. For the medical aspects of the condition see:—Neale, "*Lâtah* in Java," *Brit. Med. Journ.* 1884, P-Z; Van Brero, "*Lâtah* in Java," *Journ. Ment. Sc.*, 1895; G. Ellis, "*Lâtah*," *Journ. Ment. Sc.*, 1897; Gerrard, "Hypnotism and *Lâtah*," *Dub. Journ. Med. Sc.*, 1904; Manson, "*Lâtah*"; Allbutt's "Syst. Med.," vol. ii. pt. 2, 1907; Fletcher, "*Lâtah* and Crime," *Lancet*, vol. ii., 1908. Since the above was written I have had to modify this theory, Cf. Abraham, "Concerning *Lâtah* and *Amôk*," *Brit. Med. Journ.*, Feb. 24, 1912. The latest views will be found in Manson's *Tropical Medicine.* Edited by Sir Philip Manson-Bahr. 1945.

columns and great marble floors, that I shall describe more fully in the account of Macassar.

The railway station for Batavia was here; and we noticed that all the railway clerks and officials seemed to be Chinamen. The trains in Java are very comfortable, and run at regular intervals during the day, but never at night. The engine-drivers are natives; and the Dutch do not care to trust them in the dark. Consequently when night comes all trains stop at the nearest station, and the passengers put up for the night in the Government *pasangrahan*,[1] or hotel, till the next morning, when they resume their leisurely journey onwards.

On the way back to the ship we stopped at the *pasar* nearest the harbour to have a look at the fruit stalls. The Chief insisted on addressing everyone gravely in English; and everybody smiled, taking it as a joke of the incomprehensible English sailorman. We walked leisurely through the *pasar*; and presently I noticed two bright-eyed, red-saronged brown girls were following us, each with an empty basket slung in her *selendang*, giggling. Apparently they wanted, for a small fee, to carry anything we chose to buy to our carriage. But when the Chief turned and explained in fluent Malay, which I had thought he did not know—the wily old ruffian—that we did not want to buy anything, and so would not require their services, their looks of disappointment were so deep that we compromised by giving them a cigar and five cents each, probably more than they would have earned from a native in a day, and soon saw them hurrying off delighted, smoking their cigars like connoisseurs. Then we hastened back to the ship. It was about the dinner hour, and it would be pitch-dark at 6.15 p.m.

At dinner the heat was intense, though every ventilator and port was open to its utmost. Even the succulent

1 The *Pasangrahan* corresponds closely to the *Dak*-bungalow of British India.

exotic fruits and iced lager could not make us feel cool;
and so it was with a gasp of relief that we all trooped on
deck when the Old Man signalled by rising that dinner
was over. The night breeze was just commencing; and
in the darkness we lounged back in our deck-chairs
drinking in its freshness, recklessly disregarding the croak-
ing warnings of fever and its consequences again uttered
at dinner by the Old Man, who of course had gone
ashore to a concert at the Harmonicon, and so would be
clear of it all.

All was quiet on the waters. We watched the anchor
lights of the other ships twinkling in the distance, and
the many lanterns of the sampans flitting across the harbour from point to point. From the fo'castle head came
the tinkle of a banjo, and then a voice singing in a sweet
tenor came floating down to us:

> "Sing and heave, and heave and sing,
>   Hoodah to my hoodah.
> Heave and make the hand-spikes ring,
>   Hoodah, hoodah-day.
> And it's blow, ye winds, heigh-ho,
>   For Cal-i-for-ni-o,
> For there's plenty of gold,
>   As I've been told,
> On the banks of the Sacramento."

It was the sailors having a sing-song, no watches being
kept in port except the gangway watch, which is stationed at the top of the ladder to question all strangers
coming on board before admitting them. No one saw,
however, that on this particular night the man supposed
to be on watch had been seduced from his post by the
music; and no one noticed, either, that a long sampan
with two lights, that had been hovering out in the
darkness had crept in nearer.

There was a faint creaking as it bumped against the

ladder, a subdued giggle, a hurrying of feet in the darkness, and then the calm was broken by some dozen brown
figures scrambling on to the saloon deck, where we were
lying in our chairs smoking in the cool night.

It was a complete surprise such as the Malay pirates
of thirty years before might have planned, only these
were women, coral-beaded, bangled on arms and legs,
saronged, redolent of *ylang-ylang*, coco-nut oil, and *boreh*
ointment.

The Mate jumped up from his deck-chair furiously.
He cursed with an appalling fluency the watch, the place,
the women. The rest of us lay perfectly still. It was the
Mate's business; and we waited to see how he would
handle it. All one could make out was the white teeth
and conjunctivæ of the dim figures, the smell of *ylang-
ylang* and coco-nut oil, the jingle of the bangles as the
women danced round the deck dodging the Mate's rushes,
and the shrill, monotonous sound of their voices singing:
"Ning ning no nae, Ning ning no nae."

With a shout the watch came tumbling back to his
duty; and the Mate and he soon hustled two of them
down the ladder again; but meanwhile the rest had scattered all over the decks, and were lost in the darkness,
where it was impossible to chase them.

"What will he do?" I said to the Chief, feeling like
a spectator at a play.

"Give it up as a bad job," said the Chief comfortably.
"As long as they don't get down to our cabins and
steal things it's all right. They'll soon tire and go away
with anything the Chinks want to smuggle ashore. That's
their main object in coming aboard."

But the Mate was cleverer than that. He went down
the gangway like lightning. The men in the sampan
saw him; but he had hold of the boat before they could
push off.

"I'll swamp you if you don't call them off, d——n

you," he shouted furiously, while we hung over the rail
watching.

It was evident they understood what he meant, even
if they knew no English; and an unintelligible shouting
soon brought heads in sight along the gunwale. A rapid
interchange of conversation followed, while the Mate
hung on grimly; and, seeing it was no use, soon the boat
was filled again, and the ladies, in no way discouraged
by their reception, with a sound of much chattering,
glided off into the night.

The watch was exceedingly apologetic; but with a curt
word or two the Mate ordered him to keep a better look-
out in future. Then he relapsed into his chair as if
nothing had happened.

"That's the last of them this voyage," he said. "I don't
think they'll try this ship again."

"It's an old dodge in the Malay Archipelago," said the
Chief. "Thirty years ago we'd have had our throats slit,
if we'd been surprised like this," he added cheerfully.
"Let's have a game of bridge, Doc."

It must have been almost ten o'clock before we finished
the second rubber, by the light of the Chief's oil-lamp,
the electric light not being on, as we were not working
cargo. The Mate yawned cavernously.

"Guess I'll turn in," he said.

"Me, too," I added; and so we stumbled out in the
darkness along the alley-way to our cabins on the starboard side.

The Mate was in front of me.

"What's that?" he said.

We listened; and a faint rustling came to us from the
far end of the alley-way, next my cabin. I put my hand
to the switch mechanically before remembering the lights
were off. Again the sound came, a faint rustling as of
a woman's garments. With a smothered oath the Mate
swung down the alley-way. It was pitch-dark. Then
his voice came back:

"Look out, Doc. She's dodged me."

I stooped, and, tackling low, in the old Rugby manner, in the darkness, caught a sinuous, panting, soft young body, that wriggled for a moment in my arms, and then was still. The heavy *ylang-ylang* scent was almost over-powering; her multitudinous bangles rattled as she moved slightly in the darkness. I could hear her rapid breathing close to me in the gloom.

The Mate struck a match; and the whites of her frightened eyes, her teeth, and the little white corded silk jacket she wore flashed distinct above the brown outlines of her body.

"She's been in your cabin, Doc," he said grimly. "Hadn't we better search her?"

"Let's look in the room first," I suggested. "Most of my things are locked up."

"That d——d watch ought to be put in irons for letting them on board again. By ——, I'll make it hot for him," he said fiercely.

We drew her along, unresisting, to my cabin. With relief I saw that nothing had been disturbed; so I did not feel compelled to search her. The Mate swore vehe-mently all the time, holding on to her; but I noticed he was very gentle all the same. The girl spoke never a word. We hurried her on deck and over to the gang-way. The watch was standing rigidly on duty. He stared stupidly at the apparation when we appeared. To the Mate's vituperation he answered with evident sin-cerity:

"I can take my Davy, sir, not a soul 'as come up this 'ere ladder since eight o'clock, barrin' the Second Officer."

To strengthen his statement we found that there was no sign of any sampan near the ladder. All the same, we sent the woman down to the bottom of the gangway, with orders to the watch not to permit her to re-ascend; and then started on a tour of the ship to find out how we had been boarded. It was simplicity itself. After

pulling off in the darkness they had rounded the stern;
and there on the port side, aft, someone, probably a
Chinaman, had slung over a convenient rope. By means
of this, and their prehensile toes, getting aboard was as
easy as falling off a log. Thus the Mate had been completely outgeneralled; and no doubt the Chinamen had
been able to smuggle ashore the opium they had been
bringing quite at their leisure. As we came down the
ladder to the main deck aft we saw two dim figures,
faintly silhouetted, climbing over the gunwale; and the
rope still vibrated when we got to it. There was a faint
sound of muffled oars in the night; and when we returned
to the gangway the little solitary figure too had gone,
picked up by the unseen sampan.

"Good riddance of bad rubbish," snorted the Mate.

I remembered, however, that she had beautiful brown
eyes. Afterwards I discovered she had managed to secrete
one of my folding silk Japanese fans somewhere in the
depths of her kabaya, and so came to the conclusion that
perhaps after all the Mate was right.

.   .   .   .

The Javanese merchant has not the picturesque stock-
in-trade of his Japanese counterpart. There is very little
in the way of native goods to be bought. They used to
come aboard with their wares in square baskets of coarse
matting, tied with a bandana handkerchief, sailor fashion.
When they offered anything for sale they squatted in the
dodok fashion, sitting on their heels, as inferiors do in
the presence of the rajah. Of native goods, beautiful
plaited mats, straw hats made of rattan filaments as fine
as a panama, cigars, native jewellery, brass betel-boxes
and swords were what one saw mostly. The Malay
sword, or kris, is a murderous-looking weapon with a
beautifully carved handle and a wriggly blade made of
alternate layers of hard and soft metal, the soft layers
eaten into lines by lime-juice and arsenic. This weapon

they wear behind, concealed in a fold of the sarong, ready for immediate use, night or day.

Quite good cheroots could be bought for tenpence a hundred; but they were very strong, and could only be smoked in the tropics. We bought a lot of Manila cigars on the morning after our night adventure; and then as Jimi came on board, smiling, and wanting to know if he were needed, the Chief and I decided to pay visits to the other ships of our company. On one of these I found a doctor who had been a fellow student of mine, and had disappeared from everyone's ken for five years.

"Yes, I've been at it ever since," he said. "Can't help it now. I'm used to it. I'm miserable and chilly in England. I know everybody worth knowing in Java. I'm a member of all the clubs in every port. All my friends are here. I'd be no use in a shore billet now." He was silent for a moment and then continued: "You chuck it, old man, after this voyage, or you're done for. The fascination of it will get hold of you. Chuck it, if you want to do any good. I can't now. Have another drink?"

He asked me eagerly about old pals: What was So-and-so doing?—Where was So-and-so?—Was So-and-so married yet?

I could not get away from him once he was started. We talked about the old times, the never-to-be-forgotten times, when we were undergrads together.

"Yes, yes. These fellows are a very decent crowd. I've sailed with the same captain for two years now; but sailors, you know, are not like your old pals—very decent fellows, but not——"

I think seeing me somehow made him feel the years that the locusts had eaten.

"Fever! Oh, yes! I know all about the fever. Had it myself. Wrote a thesis on it once, but never presented it. Thought it wasn't good enough. Mind you, there's

a lot to be done on Java fever. Have another drink?
What, no? Oh, yes, you will, just for company. Steward!
Steward!"

The almond-eyed Chinese steward came silently to the
cabin door.

"Two more iced lagers."

The steward nodded silently. "I savvy," he said.

Next day I began to think I must have a special knack
of discovering derelicts; but later on I found that other
people had had the same impression too; and so came to
the conclusion that perhaps it is only when one happens
to get to the out-places of the world that one comes
across them.

We were shipping molasses in great tubs, much to the
disgust of the Mate.

"Can't think what the company's up to," he said. "Half
the muck will leak out; and it'll have to be pumped from
the holds in Liverpool—beastly, sticky, filthy stuff. We
never shipped it before; and I hope to goodness we never
shall again."

It certainly was filthy. It leaked from the tubs when
it was being raised from the lighters, and trickled down
the ship's side. I had to screw up my port-holes hermetically to keep it out of my cabin. The decks too were
sticky with it.

An exceedingly active shipping master was in charge
of the coolies who were putting it aboard. His beautiful
white ducks were filthy with brown stains.

"That's the most active fellow for a Dutchman I've ever
seen," said the Chief casually to me.

He overheard the remark, and turned on the surprised
Chief.

"Dutchman! I'm no Dutchman," he said truculently.
"I'm an Irishman, and I don't care a d——n who knows
it."

"So am I," said the Chief placidly. "Shake." They
shook.

"So am I," I echoed, and we shook again.

He turned out to be an exceedingly charming fellow. To ourselves then, and afterwards, the Chief and I always called him the "Treacle Man," for we never knew his real name.

He had been everywhere—Australia, South America, South Africa, with De Beers as an engineer, in India, Singapore, in Batavia, and here. He could speak Dutch like a Dutchman, and had a fluent flow of vituperative Malay. He was obviously a gentleman.

The Chief lent him a clean suit to go ashore in; and in return, when he discovered we were pestered by mosquitoes at night, he next day appeared with a dozen of what he called "Japanese stinkers," burning one of which in one's cabin completely cleared it of mosquitoes. Though they did not bite me, the sizzling noise of them was most annoying when I wanted to sleep; and so it was quite as much a relief to me as to the others to find the stinkers worked like a charm.*

We tried them that night, and were so pleased with the result that we asked him specially to breakfast next morning.

It was in a moment of expansion then that he said, "Fancy taking me for a Dutchman! I was born in a little place in Ireland I don't suppose any of you ever heard of."

"Where?" said the Chief.

He mentioned the place; and, with a start, before I had taken time to consider, I said, "But I was born there too."

Then he shut up like a clam. There were no more confidences. I fancied even that he tried to avoid me afterwards, fearing I might question him. Still, he was very pleasant. I got the Chief to ask him his name. He gave one that had never been heard of in the place; so I said, "Don't bother him about it." After all, it was his

*Pyrethrum powder is the basis of these "stinkers."

affair. We heard things about him, and all of them to his credit. There was a story about a Dutch girl (perhaps I should have mentioned that he was very good-looking)— it was almost an idyll. I should like to tell that story some day with all the local colouring. At the time it made me feel choky. As I have said, we called him the "Treacle Man" to ourselves for months afterwards, wondered who he was, what he was doing, how he was getting on. He had the knack of impressing himself on one's memory.

. . . .

That night I saw a kind of fishing that was new to me. It was the Mate who first drew my attention to it as were were sitting in the dark on deck at night. There were a number of sampans moving about in the calm water of the bay, each with a very bright light hung over the bow almost touching the water. One came close to the ship; and then we saw that in the bow a man was standing with a poised trident in his hand, whilst another aft, held a square landing-net on the end of a long pole half buried in the water. The boat was allowed to glide almost at its own will; and the bright light shone clearly on the water, sharply outlining the long sampan and the tense figures of the expectant fishermen. It was the light that drew the fish; and when one appeared it was skilfully speared by the man in the bow. The net was then brought under it by his companion in the stern, and another struggling glistening fish added to the increasing heap already in the bottom of the sampan. It was a parable on the danger of curiosity.

. . . . . .

The Mate had been right when he said they wouldn't know what to do with us when they got us to Java; and so a crop of rumours used to arrive daily with the Old Man as to our next destination: Tjilitjap on the south coast through the Straits of Bali, Batavia for orders, Semarang, Cheribon, Deli in Sumatra, all had their moments.

At length we gave up bothering about our destination. "The agents don't know themselves, so it's no use our worrying," said the Chief. "I want to go to Macassar; but it's hardly likely we'll be sent back there, as we passed it on the way down."

As our stay was so uncertain, we determined to make the most of the time we had; and so we went ashore nearly every night. One evening a little Dutchman asked the Chief and myself up to his place. He had a pale little wife, who dressed in the house, as most of the Dutchwomen do, native fashion, in a white jacket, sarong, and sandals. In the verandah he had rigged up a gramophone; and there we sat in the torrid air listening to the music it brayed forth. In the dusty road outside a crowd of Javanese had gathered to listen. We could only see the whites of their eyes as they stood immobile in the sweltering night. One of the tunes, I remember, was "My Irish Molly O"; and I have often wondered what they made of it all.

Afterwards we drove up to the centre of the city, and sat in one of the open-air cafés in front of the hotels, amongst the close-cropped Dutchmen. Everyone was out promenading the brilliantly lighted square where the Simpang Club, the Hellendoran, and Grimm's Hotel stood.

Social life in Java begins after sunset. During the day the heat is so enervating that even activity of mind, not to mention body, is somewhat of a strain. But with sunset comes a welcome coolness; the ladies put aside the native costumes they have been wearing during the day, and array themselves in the latest Parisian modes; the men don official uniform; and At Homes, musicales, dances, or dining-out fill up the evening.

At the little marble tables outside Grimm's Hotel we found ourselves seated, like many others, watching the white-robed crowd promenading up and down under the brilliant glare of the electric light. It was a courtly kaleidoscopic crowd; the subdued music of the band, the uniforms of the numerous officers, the toilettes of some of the ladies, making for an air of European gaiety that continually clashed with the presence of the purely exotic all-pervasive, silent-footed Javanese waiters, moving around continuously, supplying the material wants of the spectators, and the dark faces of the turbaned coachmen and grooms, who stood beside the splendid waiting carriages in the background.

After an interval the Chief and I suddenly tired of it all, feeling that the pathetic earnestness of the attempt to represent home amongst these exiles was not in keeping with our mood.

Quietly at random we wandered into the darkness of a side street; and there quite accidentally we came across a Javanese theatre. Then the feeling of loneliness left us. We were no longer exiles playing at make-believe. We were curious sightseers looking upon a profoundly interesting product of the country we were travelling in; and the effect on our spirits was immediate.

Witnessing the performance of the *Wayang* marked, in addition, a change in my attitude of mind towards the people whose national character had evolved it: for one is apt to look upon the native, in spite of his intelligence and his exquisite courtesy of manner, as of a race on a vastly lower intellectual scale than one's own, so much do the external material things of civilisation—clothes, buildings, the impedimenta of scientific accessories—colour one's ideas of comparative anthropological position. The *Wayang* made this comfortable philosophy impossible; for it forced me to see that we were not dealing with a race emerging from illiteracy, but rather with one with the records of a great and ancient, almost forgotten civilisation behind it, a civilisation which had suffered an eclipse, but nevertheless had left its impress upon the people, and caused them to retain an enormously unsus-

pected proportion of the instincts developed under its
never-forgotten traditions.

There are two main varieties of national play extant in
Java, the *Wayang-wayang (Wayang-poera)* and the *Topeng*.

The *Topeng* is played by actors disguised in hideous
emblematic masks; but it is the *Wayang-poera* which is
most characteristic of, and most beloved by, this intensely
susceptible and highly artistic race. To the English mind
it may be described as an elaborate—most elaborate—
combination of a Punch and Judy show and a shadow-
graph, for all the actors on the stage are puppets. In
front of the miniature stage is the *Gamelan* or native
orchestra. This *Gamelan* is characteristic of the Malay
people. It consists of about a dozen performers. The
most striking instruments are a number of bells, shaped
like round pudding-dishes with covers. In addition there
are usually one or two tom-toms, a Persian viol (rebab),
a zithera, and one or two reed-like flutes. The music is
curiously melancholy and disturbing. There is a feeling
that it is the elemental music of the world, a music
known and loved in forgotten æons before the present
incarnation came to blur one's memory of its subtleties.
Following the overture come the women dancers. They
glide in, clothed in the shimmering traditional costumes
of ancient Java before the Mohammedan conquest, tiara-
crowned, multi-jewelled, their gorgeous trailing robes
caught at the waist with a silver buckle, their shoulders
bare and scented with boreh, their soft round arms and
slender fingers a mass of bracelets and jewelled rings.
The dance is a series of slow graceful posturings and
swaying movements of the arms and body, like the bend-
ings of the young bamboo before the wind, or the rice-
fields swaying beneath the sunny autumn zephyrs. All
the while they dance, a singing monotone, kept up
around, explains the meaning of their movements. This
is the prologue to the play.

The stage is a simple screen of white batik cloth, with a soft banana stem in front into which the sharp ends of the puppets are fixed. The puppets themselves are elaborately cut and gilded figures, all presented in profile, each characteristic of some person or thing, and all recognised and capable of being named by the audience. A light is so arranged that the shadow of the figures is cast upon the screen; and by immemorial custom the men sit in front and look at the puppets, whilst the women sitting behind see only the shadows. In the centre of the screen is a dome-shaped conventional representation of a hill. This is the *Gunungen;* and it represents the idea of locality, a hill, a palace, a river, anything mentioned in the play, the Javanese mind accepting it as an abstract reminder of the idea of place without difficulty. In addition to the figures there are miniature swords, spears, chariots, horses, and all the other paraphernalia of life, each carefully and elaborately accurate.

The puppets are manipulated entirely by the *Dalang,* or manager, who must be a protean artist. He has to recite all the dialogue, some of it in *Kawi* (ancient Javanese); he must know all the intricacies of court etiquette, and forms of etiquette are more elaborate and more stereotyped amongst the Javanese than even in Japan; he conducts the *Gamelan,* and regulates the dancing. As these plays sometimes last a fortnight his memory must be prodigious. In addition he must be able to improvise poetry to suit any situation, and occasionally enliven the play by witty topical remarks. It is obvious then that to become a good *Dalang* requires years of careful training, and but few can hope to aspire to the position. As a consequence, therefore, the *Dalang* is held in almost regal honour; native rajahs vie with one another for his presence; his triumphal progress through the country is like that of a sultan; and the common people almost worship him. He pays no taxes, has all his wants provided for without the asking, and holds a position the greatest man of letters in this country might envy.

To understand the plays requires a minute knowledge of Hindu mythology. What we saw that night was an episode in the great drama portraying the fight between the Titans and the Gods, a story which occurs in each of the classic religions, Hindu, Greek, Semitic, and one which appears to be a great favourite with the Javanese.

The episodes were interminable. The play had been going on for some days, and would be continued all the rest of the week. The people sat enthralled as the *Dalang* intoned the high-sounding eloquence of the heroes in love, in war, in triumph, and in defeat.

"I'd rather have the *Topeng*," said the Chief with a yawn. "It's much funnier to an outsider."

Driving back in the purple night under the multitudinous stars, we fell into a silence of mutual content, in keeping with the stillness of the world around. The air was slumbrous with the scent of unseen exotic flowers. Not a leaf stirred. Occasionally we passed silent groups of natives around a brazier, a face, an arm, a turban showing fiery-red in the half-revealing glare of the glowing charcoal.

Once a hoarse challenge echoed to us in the night; and turning to look, we saw the dim shadow of a hut, with two sentinel figures, standing erect, holding what looked like gigantic catapults against their right shoulders. The driver answered in an unintelligible melodious cry; and we passed on unchecked. They were the night watchmen calling to know the fare and destination of the driver; and the catapults were long forked poles with which they could chase evildoers, or possible Amoks, and pin them against a tree or wall.

Smoothly the big comfortable carriage rolled on behind the two little sandal-wood ponies that drew it; and gradually we became more and more somnolent. It was therefore with quite a start that we found ourselves abruptly stopping at the landing stage.

The water was a mass of phosphorescence; the riding lights of the ships looked like low-lying comfortable stars. To our call in the night there came an answering cry: "Heah! Tuan. Commin!" and we could hear first the sound of wood upon wood, and then the splash of sampan oars as Jimi glided like a shadow to the steps.

Presently with swift, sweeping strokes we were heading for the ship, and sleep.

．　　　．　　　．　　　．

On Friday morning we were ordered to be ready to sail for Semarang at five o'clock. This was altered to six o'clock on Saturday for Batavia, and finally to four o'clock on Sunday for Macassar.

"Macassar," said the Chief. "Hooray!"

Everyone was delighted. Up went the Blue Peter on Saturday afternoon; and the rest of the evening was spent in a mad rush round the city buying things, finishing up by having supper in an Indian restaurant, where we ate all sorts of curious "chow," and found at the end that everything we had left of each course had been carefully kept, wrapped in paper and gathered together to be presented to us when we were departing. Jimi got the parcel, to his huge delight; and so we had not to offend the susceptibilities of our host by rejecting it.

The length of our stay in port had by this time made us all very hard up; most of us had overdrawn our pay; and no one had the courage to corner the Old Man for another advance. Getting to a new port, however, would be a colourable excuse for approaching him again; and so it was with huge delight that on the Sunday we pulled down the Blue Peter at noon, and steamed slowly out of the roadstead.

The "Treacle Man" shouted farewell from his launch; a party of eighteen people whom the Old Man had had to breakfast raised a cheer from their tender; Jimi, resplendent in a cast-off white suit of mine, grinned from ear to ear from his sampan; and we were off.

It was grand to be rid of mosquitoes, to be clear of the sweltering heat, to feel the cool sea-breeze sweeping over the decks again.

The Third Officer, pyjama-clad, grinned cheerfully at me from the edge of his bunk, from which he had swept his mosquito-net.

"I'm sorry for the poor people ashore," he said.

"After all, there's nothing like being at sea," I answered.

CHAPTER IX

MACASSAR IN CELEBES

WE were bound for Macassar. Dim recollections of short legs dangling from a chair in a many-a-year-forgotten drawing-room, and of a fearful thing of crochet-work that would keep slipping down, stirred at the sound of it.

Going there, ridden by this obsession, I found it difficult to associate the name with anything like a definite geographical place; now, looking back, my mind crowds with rainbow recollections that are too evanescent for mere words, leaving, as it were, a lingering savour of sweet things on memory's palate, too subtly ethereal for concrete expression.

Macassar is the main seaport of Celebes. There is deep water right up to the wharf; but it is surrounded on all sides by numbers of little islands, atolls, and coral reefs, so that there is only one good channel running north and south.

To reach port we had to retrace our steps a little, as we had passed it on the way down from Japan—too far out, however, for any sight of land. Returning then, we greeted Hastings Island as an old friend when it once more rose above the horizon; but it was not till "six bells" (7 a.m.) on the Monday morning that they called me, saying port was in sight.

Sailors and Swiss peasants do not rhapsodise on scenery; but deep down somewhere the sailor, at any rate, has an inarticulate understanding; and everyone on the ship, I noticed, had been glad when we got the orders for Macassar.

Looking at the panorama as it unfolded itself to me

230

that beautiful clear morning, I think I understood why they liked it so much; for the approach to Macassar is one of the faery visions of the world, and years after the inward eye can ruminate on it and return anew.

Imagine to port an opal sea, pellucid, mirror-like, studded with a thousand little atolls, each with its silvery beach and fringe of dark green palm trees, smiling under a sky of purest ultramarine shading gradually to a pearly-grey as it touched the horizon. Landward the silver shore ran sinuous in little sparkling bays and inlets, fringed, far as the eye could see, with feathery groves of slender coco-nuts, backed by serrated blue mountains shimmering in the hinterland.

Gradually as we approached native huts could be made out, nestling amongst the njamplong trees, each house a framework of bamboo standing on props, with walls of latticed yellow rattan, and dark brown palm-thatched roofs. Dilapidated boat slips, a patchwork of blistered stakes and warped tinder-like planks, ran up to some of the stilted huts projecting into the water; and sampans and dug-outs, some with, some without outriggers, lay bleaching on the strand, just beyond the lazy ripples.

On the intervening water other fishing praus were shooting about, with their peculiar-looking lozenge-shaped Bugis sails swelling in the light morning zephyrs. A lotus-air of immemorial calm lay over everything.

Then came signs of civilisation—a long white red-tiled building close to the shore with a square green behind; next a dazzling black-and-white lighthouse flying the Dutch tricolour; nestling beneath it, glistening in the morning sun, lay a little white jetty for yachts; and then came the long straight reach of over half a mile of black tarred wharf, almost devoid of shipping, with a row of yellow bamboo rattan-latticed godowns behind, and again behind these the huddled red-tiled roofs of the city itself.

Several river gunboats lay anchored off the pier; and

from the red-roofed building we had first noticed a burst
of military music floated to us on the morning air. It
was a regimental band playing outside the officers' mess
at breakfast.

.   .   .   .

It was quite a pleasant change to be moored alongside
the wharf—this port, Singapore, Tanjong Priok, and
Tjilitjap being the only ones in the Far East our large
ships could get alongside. Everywhere else one always
required a sampan in and out, and consequently felt it
was hardly worth while going ashore unless one had the
whole day free. Here, on the contrary, one could go off
for half an hour before breakfast, come back, run ashore
again for ten minutes to get something before lunch, or
go off for the entire day, with equal facility.

We were moored before breakfast; and so shortly after,
before it grew hot, I strolled ashore to get the lie of the
city.

It consisted for the most part of three long narrow
streets, parallel to one another and also to the shore.
That next the sea was the main business street; but,
instead of the first row of houses facing the sea, they had
their backs to it, some of them even projecting out on
props into the water, whilst their fronts faced on to the
street.

The shops were of the usual bazaar type found all over
the East—shops for buttons and cheap jewellery, sarong
stores, shops selling basket-work, mats, odds and ends of
ironware, fruits, carved sticks and kris heads, etc., etc.
At the far end the street dwindled into the open country;
at the near end there were a number of European stores
owned by Dutchmen and *Paranaks*. At this end also the
main street opened on to a gravel-strewn square (Prins
Henrik Plein), surrounded by a line of beautiful waringen trees. This square, with the shady road leading
from its inner side, formed the Rotten Row of Macassar.
The Club—the Societat Harmonie—was in it; and

opposite the Club was the bandstand. The Governor's palace, the military cantonment, the residences of the big Government officials were close by. The two principal hotels were also near. Obviously the square was the centre of life.

After tiffin the British Consul called on us, and arranged to have the Old Man, the Chief, and myself made temporary members of the Club.

"That's all right," said the Chief. "They keep the best iced lager in the East, and one gets it at half the hotel prices—that means something in a country where iced drinks are a necessity, not a luxury."

In the afternoon we hired a carriage; and the Old Man, the Chief and I drove out into the country. It was a typical Malay scene. The ricefields were brown and fallow, with here and there the bare expanse relieved by a tope of lofty palms sheltering a few brown native huts, and ever in the background the mountains of a marvellous blue. Every now and again we would come across a group of fearsome huge horned buffaloes rolling in the shallow mud pools, or being driven along the paddy tracks by diminutive naked boys, who rode on their backs and belaboured their tough hides with rattans, accompanying each stroke with shrill vituperations, both of which the animals received with the ruminating stare of perfect indifference.

"It looks very quiet and peaceful, doesn't it?" said the Old Man. "But out there in the mountains there's fighting going on. The Dutch have got a little war on. They've killed the old rajah."

"Not the old fellow I saw on my last voyage!" said the Chief. "I thought he was a perfectly harmless old stick."

"Yes, he wasn't a bad old fellow," replied the Old Man. "I've known him off and on for years. He took a great fancy to a map of the world I brought the Consul. It had all the British possessions coloured red; and he was heart-broken when the Consul refused to let him have it. I think he went as far as to offer him one of his wives for it. He could afford to, as he had forty of them."

"But how did he get killed?" I said.

"Sheer foolishness. He was quite content to go on as he was; but some of the young bloods of sons weren't. They raised trouble—knifed a sergeant or something—had to fly, and started a rebellion in the interior. It was a failure because they had not the authority of the rajah; so they had to induce the poor old fellow to give them his physical as well as moral support by flying from Macassar. They got him to do it eventually by working on his fears as to his own personal safety now his subjects were in rebellion. So the rajah fled with his harem. It was the harem spoiled it. They were pursued and captured, of course. The rajah managed to escape in the confusion; but was shot accidentally in a nullah in the pursuit. Nobody wanted to hurt him. It was quite an accident. They wanted to bring him back; but he's as dead as salt pork now. His eldest son has proclaimed himself rajah; and now he is kicking up the devil in the interior, burning villages and torturing people in the good old Malay fashion."

"So that was why the Consul warned us not to go out too far?" I said.

"Yes. They're sniping quite close to the town," he answered.

"I feel sort of sorry he's dead," said the Chief.

"Oh, I dunno," said the Old Man. "He was a pretty tough old ruffian when he liked. I remember when I paid him a state visit some years ago he had a Hindu interpreter, whom I tipped a couple of guilders when I left. Going back to find my gloves, which I had left behind, what did I see but the rajah on the top of the unfortunate man, guzzling him on the floor till he compelled him to fork out the two guilders."

On the way back, just before we got into the square, we passed the Governor's palace, a fine building with

a courtyard in front, in which were a couple of very ornamental cannon, once the property of the Sultan of Goa.
Around were the houses of some of the more important
Government officials, the two principal hotels, and the
church.

When a Dutchman leaves his beloved Warmoestraat
to go East, he does so with the lofty ambition of having
a good time and making himself as comfortable as the
climate will permit. He does not yearn to elevate the
native to the bomb-throwing standard of British India.
He is quite content to leave him alone; and the native
is perfectly happy to be left to enjoy his betel-chewing
lethargy according to the immemorial customs of his
fathers. For his Dutch rulers he has the profound contempt which every true son of the Prophet bestows on
the infidel; his intelligence is not disturbed by the leaven
of discontent stirred up by the average missionary; and
so the Dutchman waxes fat and comfortable, and the
Malay multiplies exceedingly in a land so fruitful that
one day's work supplies food for a month. What more
could one possibly want?*

The Dutchman has his beer sent out, packed carefully
in ice, from Amsterdam, so that it never has a chance to
get warm. His tobacco he grows himself or imports from
Manila. His house is large and spacious, marble-floored,
marble-walled, with a great white portico built like a
Grecian temple, embowered in luxuriant palms, Madagascar flame trees, and gorgeously coloured vines. The
cool evening breeze sweeps through the whole house,
screened off into chambers only by hanging bead-net or
rattan curtains. With the lamps lit at night in the
portico, which serves as drawing-room, dining-room,
smoke-room, and lounge, each villa looks like a sparkling
jewel set in a frame of jet as one passes in the darkness.
When the lights are lit anyone is at liberty to call; but

*The Japanese invasion and the anarchy following on their
defeat has changed all this.

when they are out Mynheer is "not at home," and lies
in his cane lounge in the cool darkness, smoking contentedly in *deshabille,* knowing he is free from visitors.

Hospitality does not consist in dinners, but in musicales; and there are fine native bands in every station. In
every town there is a magnificent Club, subsidised by the
Government; and weekly concerts are given all the year
round.

In material things, and in the running of colonies,
we might learn a lot from the Dutch. Java has been a
gold-mine to them. When we had it we threw it away
like a rotten orange, and incidentally broke the heart of
the greatest man England has ever given to the Far East—
Sir Stamford Raffles, the founder of Singapore.

The Dutch colonial house is built essentially to suit
the requirements of a hot climate. It is a triumph of
architecture because it is not only eminently suitable for
the purpose it is designed to meet, but also at the same
time manages to be beautiful to the eye.

Nothing, I think, struck me so much in the Far East
as the extreme beauty of the Dutch colonial home,
coming as it did as a complete surprise to find it amongst
these eminently practical people.

Its appearance irresistibly reminds one of the classic
architecture of ancient Greece, of Rome in the golden
era of the first Emperors.

In the front of the house is a marble-floored loggia,
approached by one or two broad flights of steps, and
supported by tall white Doric columns. In the centre
of the loggia is a doorway, always open, which leads
into an inner marble hall, leading out of which are
numerous bedrooms. The further end of the hall opens
into yet another loggia at the back of the house, larger
and more imposing than that at the front. It is in this
that most of the meals are taken, and the long hot hours
spent.

The Great Temple at Boro-Boedor

Facing Page 236

The Native Village, Tanjong Priok

All around the house is a wide sweeping verandah, keeping off the hot rays of the sun during the day, and sheltering one also during the seasons of torrential rain. There are very few punkahs in Java or Celebes.

Behind the house is a garden compound, surrounded on three sides by the servants' quarters, the bathrooms, kitchen, stables, etc. Connected with the main building by a covered portico is the all-important, in Colonial eyes, pavilion known as the guest quarters; for hospitality is, in these countries where white men are so few, an exceedingly pleasurable virtue.

All one's meals are taken in the open air, an experience which the new-comer finds rather embarrassing at first, owing to the feeling that invisible eyes may be watching him all the time, but one which he soon gets accustomed to when he acquires the feeling that natives are no more to be regarded than the furniture around, or the footmen or maids who wait upon him at home. The marble floors are not for display, but comfort. They are not carpeted—again for coolness' sake—but occasional mats or rugs are sometimes spread upon their snowy whiteness. The chairs too are always cane-bottomed; and no one can realise how much these apparently trivial details make for ease until he has sat on an upholstered sofa or in a room with carpets in such a climate, and felt the insufferable stuffiness of the difference.

The bathroom is probably the second most important room in the house. It, too, is marble-floored, with plain whitewashed walls. It is windowless, save for a little grating over the door; and, standing on the cool white floor, one sluices the icy water over one's weary, heated body, till a feeling that all the cares of the world have been washed away and a calm content comes over one. The bath is almost a fetish in the Far East.

At the Hotel Der Nederlanden the Old Man cried a halt; and we were exceedingly glad to get out of the afternoon glare into the cool shade of the café lounge.

A courteous old Dutch gentlemen, smoking lazily, talked with us while the ice tinkled in the long glasses. There was not a sound in the stillness of the afternoon, the leaves of the trees hung motionless. Suddenly and unexpectedly, shattering the stillness, there came a sound as of two men sawing wood with feverish haste. We all looked up.

"It iss zee cicadas," said the Dutchman placidly.

"He ought to be locked up," said the Chief solemnly.

"It iss not possible. He iss a beedle," the Dutchman explained with unmoved countenance.

That evening we forgathered at the Club. The presence of three river gunboats lent an air of special gaiety to the night; for the officers, free for a few days from the river campaign, were celebrating in the Club. One particularly amusing person's only grievance was that he had not been able to have a decent bath for six months, while he was ashore with his contingent in the jungly swamp man-hunting. The toil, the danger, the heat, the risk of river fever, the chance of sudden and violent death, were all in the day's work; but not being able to have a bath—that was a grievance for which he claimed our sympathy. He was quite bald-headed; but behaved like an irresponsible boy. He had had only two days' leave; and that was up the next morning at six o'clock. He and his men, with their little flat-bottomed boat and its two spitting Maxims, mounted fore and aft, were to be off before we were awake in the morning; but, all the same, he invited me to breakfast with him, or invited himself to breakfast with me—he was not quite sure which, and I did not bother him to explain.

Anyhow, it appeared we were bosom friends. We were playing billiards, as everyone does in the East; and the tables were of the rockiness invariably found also in the East. When he missed he laughed loudly; when anyone else missed he laughed, if possible, more loudly still. I dragged myself away from him at 1 a.m., promising all sorts of things at his earnest entreaty.

In the morning his boat was gone. I could not remember his impossible Dutch name. I'm sure he didn't know mine. It is vastly unlikely we shall ever meet again; but I can see his shining cranium under the lamp-light still. I wish I could reproduce the vagaries of his English—it was an extraordinary mass of unexpected-nesses. Sometimes I wonder has he been promoted for some piece of cool dare-devilry; or, steaming slowly up some river, did he find his quietus from a sudden squib-fire from the jungle, as he lay at ease, a large white target on the deck of his little boat. Both are equally likely.

After breakfast the next morning the Chief and I went shopping in the long main street. One old Malay was making kris handles, carving with his hands, and holding the wood with his toes.

Most of the industrial work, however, seemed to be done by the Chinese. In a joss-house the boy attendant wanted to sell me a baby turtle (*Caretta imbricata*) that was swimming in a tank; but unfortunately it was too large for the accommodation we had on the ship.

Everywhere one saw the stalls of the itinerant cooks and betel merchants. We were particularly struck by the way the natives grilled their beef. Each little piece, the size and shape of a large button, was run on a sliver of bamboo till there were some three or four dozen buttons on about half a dozen sticks. Holding these in a fan-like manner in one hand over a charcoal brazier, the cook grilled them by winnowing the embers with a plantain-leaf fan, turning the segments round and round as they frizzled. Anything we bought from one of these itinerant merchants was wrapped up, not in paper, but in a plantain leaf, and fastened, not with string, but with a cactus thorn.

We wandered into a fan-tan saloon, where a number

of Chinamen were indulging the national taste for
gambling; and later on found our way into an opium
den where a few somnolent figures were dreaming their
lives contentedly away.

The Chief wanted a wicker chair, such as Hong Kong
is famous for; and we went into a Chinaman's shop,
where we picked one and gave him directions where to
send it. Apparently we did not succeed in quite making
him understand, for the chair never arrived at the ship.
However, as it had not been paid for, the Chief was
much too lazy to go after the man and explain anew;
and he never had it.

Macassar is famous for beautifully plaited mats; and we
spent probably an hour bargaining for some. The shops
of the mat-sellers were all together at the far end of the
town; and we wandered from one to another when we
found they were asking too much for them. No one,
however, would sell lower than his neighbours; and
everyone knew what we were offering, as little boys ran
before us from shop to shop carrying the news. At length
we gave it up in disgust; and told one man, who had
some particularly fine ones, that if he wished to sell he
must bring them to the ship. Eventually that was what
he did; and there we got them for one half of what he
had been asking at his shop. Such is trade.

It was on our way back, close to the ship, that we
found the Japanese store; and thereafter the Chief was
lost.

The little lady who ran it had a fascinating smile,
coquettish ankles, and sold iced lager at the same price
as the Club.

There was a man in the background who wore a
billycock hat with a kimono—a husband, or brother, or
something. But the Chief didn't worry about that;
neither did the little lady; neither, apparently did the
man in the billycock hat. As long as the Chief drank
beer, occasionally bought things, and supplied her with

cigarettes, she would sit, cross-legged, smiling and dimpling, correcting his faulty Japanese, and dimpling again. When we wanted him we soon learnt where we could find him. He said it was the lager drew him.

I told Horner, in a mischievous moment, she reminded me of Ponta; and he was over like a shot. He declared, however, that she was not in the least like her; but he went again, and, as he could talk much better Japanese than the Chief, soon threatened to cut him out. Then the Chief bought more things, and Yuki's smiles came back to him again.

The Third Officer had been ashore only once during the voyage—that was in Penang. All the time we had been in Japan and Java he had stuck closely to the ship. The reason was that he was going to be married at the end of the voyage; and as nothing clears a sailor's pockets so quickly as going ashore, he wisely decided the ship was the safest place for him. Here, however, where we were alongside the wharf, it was more difficult to keep on board; and we had ragged the Chief so much on his supposed infatuation for Yuki that the Third Officer's curiosity was aroused. Accordingly we took him over, introduced him, and watched her beginning to spread her net to make him buy. There was nothing in the shop worth more than a few shillings; but it was full of quaint dolls and lanterns, paper toys and useless little knick-knacks. We told him some of them would come in handy for decorating his walls when he set up house, and that here he could get them at one quarter the price he would pay in Liverpool. He hesitated, somewhat doubtful of our blandishments; then Yuki smiled on him, and he was lost. Next the Mate was drawn in; and soon the little divan behind the shop became a sort of ship's club. Before we left even the Old Man had been added as a customer, departing one day laden with toys for his children.

She was a clever little woman, and made us quite

forget the man in the billycock hat and kimono.
Probably he knew her cleverness a great deal better than
we did.

· · · ·

One day the Chief and I took it into our heads to go
shooting. We didn't much mind what we shot; only the
Chief drew the line at monkeys.

"I shot a monkey by mistake once at Tjilitjap," he said.
"It was only wounded; and it cried like a baby wailing
in the dark. I could not get at it to put it out of its
agony; and so it wailed on. It made me feel like a
murderer—couldn't sleep for a week. No more monkeys
for me, thank you."

We hired a dilapidated carriage; and armed with shot-
guns drove off, calling on our way at the comprador's
with a message from the ship. I wanted to inspect the
inside of a typical Malay hut; and so the comprador—a
greasy Bengali—took us out into his plantation, in the rear
of which he kept his native wife and family. The coco-
nut trees had notches cut in them for convenience in
climbing; and a boy was sent up to pick some fresh ones
for milk. Pineapples, pomelos, plantains, and durians
were growing in the plantation. The native hut was at
the far end; and, like all Javanese houses, the ground
floor, of split bamboo, stood on props about five feet
above the soil. It was approached by a short, roughly
constructed ladder that led to a narrow verandah which
was the sitting-room and guest-receiving room of the
house. Inside was a large apartment almost devoid of
furniture, cool and shady, light filtering into it through
the walls of interlaced cane. This was the sleeping-room
for the whole family; and there was a sort of kitchen
tacked on behind. The whole building had a high
peaked roof, thatched with atap.

The Malay woman scuttled into the kitchen on our
approach; but two little brown imps, a boy and a girl,
playing on the verandah, were anything but shy, and

kept close to us, smiling and laughing, and evidently quite accustomed to receiving copper coins from visitors, judging from the practised way in which they grabbed ours.

Leaving the comprador's, we rattled along the beautifully shaded roads, stopping whenever we saw anything strange or curious, till at length we came to a place where the road crossed a lake by means of a chain-ferry. On the Macassar side the Dutch, always mindful of their comfort, had built a *Pasangrahan*, or Government rest-house, which was an excellent little café-restaurant such as one might expect to find on the outskirts of Paris. We noticed, however, that though it looked so beautifully suburban, it was loopholed for rifle fire, and placed in such a position as to command the approach to the ferry completely.

It was kept by a half-caste, was beautifully clean, and supplied delicious iced lager. The view over the lake to the approaching ferry was temptingly cool; and some natives in sampans out fishing looked particularly comfortable under their big sugar-loaf hats.

"For two pins I'd swim across," said the Chief, mopping the perspiration from a very red face.

The proprietor of the *Pasangrahan* knew only a little English; but the Chief's sweeping movement interpreted itself. At any rate, the proprietor smiled grimly; and, pointing to what looked like a number of half-submerged logs on the near side of the ferry, made a peculiar snapping sound with his teeth.

"Crocodiles?" I said; and he nodded intelligently.

"Stuff," said the Chief; but all the same his ardour had evaporated.

The big wide ferry-boat had reached our side by now, disembarking a bullock-wagon-load of fruit and some half-dozen natives.

We decided not to take our carriage over, but to tramp on foot in search of anything we could find. A few

natives hung back till we entered, and then followed us
gingerly. The windlass began to work; and we were
soon at the other side.

Close to the landing stage there was a *worong*, or native
restaurant, a rough open shed where some coolies were
having their afternoon meal. When we stopped to look
at them they ceased eating, and glanced at one another
uneasily. One man stealthily fingered his kris. Moving
along slowly, we looked on all sides for something alive
to shoot at. Every time we moved there were sounds
of soft padding footsteps behind us. Every time we
stopped the sounds ceased. Looking back, then, we
noticed a man following us with a gun. He had been
on the ferry with us, but had studiously kept in the
background. Squinting behind, I soon satisfied myself
that he moved when we moved, and stopped when we
stopped, keeping always about a hundred yards behind
us. Then it dawned on me that we were in the disturbed
district, and our guns were probably a source of anxiety.

"The poor beggar is afraid to pass us," I said.

"Let's motion him on," said the Chief.

We did so; and he passed us slowly, rolling the whites
of his eyes.

Neither of us noticed that in a few minutes he was
lost to sight completely, though the road led straight on
for miles through the swamp. We trudged along.

It was the time of the *siesta*; not a sound was to be
heard; not a single living thing showed. The swamps
stretched endlessly on either side; the mountains rose
blue in the far, far distance ahead.

It was very hot, and we began to repent that we had
not had the carriage over. Everything was so still, we
instinctively drew together for mutual company. The
Chief hummed the air of a music-hall verse almost in
bravado.

Then a large white cockatoo flitted across the road in

front of us into the scrub in the surrounding swamp; and
that somehow broke the spell of the brooding silence.

"I'm after that," said the Chief.

"D'ye think this ground will bear your weight?" I
said.

"I'll try it," he said, swinging off the road.

I followed him slowly, stepping carefully from clump
to clump of what looked like firm ground. The bird
kept persistently beyond range. We followed it further
and further into the swamp.

At length it perched on a low shrub about sixty yards
away. The Chief took a careful aim and fired. Almost
simultaneously there was a second report on the left, and
a bush a few yards in front of us was rattled as if by a
shower of hail.

The bird had tumbled over with a last flutter. The
Chief looked at me.

"I wonder was that shot fired at us?" he said.

"I wonder," I echoed.

"Anyway, he's a d——d poor shot. Let's get the bird,"
he said.

"Keep low, then," I suggested.

We crouched forward to where we thought the bird
had fallen; but not a sign of it was to be seen. Then
we searched all round, keeping a careful look-out for
any other sportsman, and especially for our friend of the
shot-gun; but not a sign of either did we see. There
was neither bird nor human being apparently within
miles.

"Perhaps it was a phantom bird?" I suggested.

"Intended to lead us off the track to our death, I
suppose you mean?" he queried.

He looked at me solemnly to see if I was trying to pull
his leg. Then his eyes twinkled.

"I don't think that second shot was a ghostly one,
at any rate; and if I catch sight of that ——," he added,
his anger beginning to rise at the thought of it, now he

had got over his eagerness to find the bird, "I don't think I'd think twice about tryin' to make a ghost of him."

"Possibly he was after the same bird, and it was quite an accident. His gun may have gone off in the surprise of finding us so near," I suggested.

"No," he said. "I can't swallow that, Doc."

"Well, at any rate, you'll agree this place is none too healthy for us. Let's get," I said.

"Right ho," he answered, removing his helmet slowly and mopping his brow; "this is too hot by far for my comfort."

We made our way back to the road, and turned again for the ferry. It was stiflingly hot. Before we got in sight of the lake we were both almost melted. Beads of sweat kept dripping off our eyebrows; our clothes stuck to us; and the distant vision of the *Pasangrahan* across the ferry was a welcome sight.

But the Chief was still thirsting for something to kill. He grumbled all the way about losing that cockatoo.

"Why not have a pot at the crocodiles?" I suggested.

We were in midstream at the time; but when we tapped the barrels of our guns, and pointed to the inanimate crocodiles, the ferryman understood, grinned expansively, and stopped the boat.

The range was about eighty yards, and even if we hit them we were not in the least likely to do them any harm. Still, they were living targets, and we satisfied our thirst for letting off things by plugging at them. As a result three of them were sufficiently annoyed to move lazily under water.

On the way back to the ship we passed a Chinese graveyard, with its curious cupola-like head-stones, so like the plastered brick domes one sometimes sees over wells in the country near out-of-the-way villages. As we were passing, a little kid of about a month old ran bleating across the road looking for its mother. As soon as he saw it an intense desire to have it as a ship's pet entered the soul of the Chief; and he immediately offered the Malay driver, and the ragged little urchin who accompanied him on the box, a guilder for its capture. They promptly left the carriage in the middle of the road and chivied after the kid; and in a moment the Chief followed. But the kid developed unexpected powers of feinting: it dodged, it ran back, it squirmed, it slipped through their hands again and again. Then suddenly it bolted through a hole in the hedge into the Chinese graveyard; and the pursuit was carried on amongst the tombs. Here again the kid was too able for them all. In some mysterious way it disappeared. Another kid, however, somewhat older, had now come into evidence; and this the Malay boy had no difficulty in capturing. But the Chief would have none of it. He demanded the first and no other. It was useless; the kid was lost; and we were compelled to return without it. The Chief was quite inconsolable.

"But the kid wasn't theirs to give," I expostulated.

"What odds?" he retorted carelessly, with the true contempt of the white man for the brown man's rights.

That night the Old Man and I dined in state with the British Consul, and afterwards gravitated with him to the Club.

It was a band promenade night, and the Square was brilliantly lit. Everyone knew everyone else; and everyone sat out in the cool night at little round tables in front of the Club.

Men and women alike were dressed in white; and in between the groups the silent-footed, brown-limbed, gaudily turbaned and sandalled waiters passed noiselessly with the many-coloured little liqueur-glasses and coffee-cups tinkling on trays.

The band played softly; the sound of light laughter was everywhere; the stars twinkled brightly in the cloudless night.

Heavy tropical scents came out and floated clingingly around us.

Across the Square a tall equerry came with clinking sword, and secured tables a little apart. Then everyone rose; the band stopped in the middle of a bar and struck up .the Dutch National Anthem; and the Governor-General and his suite came slowly up on foot and took the places reserved for them. Then everyone sat down again, and the interrupted laughter recommenced.

      .   .   .   .

We were shipping copra for Marseilles; and already the decks were all-pervaded with its sickly sweetish odour, and the copra-bug had taken possession of the ship. He is a little black fellow about the size and shape of a lady-bird, and wherever the copra goes he goes. Luckily he has no bad habits, and so one soon accepts his presence without resentment. Occasionally snakes also found their way on board with the copra. These we did not appreciate at all.

On the morning after the band promenade the sound of tom-tom beating drew me along the quays towards the old native harbour. This lay at the far end of the wharf, away from our moorings.

There I found a fleet of Bugis sailing praus coming into port; and, as was the custom, on the bow of each, standing outlined against the sky, was an almost naked little boy rattling a tom-tom, slung round his neck, with all his might and main.

Macassar is one of the greatest emporiums of the Far East. To it comes rattans from Borneo, sandalwood and beeswax from Flores and Timor, trepang (beche-de-mer) from the Gulf of Carpentaria, oil of Cajuputi from Bouru, nutmegs, spices, and pepper from the Spice Islands, mussoi bark from New Guinea, mother-of-pearl, tortoiseshell and pearls from the Aru Islands, edible birds'-nests for Chinese consumption, and agar-agar for the bacteriological laboratories of Europe. According to

Wallace, to whose delightful *Malay Archipelago* every scientific reader is indebted, the first Bird of Paradise skins ever seen in Europe came from Macassar, and were described by the great Linnæus.

The sailing praus had come to anchor when I got to the end of the Wilhelminakade, as the European wharf is called in honour of the Queen of Holland; and stepping off it one moved in a yard back from the twentieth to the twelfth century, from the age of the steam crane and the Parsons turbine to that of Sir John Mandeville and the Great Cham of Tartary. One could well imagine that when the Arab conquerors first invaded Java in the fifteenth century, and forced their militant faith on the mild-eyed Buddhist population, they must have found the native harbour of Macassar much the same as I on that bright morning.

Imagine a number of crazy wooden piers, short, long, and irregular, built of sun-dried multitudinously patched pieces of plank, full of holes and cracks, supported on irregular rows of stakes driven into the shallow water, shaking as one walked on them, ready to drop to pieces, dry as tinder in the hot sun, spread here and there with masses of trepang (sea-slugs of the Holothurian type), bales of sun-dried fish, odoriferous buffalo hides, piles of dried seaweed, and edible birds'-nests.

Playing over these crazy platforms were numbers of naked little brown boys, who seemed equally at home in or out of the water, climbing down the piles with prehensile toes into little dug-out canoes, and upsetting one another out of these into the warm water in play.

Here and there at the inner ends of the piers, where the backs of the houses projected into the water, quiet Chinese merchants, loose-robed, pigtailed, were conning over the cargoes coming in and going out; whilst creaking against the ends of the piers, swung by ropes of twisted rattan, were the praus just arrived, some with sails furled, already discharging their cargoes of dried fish and other

commodities, others still full up, one with the captain's
wife cooking the midday rice.

As these Bugis praus are the swift-sailing ships of the
once-dreaded Malay pirates, a description may be interesting. They are of about seventy tons' burden, carry a
crew of from thirty to forty men, and are credited with
a speed of twelve to sixteen knots. The deck slopes
from stern to bow; and the steering is done by two large
tillers, slung in rattan slings, one on either quarter, let
through square holes from a sort of lower half-deck into
the water. It looks a dangerous arrangement, as one
would expect a following sea to gurgle through the holes
and swamp the ship, but apparently the Malays find it
quite satisfactory. The poop, aft, is three feet six high,
so that one can sit comfortably under it, Malay fashion.
In the centre of the ship is a deck-house with a palm-leaf
roof, and low sliding doors of thatch on either side. There
are two masts; and the main yard is about a hundred
feet long, made up of two or three bamboo poles neatly
lashed together with rattans. The sails are oblong or
triangular, hung from the centre of each mast so that
the short end is down on deck and the long end projects
into the air. The main sail is made of matting. There
are two jibs, and a fore-and-aft sail of batik astern.
Wallace made a voyage, from Macassar to the Aru Island
and back, or a thousand miles in one of these praus, and
states that they are magnificently speedy and very
comfortable.

I was looking at one that was discharging a cargo
of dried fish when the old Chinese owner came along
the crazy gangway, and, seeing my evident curiosity,
motioned me to go aboard. Nothing loth, I dropped on
the deck; and he followed down more cautiously. Neither
of us could speak a word to one another; but he motioned
me aft, and we squatted on the poop. There he produced an earthenware jar of hocshu and two earless
cups, smiling and pointing to the buttons on my tunic,

which were of mother-of-pearl stencilled in silver with the Chinese for "Good luck." He filled up the cups, handed me one, we both said "chin-chin" solemnly, and drank. It tasted like very mellow arak, and was distinctly heady, as I found when I bade him farewell after an inspection of the ship which I could not make as complete as I should have wished owing to the overpowering odour of the cargo. In spite of the smell, however, I took my time, shook hands, and bowed myself slowly away, feeling very flattered by the old man's kindness, and wishful therefore to let him know it.

When I told the Second Engineer about it after tiffin, he roared with laughter.

"Fancy shaking hands and bowing to a Chink. I guess he knew you were no Dutchman, Doc."

"I'd like to have tasted that 'hocshu,' though," he added as an afterthought. "I should think the old boy must be a connoisseur. But fancy bowing to a Chink. You take the biscuit, Doc."

That evening, for the first time, I tasted the famous durian fruit. Often had I passed the native merchant with his mass of mammillated spheroids, and smelt the sickly odour arising from them as he carved the segments for sale. I had seen Malays, and even little Dutch children, enjoying them with evident gusto, but had thought it must be an acquired taste, for the smell is as the smell of rotten onions, and the fruit is not supposed to be eaten till it falls off the tree.

That evening, however, the Steward supplied some for dessert; and the evident enjoyment of the officers at length induced me to try it. Then I was sorry I had deprived myself of such a pleasure so long, for, as Dampier saith, "'Tis as white as milk, and as soft as cream, and the taste very delicious."

Afterwards I found quite a considerable literature about it, for the repellent odour and the subsequent surprise of the taste makes every traveller talk about it. Wallace calls it the "king and emperor of fruits," and quotes Linschott as saying: "It is of such an excellent taste that it surpasses in flavour all the other fruits of the world, according to those that have tasted it." Paludanus says: "It is of a hot and humid nature. To those not used to it it seems at first to smell of rotten onions, but immediately they have tasted it they prefer it to all other foods. The natives give it honourable titles, exalt it, and make verses to it."

On the other hand, Dampier, though praising it highly, gives preference to the mangosteen, as does also Miss Scudamore in her charming sketches of Javanese life. Unfortunately for my curiosity, the mangosteen was not obtainable at the time I was in Java.

"You thought I was pulling your leg the other day when I suggested we might have some when we were out," said the Chief; and I had to confess that I had indeed thought so.

· · · · ·

A day or so after the fleet of praus had arrived we had a visit from the oil and pearl merchants. The first were of the ordinary type, selling the famous Macassar oil and Kaiputi (oil of Cajuputi); but the pearl merchants were of a more interesting variety. Typical Malays of the better class, they came aboard garbed in little round basket-work skull-caps, the usual baju jacket, sarong and sandals. But in addition each wore a wide leather belt having many little leather pockets. Tied up in handkerchiefs they also brought great pearl-oyster shells as large as a dinner-plate—many of them with one or more mother-of-pearl blisters, which might or might not contain a pearl if cut into.

Squatting *dudock*, they spread the shells on the deck before us as we lounged in our chairs enjoying an after-tiffin smoke, and from the numerous pockets of their belts produced little parcels of pearls, wrapped up in thin

Chinese paper. These also they deposited on the deck. The pearls had come from Papua, and probably a good many of them had been acquired in questionable ways.

The first day they came they evidently did not expect to sell. It was only a preliminary skirmish, and the prices asked were merely for the purpose of finding out what limit we would be likely to rise to, each offer coming lower and lower, after the manner of a Dutch auction. There were all sorts and sizes of pearls, from large perfect spheres through black globoids down to irregular masses of mother-of-pearl and tiny seed pearls.

Each day the prices came lower; and each day we laughed and bargained. It was all part of the game.

"You can bet your boots," said the Chief, "they won't sell you anything at a loss, so bargain away."

Of course we knew nothing whatever about pearls and their values; but nevertheless we all bought a number that took our fancy; and afterwards when I had mine valued in London I found I had really got them cheap. Then I was sorry I had not bought more.

This constant bargaining for everything is a habit one must acquire for one's own protection in the East. The Eastern merchant has no fixed price for anything; an article is worth what he can get for it, and he has a profound contempt for the traveller who pays him what he asks without demur. In addition his rapacity is thereby aroused, and he keeps asking more and more every time, till the traveller, goaded into recognising that extortion is being practised on him, refuses to tolerate it any longer, thereby making not only himself irritable but also the vendor, whose hopes of reaping a huge profit from his inexperience have been thus rudely shattered. The moral is to bargain for everything.

　　　•　　　•　　　•

At last the date of our departure was fixed. It was for Saturday at noon; so on the Friday night the Old Man gave a supper party on the bridge-deck to which a number of Dutch ladies were invited. One fine old Dutchman was present with his grand-daughter, who appeared to be a typical full-blooded Malay. It was a curious example of Mendelism. The old gentleman had married a Malay and his Eurasian son a Dutchwoman, and yet this son's daughter appeared to be a pure Malay.

Saturday morning saw us still taking in cargo. We were due to start at noon; and as was his nature the Old Man was acutely miserable to be off. He paced up and down the bridge-deck all morning in a fume, while the Chinamen on shore kept on leisurely weighing the copra with the curious steel-yard invented before the Christian era, and bales of buffalo hides kept coming still on board.

We were carrying the mails to Semarang, and the bags, too, kept coming at intervals, much to the annoyance of Horner, in whose charge they were. The Chief had paid a last hurried farewell visit to Yuki in the morning, and had his last lager from her delicate fingers. I, too, had been rushing round in a vain attempt to obtain photographic plates from a mythical Chinaman. The whole ship's company was thus aboard, and everyone was wishing we might start.

A Norwegian barque that had been loading for a week, and had sailed that morning, was now a white-winged vision on the edge of the horizon.

But all the cargo was not yet in, and the Old Man said he would wait an hour extra and no more. At one o'clock, then, he climbed sturdily on the bridge, and immediately afterwards the siren sounded. Then a man coming slowly along the quays with a bullock wagon seemed to get excited. Vainly he tried to goad his leisurely beasts to greater speed. Nothing could make them do it.

"It's another load of hides," said the Third Mate.

"Can't wait for them," snapped the Old Man.

Then a Dutchman came furiously round the corner

waving something white. He ran panting up the gangway. It was a late letter for the mail.

Horner grimly charged him fivepence extra as a late fee, and the man began to expostulate, but a voice roaring down from the bridge cut him short. It was the Old Man shouting, "Haul up the gangway."

With a startled look the Dutchman fled.

The bullock wagon was still approaching, its driver gesticulating wildly.

"D——n the hides," said the Old Man, as he rang the "stand-by."

We were off.

CHAPTER X

THE RETURN TO JAVA. SEMARANG. BATAVIA

In an hour the panorama of the land was gone, and we were steering once again for Java. Late in the afternoon we passed the Norwegian barque that had sailed before us in the morning; and so at sunset we were alone in an opal sea, that changed to red, merged into purple, and ended in a lotus-yellow in the afterglow. Macassar had become a memory: the calm of the waters fell over us once more.

All the next day we were steaming through a rippling summer sea, with the thin blue line of the Java coast faint and hazy, far to southward. A slumbrous calm lay over the ship. With half-closed eyes we lay stretched watching the bonito jump black against the sun, becoming a rippling gleam of silver as they turned and plunged again. Now and again the look-out bell sounded warningly; and we would look up to see one or more Javanese praus, with their triangular sails swelling to the breeze, crossing our track.

Night fell, and in the darkness, far to the south, came a glow as of a great forest fire.

"That," said the Old Man, standing beside me on the bridge, "is Slamat, the volcano behind Semarang. The glow is the cloud reflection of the crater. We should be under it at midnight."

It was almost midnight when we reached port. The water was very shallow; and we were obliged to anchor in five fathoms at a distance of three miles from the shore. Around us were the riding lights of the other ships; and presently the packet-boat arrived from Batavia, port-holes aglow, looking like a luminous snake as she wound gracefully to her anchorage close by.

We signalled, and in answer she sent a launch for the mails.

"I'm jolly glad to be rid of them," said Horner. "Once on a time the second mates were paid for looking after them. Now they're not, and still one has the responsibility."

I was exceedingly anxious to get ashore at Semarang, not so much on account of the place as because there are some famous Buddhist pyramids near. The centre of Java is studded with these wonderful temples, relics of a bygone civilisation. At Boro-Boedor there is one covering as large an area as the great pyramid of Gizeh; but, unlike the Egyptian pyramids, these are studded with hundreds of the most elaborately carved statues and miles on miles of bas-reliefs. This great temple was discovered by Sir Stamford Raffles during the English occupation, buried in jungle vegetation, forgotten even by the natives. The Dutch had held the country for two hundred years, and did not know of its existence. It has over five hundred carved Buddhas arranged around its walls, and is probably the most wonderful work of its kind in the world.

Legend, as is natural, has been busy with the site; and the tale told is something as follows. At the time when William the Norman was parcelling out England amongst his robber barons there dwelt a Prince in Boro-Boedor who was great and wise, very learned, and a profound philosopher. And, as is often the way with wise men, he loved the frivolous, gay, and witty daughter of a neighbouring Prince, the Lord of Mendoet, courting her with grave and stately words and most respectful manner. And she, after the manner of women, cared not for any of these stately ways, but wanted to be wooed with hot words of passion, with verses pulsing from the heart, with impetuous advances hard to be repelled—for

the maiden was young and very beautiful, and a thing
to set men's hearts afire. And so his courtship found
her cold and unaffected. But nevertheless she could
not ignore him, for his principality marched with that of
her father, she was the heiress and her father favoured
an alliance that would preserve the succession safely
after his death. And so he pressed his daughter to pledge
her troth to the Prince of Boro-Boedor in order that he
might go down to the grave in peace. At the last, then,
because of the importunity of her father, and because no
other man had touched her heart, she consented, stipu-
lating, however, that he should build a temple to the
honour of Gautama and Loro-Jongran greater than any
in Java, and in a certain definite space of time which
she made as short as was possible next to impossibility.
And the Prince of Boro-Boedor, because of his great love
for her, consented, and, stimulated by his love, hurried
on the workmen so that he had it completed within the
allotted time, putting all the sweetness of his affection,
the lofty thoughts, the noble impulses he could not give
expression to in words, into the perfect details of the
great temple. And when it was all finished he sent to
let the maiden know. But in the interval the Prince, her
father, had died; and she was now the Princess of Mendoet, and had repented of her promise.

Nevertheless she came and gazed on its wonderful
loveliness, saw its vast perfection, and knew it had all
been done for love of her. Yet was her heart not touched.
She turned to the Prince, waiting with tense desire for
her answer, and said:

"Truly, O Prince, these images are beautiful; but they
are dead. I cannot love you any more than I can them."

And the Prince bowed his head and said never a
word, for he loved her greatly, and knew by this that she
was unworthy.

Such is the story.

The great temple is near Djokjokarta, on the southern

side of the island; but there was one, not so grand, but still very imposing, near Semarang; and it was this I wanted to visit.

"There's no chance of getting ashore, Doc," the Old Man said in answer to my query. "We're ordered off at midday to-morrow."

To-morrow, however, found us loading sugar all day. The lighters came continuously. There seemed no end to the sugar that was waiting to be loaded. Someone seemed to have blundered in the head office at Batavia. All day long the round canvas bales kept coming on board; and all day long the monotonous chant of the coolies came up from the holds as they swung them into position, crooning: "Amma-ti-ra-ta-huh—amma-ti-ra-ta-huh."

One could see nothing of the town except the Pharos at the mouth of the canal leading up to it. Not a sampan came near us. It was steamingly hot, and the water looked temptingly cool; but the number of sharks nosing round the ship checked any idea of bathing. Finally the Third Steward took it into his head to fish for one with a grappling hook and lump of pork. We wandered over casually to watch; and presently one big fellow came along, nosed it, and then proceeded leisurely round the ship.

"That fellow's as good as caught, sir," said the boatswain, who was passing at the time. "Once they smell salt pork they're done for."

In a few minutes he appeared again, nosed it, and again swam leisurely round the ship. The steward had hitched the rope holding the grappling hook round his body, and then around a stanchion for further security; so, when for a third time the shark nosed it and left, he exclaimed disgustedly, "He's as partikler as a Chink about his pork, he is."

He turned his head for a moment, and then suddenly

he was jerked against the rail with great violence. The rope tightened around his body. His face was white.

"Lor, he's swallered it. Help!" he gasped.

Everybody rushed to his aid to take the strain off his body. He unwound himself, gasping while we pulled and stumbled against one another checking the shark's mad rushes. The boatswain's voice rose cheerfully. "Now then! All together," and we pulled steadily. The water alongside was lashed into foam. He dashed madly to and fro. It was a tremendous pull. Even when he was half out of the water the power of his tail was surprisingly great. Once he was clear of his element, however, his strength seemed to go from him. At length we got him on to the deck; and then he appeared to come to life again, jerking and snapping like a wolf. A blow from the carpenter's adze settled him, however; and then he lay an inert mass, with now and again a quiver while we gazed at him triumphantly.

It was the Third Steward who had captured him; and the spoils therefore were to him. The carpenter made a walking-stick out of his backbone, which the steward offered to me. I refused it, however, as his was the capture, and I could see he was very keen to keep the trophy. The carcase was given to the Chinamen, and they cut it up into strips and ate it. A Chinaman will eat anything. It was a fitting end.

.   .   .   .

Towards nightfall we were still loading, more and more lighters coming out; and then the orders for sailing were countermanded from Batavia. It was the agent who came aboard with the news; and immediately I took the opportunity of asking for the loan of his launch to take me ashore on the morrow.

It was almost sunset at the time, and leaning on the rail, we saw a sight possible only in this country. It was the Semarang fishing fleet coming out against the setting sun. They spread all about us in boats shaped like gondolas, each rowed by ten long sweeps; and as they rowed the tinkle of innumerable little bells came from them, for all along the boom each boat was thickly strung with rows and rows of them, their tinkling being supposed to draw the fish as if by enchantment. Overhead, in a sort of crow's nest at the masthead, each boat had a lookout man stationed, his body and his cone-shaped hat outlining themselves against an amber sky. From his position he could see where the shoals were; and from there he directed the steersman with a low, sweet musical call. There must have been about twenty of them; and the sea was literally alive with fish. When each boat had picked its moorings the men stopped rowing and rapidly threw out their nets, floated with pieces of bamboo, a boy being sent out with each net to square it properly, kicking all the time to keep the sharks from seizing him.

It is difficult to express how intensely beautiful it all was in the still tropical evening. We watched it spellbound till the swift darkness fell like a drop-curtain and hid it from our sight, only a blotch of phosphorescence being left to mark the position of each boat.

.   .   .   .

Semarang, like most of the ports on this coast, lies inland, connected by a canal and a steam tramway with the coast. There is the usual lighthouse at the mouth, and the usual praus and launches in the canal. I asked the British Vice-Consul about going to the temples, and he informed me it would be necessary to get a passport if I wished to go inland, the Dutch being very jealous of strangers wandering at their own sweet will about the country. That knocked my plans completely on the head, and so I decided to see the town and return. The ship's comprador gave me a half-caste clerk as a guide, and together we drove round to see the sights. The town was greatly excited, I found, by the advent of an English musical comedy company, playing "The Cingalee," "The Dairymaids," "Florodora," and "The Spring Chicken"; and going into the Hôtel Du Pavillon for something

with ice in it, on making my request in English, I was
promptly seized upon by the leading lady to explain my
presence in this "one-horse country," and compelled to
listen to her tale of quarrels with everyone and everything. She was obviously suffering from prickly heat,
and it had been too much for her temper. Consequently
I discovered that I had an engagement to have *rijst-tafel*
at the opposition hotel, the Hôtel Jansen, and fled; for a
discontented white woman in a hot country is something
to run from. It is hard enough for a man to keep equable
at times in the heat. It must be almost impossible for
a woman, especially a woman dressed in European
clothes.

The Dutchwoman manages to keep cool and placid
in Java by the very simple expedient of doing nothing,
and wearing almost nothing.

It is very disconcerting at first to the fresh arrival,
until he gets used to it, to see the startling *deshabille*
they affect, even in public. At the Hôtel Jansen several
of these "abandoned creatures," as the leading lady, stiffly
uncomfortable in European clothes, called them, were
lolling about in the inevitable cane lounges in the public
verandah.

Imagine a lady in the corridor of an hotel lying at
full length, bare-headed, dressed in a *kabaya* of white
batiste—a thin white loose upper garment like a dressing
jacket coming to a little below the waist—fastened in
front with ornamental native pins and little gold chains,
a sarong, very gorgeous in native colours, dropping to
about six inches below the knee, bare legs, bare feet, and
sandals or high-heeled shoes, and you have the Dutch
East Indian lady clothed for the public eye.

After lunch I wandered back to the comprador's office.
There I met the captain of a steamer trading to and from
Singapore. His ship was anchored not far from ours;
and he invited me on board on the way back. When he
told me he had a European leper as a passenger I accepted

at once. The victim was a Dutch tobacco planter from Sumatra, and how he got the disease was a mystery. He said he had exhausted European treatment, and now was in the hands of a Bengali who was dosing him with the powder of precious stones collected in the mountains and heated in a flame for fourteen days. He was pathetically anxious to get well. His English was perfect. He told me he could speak six European languages with equal facility; he was passionately fond of music; and he was a leper. He said the powdered precious stones were doing him a lot of good, and asked me if I did not think so too. I agreed at once, he was watching me so anxiously; and then he brightened up surprisingly. After a bit I asked if I might see the powdered precious stones; and he produced a tiny phial from his pocket, and ran a few of the precious grains out into the palm of my hand. It was ordinary crude sulphide of antimony; but I was careful not to tell him so. As long as he was happy why should I destroy his dream, poor beggar?*

I must have spent a longer time than I had thought with him, for presently the sound of the siren came booming across from our ship, and I knew the Old Man was hooting for me.

With a hasty farewell I left him. He did not offer to shake hands. I wished afterwards I had volunteered to do so. After all I could easily have disinfected mine afterwards, and he had probably not shaken hands with a white man for years.

When I got back all was bustle on the ship, and in half an hour we had sailed. Across our bows as we started two big water-spouts curled north by east about a mile in front of us, and then broke up in the offing. A deluge of rain fell on the ship; and the air afterwards was like an elixir following the stuffiness of the Semarang anchorage.

---

*Actually antimony is used with some success in the treatment of leprosy.

For the next few days we were cargo-lifting all along the coast towards Batavia, raising the stuff from lighters at sea three or four miles from the coast opposite little ports of which we only saw the outline, and sometimes did not bother even to know the name. Sometimes we would stop as often as three times in the day. The ship would be going along monotonously, with not a sight of anything; and then a number of little specks would appear right ahead; we would slow down; and the specks, turning out to be a dozen or so lighters sent out to intercept us, would transfer their cargo to our holds. Sometimes we would be as much as six hours at one of these ports—Pekalongan with its volcano, Tegal with its curious outrigged boats, Cheribon with its large conical mountain in the background. When we were compelled to stop any length of time the whole white population, numbering perhaps half a dozen souls, would find some excuse to come aboard, just to look at a fresh face and speak to someone different. It must have been a ghastly life for those fellows, out there merely to make a living, caring nothing for the habits, customs, language, or folk-lore of the people, simply tied to a stool all day making out indents of cargo for some big firm in Amsterdam hardly conscious of their existence, drinking much beer during the day, and going home at night to the un-interesting society of the native women whom they euphemistically called wives, to try to sleep as much as the heat and the sizzling mosquitoes would permit.

After we had been moving along for some days at this slow rate it was a great relief to everyone when the orders came to hasten to Batavia. We all drew a sigh of relief. The heat was beginning to affect us by now; we were anxious to get out of the steaminess of it, and be once more in the wide sweep of the Indian Ocean.

"A week in Batavia," said the Mate, "and we shall be homeward bound."

.   .   .   .

It was one o'clock on a Saturday afternoon when we
sighted Idam Island, with its white tower high above the
green; and soon every eye was fastened on the rapidly
approaching land, the Mate picking out the familiar spots
as we approached along the green-fringed shore.

A long white breakwater with three great Dutch
cruisers inside, and then a mass of shipping, came rapidly
in sight.

"That's Tanjong Priok. We'll be ashore in half an
hour, Doc," he said.

Slowly, under the guidance of the pilot, we steamed
between the two great breakwaters, passing and dipping
to the Dutch men-o'-war, sliding past the fort, the time-
flag tower, two of the magnificent Rotterdam-Lloyd mail-
boats, and one of our own ships, to which we waved
furious greetings.

We were moored eventually at what is known as the
coal-wharf, and then the heat fell on us, for we started
coaling immediately, and all the ports had to be hermetically shut to keep out the dust.

It was stifling. The Old Man had already started
for Batavia; but no one else was able to be off duty.

It was impossible to stay on the ship. Already bamboo
platforms had been erected, and the coolies were
swinging up the coal.

"I'll be off duty in half an hour," said the Chief.

In the meanwhile I wandered round the great square
basin dredged out of a swamp by the marvellous engineer-
ing patience for which the Dutch are famous. This great
basin is known as Tanjong Priok. It is the harbour of
Batavia, which is six and a half miles distant. The
original harbour began silting up after the eruption of
Mount Salak in 1699. The eruption dammed up the
river, Tjiliwong; and this, when the waters broke
through, sent a stream of mud and sand into the harbour
till it gradually became useless.

The dredging of the new harbour at Tanjong Priok

and the building of the breakwaters cost 26,500,000 gulden, or over two million pounds sterling. Before, it had been a mangrove swamp; and the stirring up of the mud when it was being dredged cost some thousands of lives from Java fever. Now, however, it is comparatively healthy; and as a harbour it is one of the finest in the world. But it is certainly also one of the hottest.

The Chief and the Second hailed me as I was coming back along the coal wharf.

"Come on. We're going to the Petit Trouville for a swim."

The very idea was exhilarating. I joined them at once. We crossed the railway tracks and over a large field where a crowd of Dutch men-o'-war's men were kicking a football about in the broiling sun. It looked suicidal; but they appeared to be flourishing on it. Coming on to a shady road, we crossed a bridge over a creek and debouched on the native village of Tanjong Priok. At the near end, next to the bridge, everybody seemed to be selling fruit, those who did not making up by displaying sherbet and "limonade."

It was the time of the *siesta*; and as we progressed the village became more and more deserted. Everywhere we saw limp, somnolent figures asleep on the *balai-balai* (string mattresses) of their verandahs.

Turning down a bridle-path arched over in a deep sea of green caused by the light filtering through the broad banana leaves, we followed the winding track, past native huts and small plantain walks, patches of yams, jack fruit, and betel trees. Suddenly we came on a graveyard, and I stopped. It took me quite by surprise. It was a European graveyard, started probably when the harbour was being made, and now used for those foreigners who had strayed to this far-off, forgotten land and died. Many of the names we noted on the gravestones were English; some of the graves showed signs of care; others (the great

majority) were neglected; many of the oblong mounds
were nameless.

"Let's go on," said the Second suddenly with a shiver.
"We buried two fellows with cholera there a few years
back."

A native woman came swinging along crooning to
herself as she walked, bronzed, splendidly erect, with a
chattie on her head. She stopped abruptly when she
saw us, and turned aside into a plantain grove. Further
round two more women were dredging for crabs in a
shallow overflow from the sea. We passed through a
copra plantation, kicking the fallen coco-nuts aside as
we walked, climbed over a fence, and were in the grounds
of the Petit Trouville.

This was a most unorthodox way of getting in, and
the Chinese proprietor didn't like it; for, seeing three
strange, intrusive figures climbing over his fence, he
came running towards us, followed by his two sons.

"Hello, Wang-Chu, still alive, you old extortioner,"
shouted the Chief.

Then Wang-Chu stopped abruptly, for it was very
hot. A broad smile spread over his face.

"Wat for you no come olla way?" he said.

"No likee pay twenty-five cent," truthfully replied the
Chief.

Petit Trouville is unique. Imagine a thick plantation
of palm, njamplong, and coco-nut trees along a silvery
sea-shore, with a row of wooden bathing-huts near the
beach, and a bamboo fence some distance out in the
water to keep off sharks and water snakes. Amongst the
trees are twenty or thirty little rustic arbours with tables,
chairs, and great cane lounges. Further back is a
verandahed wooden restaurant with a billiard-room, a
dining-hall, and an open floor for dancing.

On a Sunday afternoon, when the heat is of an
intensity and the dust rises, making the eyes smart and
parching the throat, when clothes are an irritating con-

vention and tempers are frayed by prickly heat, it is then
that Batavia suddenly remembers the Petit Trouville, and
with a gasp of relief pours down *en masse* to the cool
shade of the njamplongs, the caress of the incoming
sea-breeze, and the exhilarating embrace of the long
combing rollers that tumble on the silvery beach.

Everyone is dressed in white, the women with big
straw hats, the men in pith helmets.   Merry groups are
splashing about in bathing costumes in the water, their
heads protected from the fierce sun by enormous
umbrella-like hats provided with the bathing costumes.
Others recline in the arbours, or lie where the wax-like,
scented petals of the njamplongs fall around them with
every breath of wind, and the scent of the purple lantana
is all-pervasive.   Great patches of sunlight mingle with
the dappled shade.   Everywhere one hears the tinkle of
ice in glasses, the deep bass of men's voices mingling
with the lighter trilling laughter of the women.   Everywhere silent, impassive, pig-tailed, deferential Chinamen
move around attending to the wants of the dominant race.

The sea is a great stretch of dimpled sun-lit blue,
meeting far out the olive-green of the horizon, where a
group of islets and the white tower of Idam hang like a
faery cloud picture too ethereal for reality.

The incoming tide breaks with a turquoise roll, having
a fleecy white-rimmed edge that ripples up and sinks
bubbling in the thirsty, heated sand.

Such is the picture of Petit Trouville as I remember
it best.   On that afternoon, however, we had it all to
ourselves; and soon we were splashing in the warm sea,
our heads protected from the sun by the huge regulation
circular straw hats as big as umbrellas, characteristic of
the place.   It was gloriously exhilarating.   We returned
to the ship for dinner feeling like new men.

After sunset, however, the heat was still intense, and
the exhilaration gradually left us.   The air was stagnant
and we missed the breeze created by the ship in motion.

Our clothes felt tight, every movement was a fatigue, and the mosquito already was singing his high, insistent note.

At last I could stand it no longer.

"I'm off to Batavia for the night," I suddenly announced. "I feel suffocated here. Any of you fellows coming?"

"Can't go," said the Chief regretfully.

"Nor I," said the Mate.

"I'm game," said Horner, *sotto voce*, so that the Mate need not hear, officially, unless he liked.

The train ride in the night was delightful after the stagnation of the lagoon. A cool breeze blew through the mosquito-curtained spaces that acted as windows. We lounged at ease, for our compartment was fitted with comfortable arm-chairs, and otherwise furnished as a smoking-room. The smell of unknown tropical scents wafted through to us. Myriads of fire-flies flitted with their twinkling lights in the velvet dark. Groves of bamboos whispered secrets to the night air. The stars came out and glistened in the still waters of the canal alongside the track. We could feel the collars of our uniforms growing slacker and more comfortable around our necks.

When we arrived in Batavia we called a carriage and gave the Malay driver permission by an ample sweep of the arm to take us anywhere. We rattled along through the crowded streets and watched the crowds. Troops of hilarious Dutch sailors were everywhere, singing, dancing, wearing strange masks, mafficking generally, in celebration of the birthday of the Prince Consort.

The cafés were crowded with gaily dressed people sitting at little tables and listening to the bands. We felt as if we had suddenly dropped back into civilisation—the electric lights, the tramways, the toilettes of the ladies, the uniforms of the officers, the fine buildings, the music, all tended to produce a Parisian effect, even in the bizarre Malay surroundings.

Nevertheless it felt unreal somehow, theatrical, like a Gaiety musical comedy with an exotic background.

We paid off our carriage, and ambled along on foot. Gradually we left the open tree-embowered Weltevreden (New Batavia) of the European quarter, and wandered on till we found ourselves in the older part, the original Dutch unhealthy Old Batavia of many canals, the sinister graveyard city that slew so many thousand Europeans before the days of sanitation and cholera-prophylaxis, deserted now, except for business houses and Government offices in the daytime, given over to Chinese, Arabs, Japs, and Javanese at night. The new Batavia (Weltevreden) is a wonderful garden city, with each bungalow embowered in a park of its own; the Old Batavia is a malarious place of narrow streets and stolidly built old Dutch houses that might have been translated bodily from Amsterdam.

We dropped into native *chow* houses, fell amongst the Chinese, turned into a Japanese street, where we exchanged colloquial greetings with the little kimonoed ladies, and declined innumerable invitations to come in, smoke, and drink beer.

Finally we wound up very tired at a Japanese *yadoya*, and soon were fast asleep, each in a huge mosquito-curtained square Dutch bed, with the usual great bolster down the centre that makes these beds so comfortable in a hot climate.

In the middle of the night a most uncanny yelling brought me wide-awake. I could hear the Second Mate moving in the cubicle next mine.

"What is it?" I called softly.

An eerie scream came from overhead, the sound of something falling, and then silence. The Mate had struck a light, and we both turned out in our sarongs.

"D——n," he said, "it's only a gecko. I'm off to sleep again."

What had happened was that two great lizards, crawling along with sucker feet upon the wall, had met and promptly started fighting. One had been bitten and immediately had fallen off to the ground.

According to arrangement the Jap proprietor called us at five o'clock in the morning; and so we started out on foot shortly after sunrise. It was delightfully cool as we turned towards the railway station for Tanjong Priok. There we found we were by no means the only passengers. Outside the station a Chinaman was serving delicious hot coffee and rolls from his itinerant restaurant; and several European officials connected with the dock were patronising him. We followed their example. A company of native troops out route-marching passed us as we stood, the officers saluting our group as they passed, and we returning the salute as gravely. Crowds of coolies were packing themselves into carriages like cattle vans at the back of the train; and eventually we found that everyone was waiting till we had finished our coffee to start.

The native guard found us a saloon in front; and we travelled down with a young Dutchman who bathed his head and face freely with eau-de-Cologne. It looked an effeminate sort of thing to do; but we found others doing likewise, and in a few days were trying it ourselves, to discover then it was most refreshing.

At the ship everything was peaceful; the coaling was over, and everyone asleep.

We had our baths, changed into fresh ducks, and shouted for breakfast.

"What have you fellows been up to?" said the Chief grumpily. "No good, I'm sure."

"Because you couldn't come is no reason for taking a gloomy view of life," said Horner.

"This place is enough to give anyone the jim-jams," said the Chief.

The Old Man came back just as we were starting breakfast. I found he had had me made a member of the Harmonie Club in Batavia, so I could go up whenever I liked.

"It's a nice soft job, a ship-surgeon's," said the Chief, still not sure if he were irritable or not. "Can't think what they pay them for."

"Touch wood, or you will have bad luck," said Horner laughingly, never expecting how true his words would come.

    .   .   .   .

It was that same afternoon. We decided to go to the Petit Trouville; and the Chief was in an intensely rollicking mood, by way of reaction from the morning. He absolutely refused, therefore, to walk to the place; and so we drove round, overtaking on the way a carriage holding three decorous Chinese ladies. Our man shouted to the other driver to make way, and drove to one side so as to pass him. The road, however, was barely wider than the breadth of the two carriages, and the other driver would not give way.

The Malay is an Irishman at heart—lazy, witty, intensely sporting, doting on cock-fights—and the two men rapidly exchanged a series of vituperative retorts which ended in a challenge to race. We were so intensely amused that we forgot about the occupants of the other carriage; and their driver, with the contempt of the true Oriental for women, also never gave a thought as to how they might like it. He forged ahead of us, drawing to one side, and whipped up his little Timor ponies to the gallop. Our man promptly took up the challenge; and soon we were running neck and neck, everyone whooping. The carriages lurched dangerously in the narrow, winding side-road. I caught a glimpse of two huddled figures with white powdered faces, and one splendid girl, sitting up erect, impassive, robed in grey silk, with her big almond eyes looking straight in front, the sleek black hair on her uncovered head tied in a long plait curled up behind, a pink flower over one temple. Once the wheels interlocked, and by a miracle cleared again.

The branch of a tree struck the rival Jehu on the forehead, and our man forged ahead, yelling furiously; but the other, recovering, lashed wildly at his ponies and drew level again. The gate of the bathing-place was now in sight, and the road widened considerably. We dashed on like a tornado, ending in a dead-heat at the gate. The two Malays drew up panting and grinning, and we got out.

The girl proudly marshalled her two elderly frightened companions firmly through the gate without a movement of her features, without a single look, as if completely unconscious of our rudely staring presences.

"By Jove, what a whopper!" said the Second.

As for me, I felt ashamed. I had not been long enough in the East to develop the Eastern contempt for women, especially coloured women. The Chief, too, was uneasy.

"It wasn't quite fair, was it? They might have been hurt," he said. Then he brightened up as his glance fell on the drivers. "But it was a jolly good race, all the same. Say, Mick, here's an extra half-dollar," he added to the grinning Jehu. "You're an old sport."

When we got inside they had disappeared. We did not see them again. Cautious inquiries from Wang-Chu were unavailing. He did not seem to understand. It turned out afterwards they were his wife, her sister, and his daughter. We should have liked to have seen that girl again; but Wang-Chu, very pleasant, very bland, very inscrutable, hadn't the faintest intention of letting us. Did he resent our behaviour in not restricting the enthusiasm of our Jehus? We never could find out. Did

he pay it off on the Chief? To this day I do not know.
Perhaps he did. Perhaps it was a coincidence.

At any rate he smilingly brought us bathing suits and
big straw hats, and warned us not to get beyond the
bamboo fence. The tide was out; and the water was
shallow inside the fence. Outside the waves were coming
in in league-long rollers, curling over white and glistening, pounding on the beach in one unceasing series of
straight foaming lines, like cavalry charges from an inexhaustible army. We looked at them; then we found
a dug-out canoe hauled up on the beach, also a couple
of paddles, and the temptation was too great.

Out we went into the surf; and over of course toppled
the canoe. We tried with a crew of three; we tried with
two; we tried with one; but none of us could manage
to keep afloat. Each time the combing waves reached us
we were upset. Eventually we found the best fun was
to wait till a wave reached us, grasp the canoe, and,
diving through, follow it in on the crest of the next.

Out in the offing we saw the triangular fins of one or
two sharks; but as they did not come in near we soon
got to disregard them. Long before this we had lost our
hats—that is, the Second and I had—but the Chief, having refused to dive, had kept his.

Eventually his went too; and it was while wading for
it that he suddenly gave a yell and collapsed into the
water. It is extraordinary how difficult it is to make
haste when one is wading.. Both of us dived for him;
but before we got to him he was up again, and was
swearing furiously.

"My leg," he said. "Something's stung it horribly."

There were lots of jelly-fish about; and once or twice
we had seen the flashing wriggle of a water-snake; but
none of us had paid any attention to them. We helped
him ashore, walking painfully. Then I examined his
ankle, and found a row of little red dots just above the
ankle on his left leg.

Wang-Chu must have been watching us; and apparently he knew what was the matter at once, for when we got to the dressing-rooms he was there with a pot of some sort of lotion.

"Plenty heap good fo' sting," he said cheerfully, as he wrapped the Chief's leg up in lint soaked in the stuff.

Eventually we got him back to the ship.

Next day he said he was better; and so I started off for Batavia alone, promising to meet the Old Man at *rijst-tafel* later on.

In the interval I wandered round the "old town," with its canals and its fine old Dutch mansions now turned almost entirely into offices.

Here lived the Dutch of the now-forgotten "Honourable East India Company," the Dutch who fought so strenuously for centuries to keep the monopoly of Far Eastern trade in their own hands. Here the "Lords Seventeen" who ruled this vast empire lived in their stuffy old Dutch houses, dressed in heavy broadcloths, tight knee-breeches, and silver-buckled shoes, regardless of the climate. Here their wives in heavy velvets and brocades gave state entertainments in their gardens in the afternoon, regardless of the pitiless sun; and here plague, sunstroke, cholera, and fever slew them in their thousands with sinister persistency for three long centuries, till at last a man with seeing eyes arose, Weltevreden was built and Old Batavia abandoned. Now, though it is populated during the day, no European sleeps there at night.

But there is another Batavia, still more interesting than Old Batavia; that is the Kampong Bahru, the chief Chinese quarter of the city. Here the Chinese are segregated, a reminiscence of the precautions taken after the rebellion of 1720; and here one steps immediately into a world of bustle and hurry, all the more striking when one has just left the old-world, immemorial lethargy of the somnolent Malay. For the Chinese quarter is a humming hive of industry; everyone is busy, everyone is actively doing something.

I watched a blacksmith working at an anvil making ornamental hinges, hammering away at the hot metal, streaming with perspiration, his yellow body naked, save for a sarong, in the sweltering heat. He never looked up the whole time I was watching him. He was evidently working against time. Had he been a Malay, in the remote possibility of his being found working at all, he would have stopped, smiled a courtly greeting as of one gentleman meeting another, accepted a cigarette, and conversed on things and the world in general until his visitor chose to take a leisurely departure.

The Chinaman is never idle. He is a born merchant. His mind is constantly occupied by questions of barter and exchange. It is noticeable that unless he is very rich indeed, no matter how elaborately ornamented, dragon-haunted, gilded, lacquered, his house may be, it is in addition his place of business. Shop and home are synonyms to him; the world is divided into buyers and sellers, and the things of the world into objects to buy and objects to sell.

It is little wonder, then, that with so much concentration of purpose the Chinaman is so invariably successful. The wealth of the Chinese in Java is enormous. A rich Chinaman thinks nothing of spending several thousand pounds over the funeral of a near relative; and such funerals are constant sights of interest to the traveller, on account of the procession of hanging symbolical demon figures, which are afterwards burnt, preceding them, and the hundreds of white-robed mourners by which the body is accompanied. The wife of a wealthy Chinaman has jewels the daughter of an American millionaire might envy; his son is sent to Europe to be educated; and no one is ashamed of the fact that the founder of the family fortune probably came to Java forty years before a penniless coolie.

The sporting instincts of the Chinaman are as fully developed as his business keenness. The proprietor of the *yadoya* I had previously stopped in took me to a cock-fight that morning. Legally the sport is forbidden; practically the law is a dead-letter. I found that the Chinese had relatively huge bets on some of these contests, and that all the details of the fights are worked out with scientific exactitude. The birds are carefully dieted for months beforehand; they have regular baths, and a systematic course of massage to strengthen the muscles of their legs and wings for the contest. They are matched according to age and weight, or sometimes by a system of handicapping whereby the weaker bird has its steel spurs for fighting fastened further up the leg, the higher up the spur the more deadly being the stroke.

The cock-pit was a circle of hard ground about ten feet in diameter, around the edges of which three rows of squatting Chinamen were assembled. Inside the ring a portly person was seated on a red silk cushion. This was the umpire. A number of birds were brought into the ring, each in a banana-leaf cage, its head, shorn of its comb, projecting from one end, its tail from the other. Each bird was taken out by his owner; and several of them were passed round and felt by the connoisseurs. Finally the umpire selected two of approximately equal strength; and after they had been armed, their owners holding them, they were allowed to peck at one another once or twice. Then at a signal from the umpire they were released. With a flapping of wings they were at one another in an instant. It was all very rapid and exciting. Once they jammed their beaks together, heads outstretched; but for the most part it was a whirling circle of feather, legs, and dust. Then, quite unexpectedly, it was over; a chance stroke with the sharp steel spur, and one of the combatants had an eye gouged out. That settled him; he made a blinded rush; but the other had

him at his mercy, and the owners rushed in, a sarong
cloth was dropped over each bird, and the fight was over.

The spectators sat all the while impassive. They
might have been miles away, judging from their apparent
lack of interest.

Nevertheless some had lost heavily, others had gained
equally heavily; but to the uninitiated it was not possible
to determine which was which.

There were more fights to follow; but I was due at the
Hôtel Der Nederlanden by this time to meet the Old
Man, and be initiated into the mystery of the *rijst-tafel*
(rice-table).

The *rijst-tafel* is a thing to be approached with awe,
and described with the gourmandising enthusiasm of a
Sala. It is unique. There is nothing like it anywhere
else—it is the proud distinction of Java to have invented
the *rijst-tafel*. The returned Hollander thinks of it with
longing retrospective memories when, seated in his beloved Warmoestraat restaurant, he remembers he can
have it no more. It is the one thing the loss of which
he deplores.

Imagine a long wide colonnaded loggia open on three
sides so that between the columns one could see scarlet,
white, and purple flowering shrubs, and the slender stems
of the tropical palms in the garden without. This was
the dining-hall; and here, after the luxury of a bath, clad
in spotless ducks, the Old Man and I found ourselves
seated at a little table, assembled with some eighty to
a hundred others, to partake of the mystery.

First of all a waiter brought each of us a mountainous
plate of rice. This acts as the foundation, so to speak,
of the meal. Chicken is added to this; and then the
ceremony begins.

First one waiter approaches, holding in his hands a
big circular blue china tray divided into a dozen or so
compartments, each containing some different comestible.

There were compartments with bits of fish, dry, shredded, and raw, slices of duck, beef in little buttons, curries, chutneys, spices, coco-nut chips.

Waiter followed waiter in procession to our table. Each seemed to have an array of things different from his predecessors: pickles, salted almonds, grated Parmesan, slices of egg, slices of fried banana, young palm-shoots—they kept on coming. Then there were the *sambals*. A *sambal* is anything made up fiery-hot with cayenne pepper—bits of buried liver kept till almost deliquescent, fish-roe, sweetbreads, mysterious things to which no name could be put. They kept on coming.

The Old Man kept sampling each new supply; the people around seemed all to be doing likewise. It was immense, Gargantuan.

"I shall die if I attempt to investigate any further," I said in despair.

"It's a noble death," said the Old Man cheerfully, as he helped himself to the twentieth—or was it the thirtieth?—dish. All this had to be eaten with a spoon and fork; and towards the end I gave up in despair. The Old Man went on steadily.

"You get used to it in time," he said.

Everyone else seemed, indeed, to be quite used to it; but eventually I had to strike.

To my astonishment, however, a course of meat and salad followed, which the habitués attacked with renewed vigour. This in its turn was succeeded by dessert and coffee.

"Have some coffee, Doc?" asked the Old Man.

"No, thanks," I murmured feebly.

A gentle languor was stealing over me. I watched as in a dream the fat Dutchwomen eating—eating—eating.

"You'll be all right when you've had a sleep," said the Old Man.

I feebly assented; for it was with difficulty already I

could keep my eyes open; and I felt the wings of sleep
wooing me with an irresistible fascination.

The guests were by this time beginning to leave the
hall. It was the hour of the *siesta*; and they were going
to their rooms to sleep off the effects of the debauch; for
there is something in the "rice-table" which irresistibly
woos one to slumber, and this is probably one of the
reasons for its immense popularity.

The Old Man rose slowly with a sigh of satisfaction.
"I don't feel at all hungry now," he said.

I could not even smile in response.

Slowly we went to our room, very cool, stone-floored,
with plain white-washed walls, devoid of all furniture
except two great mosquito-curtained beds and some cane-
bottomed chairs.

In three minutes I was sound asleep.

It seemed but a few minutes afterwards when we were
again wakened. The silent-footed Malay boy had entered
and called the Old Man, who in his turn had shouted
to me that tea was ready. I looked at my watch and
found to my surprise that, like everyone else in the hotel,
we had been asleep three hours, and it was now half-past
four. I also found that my appetite had returned, and
the tea and biscuits were delicious.

We had another bath and dressed. Then we took a
carriage and drove round Weltevreden (New Batavia),
the garden city originated by the great Marshal Daendels,
the Napoleon of Java.

Imagine a city in which every house is hidden in a
garden of its own, so that one feels one is all the time
in the country, and this city surrounding an immense
open space of park-land several miles square, and one
can have some idea of the effect Weltevreden makes on
a stranger. Truly it is a dream city of delight, with this
great square, Koningsplein, lined with immense rows of
kanari and waringen trees, and its beautiful classic

columned houses buried in masses of orchids, palms, and
Madagascar flame trees.

We drove past the residence of the Governor-General,
and stopped for a little at the great Batavia museum, with
its wonderful collection of Malay works of art, its price-
less native manuscripts, its relics of the old Dutch East
India Company, and, what to us as Britishers was more
interesting still, part of the collections from the first
voyage of Captain Cook.

Two things particularly impressed themselves on my
memory that pleasant afternoon. One was a wall, dark
and forbidding, enclosing a neglected, ruinous garden.
On the wall was a grim carving of a man's skull impaled
on a great spike, underneath which was inscribed on a
tablet let into the masonry:—

> "This is to perpetuate the accursed memory of Pieter
> Erberfeld, traitor to his country. It is for ever forbidden
> to plant or build upon this spot.
> "Batavia, 14th April, 1722."[1]

Such is the memorial raised to the half-caste Dutchman
who in 1722 formed a conspiracy with a number of
Mohammedans, Javanese, and Chinese fanatics to
treacherously murder every Christian in Batavia on one
dread night, and so free Java from the hated rule of the
Orang Belanda for ever.

All the plans were fully arranged, the day appointed,
everything was ready, not one of the unsuspecting victims
had the vaguest thought of danger—and then, three days
before the appointed night, a native woman, to save the
life of an officer whom she loved, told.

There was an awful panic. Women barricaded themselves in with their children and wept in an agony; men

[1] Oyten Verfoeyelyke Gedachtenisse Tegenden Gestraften
Land Verza—Der Pieter Erberveld Sal Niemant Vermoogen Te
Deeser Plaatse Te Bouwen Timmeren Met—Selen Off Planten
nu Ofte Ten Eewigen Daage. Batavia Den 14 April A° 1722.

grew savage in the grip of fear and fell on the innocent
as well as the guilty. The archtraitor was captured. He
was tortured horribly, tortured till he begged for death.
His limbs were lopped off before he was decapitated.
His house was razed to the ground, his head stuck on a
spike on his own garden wall, his body quartered and
exposed in different places to the four winds of heaven;
and on the following Sunday a solemn "thanksgiving
service" was held in the little old church close by. That
was how they dealt with traitors in the "good old days."[1]

The other thing I remember was an immense old
cannon lying on the esplanade of what had once been
the castle of Batavia. It is said to be of Portuguese
origin, and bears a Latin inscription—"From my ashes
I shall rise again." It is held in great veneration by the
Malays and Chinese, offerings of rice and flowers being
daily placed before it. It is especially worshipped by
women who long for a son to rescue them from the
reproach of sterility—a curious example of phallic
suggestion.

.   .   .   .

When we got back to Tanjong Priok we found the
quays swarming with people, for the packet-boat had just
arrived from Rotterdam. A regiment of soldiers were
being landed, and, forming up on the quays, were looking, with the round eyes of curiosity, at the bare-footed,
yellow-uniformed Malay policemen with their brass
swords, and the multi-coloured crowd of natives, Chinamen, and white-clad Europeans.

During our day in Batavia the officers had discovered
a Dutch café near the ship; and here I found them with
the doctors of the other two ships of the company in port.
The Chief, as usual, was the centre of the party. He
was in high spirits, and said his leg was all right.

1 There is a dispute about the present monument. Some say the
skull fell off and was replaced by a carving, whilst others maintain
that it is still there covered by some inches of whitewash.

That night, however, he became delirious, and on insisiting on examining it I found it frightfully swollen.

Next day he was very little better, and everyone on the ship was gloomy in consequence. To make things worse, of course, two Chinamen took the opportunity of burning themselves about the face and arms rather badly, through allowing a furnace-door to be improperly fastened.

It was distressingly close, not a breath of air stirred. The heat was sweltering, and everyone moped. Without the Chief, somehow, no one seemed inclined to think of amusement. I busied myself taking photographs in the immediate neighbourhood of Tanjong Priok. Once I elaborately stalked a policeman, to find, after painfully manœuvring to get him into a good light, that he was itching to have himself snapshotted all the time, and so my wariness had all been unnecessary. He posed himself delightedly, pulling his sword well round to the front, and then demanded "comshaw." A cigarette completely satisfied him. Once the Customs stopped me with the camera, suspecting I was carrying concealed opium.

We were told the first European port we should call at, homeward bound, would be Marseilles, and so began to change our Dutch money into French, and commenced to wish longingly for the day when we should get the orders for departure.

Everybody was getting ragged in temper; even the Old Man complained of the heat, though he spent nearly all his time in Batavia. With the Chief in the state he was I did not care to go off enjoying myself, and so I too was cooped up in the lagoon.

Then someone suggested that Wang-Chu had poisoned the Chief; and immediately, such was the irritable state of our minds, everyone jumped to the conclusion that this idea was correct, and an expedition to "bash up" Wang-Chu was organised on the spot. It was the unstable state of everyone's nerves that suggested it; and

the feverish ennui of enforced inactivity that stimulated
the hurry to retaliate.

I half-believed it myself, though in my inner mind I
knew it was a chimera of our excited imaginations, and
so had to force myself to oppose the idea vehemently,
covering it with as much ridicule as possible, otherwise
they would have smashed up the whole place and Wang-
Chu at the same time.

The idea of revenge was abandoned accordingly; and
we sank into a lethargy of waiting again.

It was on the next evening just before dinner—we were
sitting smoking on deck—that the Mate turned to me and
said, "I'm dead sick of this rotten lagoon."

I nodded understandingly.

"Tally-clerks been worse than usual?" I said.

"No, it's not that. I want to get home, to get away
from all this. I've just had a letter. My wife's had a
daughter."

He jumped up hastily before I could say anything,
answering an imaginary call, half-ashamed he had said
anything, and too shy to feel comfortable after he had
said it.

A few minutes later the Old Man came puffing up the
ladder. He had just come down from Batavia.

"You're looking very white, Doc. Guess this place
don't suit you. Eh! You'll be glad to hear we're off
to-morrow."

"Jolly glad," I answered promptly.

Every one of the crew must have been feeling much
the same as myself, for the news seemed to spread like
wildfire through the ship, and half an hour later we
heard someone strike up the old farewell chanty from the
fo'castle:

> "Our anchor we'll weigh, and our sails we will set,
>   Good-bye! Fare ye well!
> The friends we are leaving we'll never forget.
> Hurrah, my lads! We're homeward bound."

So on the morrow we left our moorings at Tanjong Priok, and steamed out amongst the flag-dipping cruisers.

A battleship target-firing off Idam Island signalled us to keep clear of the line; and we leant over the rail listening to the reports and watching the holes ripped in the floating target, blissfully conscious of the cool breeze that played about our heated brows, knowing that all the time it was converting our cabins from sweltering heat-traps to cool wind-swept havens of delight, innocent of mosquitoes, fit again for human habitation.

We watched the Bubi light winking at us at 8 p.m.; and at half-past one in the morning I was wakened to see the site of Krakatoa (scene of the awful eruption of 1883) lit up by frequent flashes of silent lightning as we passed.

"That's the last you'll see of Java. Say *Salamat* (farewell), Doc!" said the Old Man; and, standing on the bridge-deck there in the middle watch in the starlight, I did so. I raised my cap to Krakatoa, to the country, to the people, and to the memories I had acquired amongst them.

CHAPTER XI

HOMEWARD BOUND. THE AFTERMATH

WE steamed through the Straits of Sunda into the wide
Indian Ocean, making for the coast of Somaliland through
a sea of desolation where, for days and days on end,
there was never a ship, not even a sea-bird, nothing but
ourselves and the immense shimmering rim of the
horizon.

Sometimes at first I watched the flying-fish, but when
I had finally made up my mind, despite the Natural
History books, that they really did fly, I ceased even to
do that. When there is nothing to see for days one
forgets to look overboard. Subconsciously one knows
the sea is there, just as one feels the monotonous vibra-
tions of the screw; but soon active consciousness narrows
down to the limits of the ship, and one becomes oblivious
of the naked vastness around.

It was scorchingly hot at first, any wind there was
being on the port side, so that the engineers had all the
benefit of it. On the second day out, however, a big
bank of clouds appeared to starboard, the rain pelted
us like whips, and the wind veered right round to starboard. The sea was lumpy, flying fish dashed madly on
board to the great delight of the Chinese, and a delicious
coolness came with the breeze.

The Chief's leg was beginning to get better by now;
and one of the burnt Chinamen was sufficiently well,
I thought, to be put on duty. But here an unexpected
difficulty arose. The Third Engineer reported:

"The others won't let that Chink back on duty, Doc."

"Why not?" I said in surprise.

The Third Engineer waved his hands hopelessly.

"Oh! Don't ask me! I don't understand the mind of the Heathen Chinee one little bit."

I sent for the No. 1 Chinaman.

"What for this man no can go bottom side, No. 1?"

Then the little man explained:

"S'posee alleesame acciident buln numbah one, numbah two piecee men, alleesame time, alleesame medicine, alleesame doctah: two piecee men get well alleesame time. S'posee numbah one pieceeman alligh, numbah two piecee man, he say he no alligh, he sham. S'posee numbah two piecee man he no sham, numbah one piecee man he no alligh, no can come bottom side."

In plain English, because they were both burnt at the same time, both treated with the same lotion, by the same doctor, the Chinamen thought they should both get well together. If only the first one was well, then the other was malingering. If the other was not well, then, obviously, the first one could not be. The argument was a beautiful example of Oriental logic; so I took no further action about the man. It was up to the rest to do his work; and since it was a matter of principle with them I let it pass. The second man was ready for duty three days later; I signed him off; they both returned together; and everyone was happy.

The ship at this time was a regular menagerie. The sailors had been buying busily at Tanjong Priok. For'rard I found a monkey, a green parrot, a very bedraggled white and yellow cockatoo and some canaries left over from the Moji batch. In a dark alleyway I stepped on a tortoise. In the Glory-hole there were cages full of lovebirds and Java sparrows. Aft, the Chinamen had a regular poultry-run of ducks and hens, bought for cooking at about twopence each. One of the sailors had a pair of little game cocks imported to Batavia from Bantam for fighting purposes. These little fellows had to be separated, and so they crowed against one another all day from opposite sides of the poop. In addition

there were two more monkeys aft, several canaries, two
marmosets and a mongoose. Great hairy spiders and
lizards came out of the cargo at intervals, and the copra
bug, of course, was everywhere. Once we saw a snake,
and the mongoose was let loose after it. We lost him
for three days, and then he appeared again, looking very
pleased with himself. There were no more snakes after
that.

One afternoon we found a Booby bird on the fo'castle
head. As soon as it lighted it vomited three or four
small squids, and lay on the deck too tired to rise or resist
capture. We were a thousand miles from land, five
degrees below the "Line"; probably it had lost its bearings; and this was the first sight of anything solid it had
seen for days. I regret to say the omnivorous Chinese
ate it; and a similar fate overtook a Boatswain's bird
captured on the following day.

It was on the morning after that we doubled the Line,
being 1.5° N. at noon. Later in the afternoon we sighted
a lonely little tramp steamer which we all stared at
eagerly, not because she was a thing of beauty but
because she was the only sign of human life, outside
ourselves, we had seen for eight days.

.   .   .   .

A ship at night is eerily fascinating. Everything seems
touched with a silvery glamour under the dim-lit stars,
and the lights from the port-holes shine with ghost-like
eyes. I had been up late in the First watch, as we were
passing the Maldive Islands; and I thought I had better
have a look at one of my patients, a Chinese fireman,
before I turned in. He was very ill with Java fever, his
temperature in the Dog-watch had been 103° F., and he
had been vomiting.

Abaft the cook's galley I stopped. The poop was
sharply outlined against the sky; a dim light came from
the open doorway of the seamen's quarters. The
silhouette of the lifeboats, davits, blocks and tackle, was

clear in the moonlight, as if cut out of black paper on a white background; the rails looked like black lines enclosing oblong spaces of white. It was very still.

Then something moved, and I saw the dark figure of a Chinaman, pigtail loose, come and lean over the rail as if gazing vacantly astern. There was not a sound except the even throb of the screw and the faint ripple of the water alongside. I stared at the figure, and then suddenly a thought flashed through my mind:

"My Chink!"

I raced towards him, my rubber-soled shoes making no noise on the iron well-deck. To reach him I had to get up the ladder on to the poop; and as my head came level I saw he was mounting the rail. I cannot remember tripping over anything, but afterwards I found I had barked my left ankle badly. The one thing I wanted was to be in time. I was. I got him by the pigtail and the slack of his trousers. There was almost no struggle, his body coming quite limply. He stared at me vacantly as I held him, and murmured some inarticulate nonsense. He was a little chap, and I carried him fairly easily down the ladder and put him in his bunk again. He made no resistance. Waking his snoring partner in the next bunk, and bidding him keep watch, I hurried to my cabin and returned with a syringeful of morphia with which I plugged him, knowing the enormous doses these Chinamen could stand. In the morning he was still sleeping. I told the No. 1 all about it, and bade him set a watch on him; but there was no need. Towards night he was much better. Next day he was convalescing, and I decided not to report anything to the Old Man, feeling I ought to have put someone to watch him as soon as he became delirious. I said nothing about it to anyone else, though all the Chinamen knew of course.

I asked the No. 1 if the man remembered anything. No. 1 shook his head:

"He no savvy.   I tink big black debillo him catchee,
but doctah pidgin too muchee fol debillo."

That was the No. 1's explanation and we left it at that.
Three days later the man asked to be put on duty again.

.   .   .   .

It was about the time of the change of the Monsoon,
and the weather accordingly was very variable.   One
day it would be all sunshine, and then suddenly a heavy
rain squall would sweep down on us making the quartermasters run to shift the ventilators to keep the rain out
of the holds, and sending each of us hurriedly to his
cabin to turn his wind-chute and so prevent his quarters
being flooded.   All day, perhaps, the wind would be
on the starboard, with occasional shiftings between rain-
squalls; and then for several days in succession between
three and seven in the morning we would have a regular
gale to port.   This would be followed by a day of complete sunshine, generally a Sunday much to the Mate's
disgust, as it would have been an ideal day to turn his
men on to the painting that his soul loved.   Presently
we steamed out of Monsoon weather, we were in
mirrored waters again, and the ship swung in the long
slow roll that the Indian Ocean acquires in its vast sweep
from Durban to Colombo.

We were also now in the track of ships again, and
that night we more than once saw the sudden flare lit
by an Arab dhow to let us know of its presence in the
dark.

"In the day-time," said the Mate, "when we are near
enough it is not uncommon for one of them to signal us
for water; and they'll send a dug-out with half a dozen
empty paraffin tins to hold it."

Next morning we sighted a P. and O. outward bound,
and a little later two bodies floating in the water, hastily
wrapped in canvas.   Idly we wondered who they were.
Probably pilgrims taking a longer journey than to Mecca,
was the general idea, for a little before we had passed

a Dutch steamer laden with hundreds of them returning from Jeddah to Batavia.

That evening the lion head of Guardefui on the coast of Somaliland, which we had seen on the way out, gazed once more silently down on us; and I felt that for me the voyage was nearly over.

At Suez we got our mail, after a silence of two months. The Chief also had a bundle of newspapers awaiting him.

"The Australians play England at the Old Trafford a week after we're due home. Hooray!" he said. "I'll be able to see them before we sail again next voyage."

Next voyage! He spoke of it as I would of taking the tube from Baker Street to Waterloo.

"You'll be coming with us, Doc," said the Mate. "Oh, yes, you will! The ship wouldn't be the same without you."

Of course they knew I wouldn't; but it was their kindly way of making me feel we had been friends.

We were four days in Marseilles, and four in Amsterdam. Then we sailed for Liverpool; and I spent most of the time round the coast packing my precious curios.

I took all their addresses. I was to send them photographs. I was to write to them. If ever I went another voyage I was not to forget the old ship.

We had our last night at bridge together, the Chief, the Mate and I, making up the one hundred and fiftieth almost successive nights we had played; and the next day we were in the Mersey.

At the end, the leave taking was almost an anti-climax. Everyone had someone near at hand they were eager to see; and everyone was eager to leave the ship. In six hours we had scattered all over the three kingdoms. Next morning I was home in Northern Ireland. My mother said I was very brown but much too thin. A fortnight later I was back in London.

The fat old lady outside Aldgate Station was selling

flowers exactly in the same position as when I saw her
last.   The chemist's shop with the faded advertisement
of Fothergill's Pill in the window was just the same.
At the hospital, a man I knew slightly, nodded to me.

"Haven't seen you about lately.   Been out of town?"
he said.

"Yes," I answered.

EPILOGUE

SOMETIMES a weariness of London comes over me, and I feel that I would give almost anything to be on the high seas again. There are certain days and certain things that cause this feeling.

Sometimes it is only the misery of a cold raw day that sets me thinking. Often I get it crossing one of London's bridges when the tide is in and the salt tang strikes upon one's nostrils. Sometimes it is casually seeing in the Shipping Intelligence the name of my old ship that sets me off.

As a rule I try to avoid such thoughts. They are disconcerting; they confuse one's issues; they are not part of a well-ordered life. But they are difficult to get away from, even when one tries. Once I went into a chemist's shop in Bond Street for something. As I entered the faint odour of *kananga* leaves struck my nostrils; and immediately I was back as in a vision on the ship and saw the low-lying beach of Cheribon, and the lateened praus around the ship, as I lay in my chair listening to the monotonous "amma-ti-ra-ta-huh" of the coolies swinging bales of Java sugar in the hold.

Then a suave voice said, "What can I get you, sir?" and I was back again in London.

Once, a year later, I saw the ship's name amongst the arrivals at the Royal Albert Docks, and made a special pilgrimage to see her. I knew her ugly old black hull amongst them all long before I could read her name.

The Chief was standing on the saloon-deck when I climbed aboard.

"Hello," he said quite casually, as if I had just come up from my cabin.

"Hello," I answered.

There was a milkman standing near; and the Chief continued the conversation I had interrupted.

"How much milk did you say you had left us?"

"A quart, sir."

"A quart!" the Chief echoed in surprise. "That's not nearly half enough. There are five men in the mess. Bring all you've got."

The man departed; and we gravitated, as was natural, to his cabin, and were soon deep in reminiscences. They had been to Port Arthur; and he had been arrested as a German spy, for some unknown reason, by the Japs, and had had quite a bother getting off. He was telling me all about it when a tap came to the door.

"I've done it, sir," said a voice. It was the milkman.

"Done what?" said the Chief.

"Brought up all I've got."

"How much?" said the Chief.

"Eight gallons, sir."

"Holy Moses!" said the Chief. Then he laughed. "Doc, you'll have to stay all night and help us use it up."

"Better send it across as a present to the hospital," I suggested.

It never occurred to either of us to ask the milkman to take it back, as of course he would; and so the hospital authorities got it, and no doubt wondered who on earth sent such a curious gift.

"When are you coming back to us?" he said casually.

"To-morrow if I could," I answered promptly. "But——"

"I know," he said. "It's a good thing for you, Doc, there is a 'but.' I was like that once. I could have broken off after the first voyage or two; but I thought I'd stay two years and then take a shore billet. I had a good one offered me—manager in a cotton-mill—better pay, better everything—but I couldn't do it. I tried it for a month. It was no good. You're much the same as me, Doc; and I can tell you you've just got out in time."

"D'ye remember what you said to me at the beginning of the voyage when we were going out from Liverpool?"

"Lord, no. I say such a lot of rubbish. What was it?"

"We were leaning over the rail, and you said you were always glad to get back to England, and always glad to get away again. When you were in the East you were sorry for the poor devils who had to live there, and knew they were envying you all the time they were talking to you of home. You said that when one passed the 'Rock,' homeward bound, one counted the hours till one got to England; and when one had been there a fortnight, and seen the people that mattered, one was itching to be off again—off to the long calm days, the quiet of the deck, the hot kiss of the tropical sun, the soft velvet of the tropical night, the warmth of colour and costume denied one's eyes in Puritan England. You told me I should know and feel it all. I want to tell you now that I do—every bit of it—and more."

The Chief nodded quietly: "I know, old chap."

. . .

So the Pathologist and I sit opposite one another, with our feet on the mantel, smoking many pipes; and sometimes when he is particularly aggravating I try to tell him of what he has missed.

Sometimes he says: "If it's as good as all that, why the deuce don't you go back?"

But as a rule he merely grunts, and shifts the conversation to theories of immunity.

We are getting more and more guinea-pigs. I hate them; but habit is gradually dulling that. I have often threatened to leave him, but he knows I do not mean it; for if I did he would be compelled to marry someone who would remember to send his things to the laundry. Then I should be without a friend of—I decline to think how

many years—and Science would have lost one of her most
enthusiastic votaries. So I remain.

.   .   .

Nevertheless, I feel that I shall always be under an
obligation to him: for it was he first suggested the idea
of the voyage, and, curiously enough, as I shall presently
relate, also the method of quieting the unrest produced
by it.

He is subject to illuminating ideas at times; and these,
and his helplessness in the everyday affairs of life, are
part of his great charm for me. So much so is this the
case, that I am constantly haunted by the thought that
in spite of my care one day some woman will come across
his path, discover the charm, and spoil him for me by
insisting on marrying him—for there is nothing so absolutely fascinating to a woman as a helpless man, except
perhaps a baby, probably because the same primitive
instinct is at the bottom of her inclination towards each
of them.

It was one evening, when the wind was howling
around the chimney-pots, and the driven rain tapping
with soft wet fingers on the window-panes, that the
idea came to him.

I suppose the weather made me particularly aggravating. At any rate he said, half querulously, after some
forgotten remark of mine:

"Why don't you write the whole damn thing down,
and so get rid of the weight of it? Putting your memories
on paper would lighten them in your mind. I wish you
would; and then we might have peace."

That is how the book came to be written.

.   .   .

It was only when the pile of author's copies arrived,
and we were staring at them, that a certain doubt came
to me. It must have been more or less in the Pathologist's mind also, for he suddenly said:

"Shall you send copies to your old messmates?"

The question somehow seemed to crystallise the doubt in my mind; and I began to wonder, when it was too late, how they might like being thus exhibited before the great unknown public. An uncomfortable feeling that perhaps they might not take it as kindly as it was meant assailed me.

"I don't know," I said dubiously.

Hesitating about the matter for some days, I finally came to the conclusion that on the whole it would be better not, comforting myself with the thought that sailors never read expensive books of travel, and that these old comrades of mine were away from England so much they might never hear of the liberties I had taken with their personalities.

But the success of the book defeated me; and when I found that a Colonial Edition had been issued, I knew it was only a matter of months before I should hear from some of them.

It was the Chief who, characteristically, broke the silence, set my mind at ease, and gave me all the news. One morning I found a letter with a Japanese postmark awaiting me.

> "S.S. 'Erymanthus,'
> Kobe, Japan.
> Feb. 9, 1912.

"Dear Doc,

"So you've put us in a book—have you? Funny thing that none of us ever suspected you. But surely, surely you might have sent a copy to the Chief, with the author's compliments, and not have taken me by surprise like this. We were in Singapore; and I had gone on board a coast-boat called the *Pulo Wei* to see the Chief Engineer. As soon as I got to the top of the gangway the mate came along, looked at me, ran below, and presently returned, in a state of great excitement, with a book open at an illustration, saying: 'So you're the Chief of *The Surgeon's Log.*'

"To tell you the truth I thought he was dotty till he showed me my own face staring at me from the page.

"Well, I've read it on the way up here; and there's no doubt you've got us. I read an extract to our present Captain. He grinned all over his face, and said: 'That's Tucker, all right.'

"But there are a lot of changes since your time. The Old Man has been promoted to a bigger ship; and Bruce the Steward is still with him. The mate's been made a captain; and Horner is now a first Mate, and married—I don't believe a single word of that yarn of yours, by the way. I, too, have had promotion. My present ship is a flier—fourteen knots—always in the tea, rubber and tobacco trade. No treacle loaded in this ship; and no Java—thank you very much all the same.

"Yesterday I went up to the waterfall to see Sono-San. She pretended to remember you, and said she 'wait long time for you, but you no come.' I told her I should fetch you next voyage; but I suppose the East has finished calling you by now. At any rate I hope everything is doing well with you. I won't say I am well—only fifteen stone five.

Yours sincerely,
M. HALAHAN."

After this, I need scarcely say, his copy was waiting for him on his return. And so it all ended happily.

.   .   .   .

I never expected to see Port Said or Suez again, for I had settled down to consulting practice and the sky of 1912 was an untroubled blue. But the First World War came; my life like that of millions of others was dislocated; and, after some thrilling Service in the Balkans, I found myself eventually, as A.D.M.S. Communications, responsible for transporting sick and wounded across the Canal to Cairo, outward from Suez to India, homeward from Port Said to Malta and England.

Early in the war I knew that my friend the Pathologist had been killed in France; and when I came back in 1919 I heard that the old ship had been sunk by enemy action. Captain Tucker, I learnt, however, was still alive and had been decorated for several gallant actions. The Chief, too, had survived, but not the Mate.

The knowledge that the ship had gone used to sadden me a little at times; and then one morning in 1920 I got a parcel from Shanghai. It was a beautifully embroidered Chinese tablecloth from the Captain and Officers of the *Clytemnestra*—the new *Clytemnestra* that had taken the place of the old—and it had been sent as a present when they saw a notice of my marriage in a two month-old copy of *The Times* at Hong Kong.

The names, written on the ship's menu card accompanying the present, were unknown to me; but the unexpected kindliness of it all brought back sharply many happy memories; and the fact that *The Log* had not been forgotten in the new *Clytemnestra* made me feel that the spirit of the old ship still lived in her successor.

FINIS

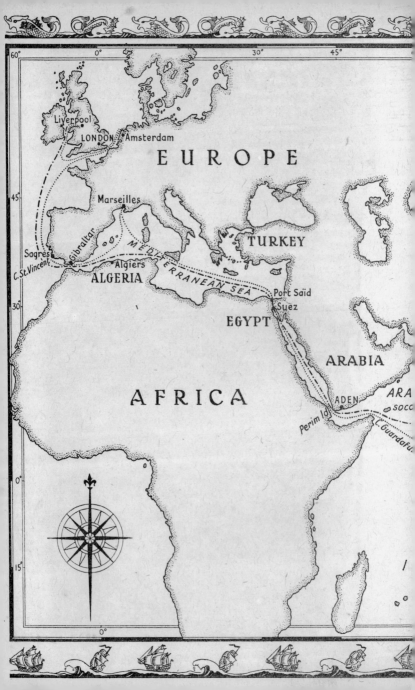